Liberating Letters

From a Mother To a Daughter
to Restore Liberty

Volume 2

Written by Pamela J. Adams

Edited by Brent N. Adams

Printed in the United States of America
First Printing, 2016

ISBN 9781533399809

This book is dedicated to the citizens of America as well as the world. The only way to succeed in the future is to know, understand, and learn from the past.

It is also dedicated to my husband who has been not only supportive but extremely encouraging in my research and writing of these letters.

Lastly, I dedicate this book to my precious daughter, Trinity Grace. The more letters I write the more I realize how important this knowledge is for your generation. Liberty and Freedom are principles that if not fought for and preserved, will be quickly and quietly taken from you. Knowledge is power, use it.

Table Of Contents

January 1, 2015

Dear Liberty,

Many cultures from the beginning of time have developed their own calendar systems. Calculations were done in regard to moon cycles and planets to determine how many months  would be in a year and how many days in a month, which scientists can replicate with countless mathematical equations. However, when asked why we have 7 days in a week, most will claim that there really is no reason for it. Could it be because of where the truth actually lies?*

In Genesis 1, God informs us how he created the universe and all in it, describing his work for each of the six 24-hour days. Many try to argue it is unknown how long the "day" in Genesis really is, claiming possibly millions of years, allowing it to conform with an evolutionary world view. However, the text clearly says "And there was evening, and there was morning" after each description of the day's work, unmistakably meaning a 24-hour period. Yom, Hebrew for "day" in Genesis, is also used in the Bible 357 times outside of Genesis. In all those cases it means a 24-hour period. It is highly unlikely it would mean something else in Genesis.

God also explained that on the seventh day He rested.

"By the seventh day God had finished the work he had been doing; so on the seventh day he rested from all his work. Then God blessed the seventh day and made it holy, because on it he rested from all the work of creating that he had done." (Genesis 2:2-3)

People from the time of Adam and Eve would have known this and followed God's example of resting every seventh day, or the Sabbath Day. It is also a day which should be spent in worship and study of God's Word. When God gave his Law to Moses, He commanded, "Remember the Sabbath day and keep it Holy," clarifying that one should work six days and rest on the seventh.

"Remember the Sabbath day by keeping it holy. Six days you shall labor and do all your work, but the seventh day is a sabbath to the Lord your God. On it you shall not do any work, neither you, nor your son or daughter, nor your male or female servant, nor your animals, nor any foreigner residing in your towns. For in six days the Lord made the heavens and the earth, the sea, and all that is in them, but he

rested on the seventh day. Therefore the Lord blessed the Sabbath day and made it holy." (Exodus 20:8-11)

He instructed the Jewish people to also give the land a year of Sabbath. During that year the land was not to be reaped, sown or harvested. After seven cycles of seven years, or in the fiftieth year, properties were returned to original owners and debts were to be forgiven. It was to be a year of rest, restoration and liberty for people and land.

The Lord said to Moses at Mount Sinai, "Speak to the Israelites and say to them: 'When you enter the land I am going to give you, the land itself must observe a sabbath to the Lord. For six years sow your fields, and for six years prune your vineyards and gather their crops. But in the seventh year the land is to have a year of sabbath rest, a sabbath to the Lord. Do not sow your fields or prune your vineyards. Do not reap what grows of itself or harvest the grapes of your untended vines. The land is to have a year of rest. Whatever the land yields during the sabbath year will be food for you—for yourself, your male and female servants, and the hired worker and temporary resident who live among you, as well as for your livestock and the wild animals in your land. Whatever the land produces may be eaten.

" 'Count off seven sabbath years—seven times seven years—so that the seven sabbath years amount to a period of forty-nine years. Then have the trumpet sounded everywhere on the tenth day of the seventh month; on the Day of Atonement sound the trumpet throughout your land. Consecrate the fiftieth year and proclaim liberty throughout the land to all its inhabitants. It shall be a jubilee for you; each of you is to return to your family property and to your own clan. The fiftieth year shall be a jubilee for you; do not sow and do not reap what grows of itself or harvest the untended vines. For it is a jubilee and is to be holy for you; eat only what is taken directly from the fields.' " (Leviticus 25:1-12)

Once Christ came, Christians chose Sunday as their Sabbath for several reasons. Christ was not only resurrected on Sunday but the Holy Spirit came to the disciples on the Sunday celebrating Pentecost. Since Jesus said, "The Sabbath was made for man, not man for the Sabbath," (Mark 2:27) and proclaimed, "The Son of Man is Lord of the Sabbath" (Luke 6:5), the apostles understood this change would not be a sin in the eyes of the Lord. It's not surprising the Russian word for Sunday actually means Resurrection.

All this along with the understanding that God uses seven throughout the Bible to denote completion and perfection, it's pretty easy to see where the seven-day week originated. It also explains why Saturday (the Jewish Sabbath) and Sunday (the Christian Sabbath) are designated the "weekend" with many businesses and schools being closed.

So, Liberty, we know the moon and the stars (which God designed) determined the number of days and months in a year. We also know that God plainly instructed that man observe a seven day week. If that is true, then what event happened that centers our yearly count, giving dates either a BC (before) or AD (after) label?

After the Roman Emperor Julius Caesar assumed power, he reformed the common Roman calendar in 46 BC. This calendar became known as the Julian calendar and was based on the number of years after the founding of Rome. Other methods reflected the current ruler at the time and his year of reign.

During this era, Christian churches throughout the civilized world were celebrating Easter on different days as they did not have a consistent chart to properly calculate the correct date for Christ's death and resurrection. The First Council of Nicaea in AD 325 unified the Easter Celebration, connecting it to the spring equinox by making the following Sunday the day of observation. (see Yes, Liberty, There Is A Santa Claus-Vol.1) Dionysius Exiguus, a sixth century Scythian monk, went even further, seeking to formulate a table that would allow all Christendom to worship Easter at the same time. In AD 525, he developed a table to calculate the proper date for Easter for the next several decades as the previous table would be ending soon.

The expiring Easter table had been designed in the Diocletian Era and named after the Roman Emperor Diocletian. It followed a numbering system which began with his first year of reign. During his emperorship, Diocletian organized the last major persecution against Christians. Dionysius saw an opportunity to replace this period and erase Diocletian's name from history by introducing a system that labeled the years "since the incarnation of our Lord Jesus Christ." His efforts resulted in the Anno Domini era, which was adopted by the Julian calendar.

Using Christ's birth as the epoch, or starting point, the years after this event were noted AD from the Latin Anno Domini meaning, "In the year of the Lord." More specifically Anno Domini Nostri Iesu (Jesu) Christi ("In the Year of Our Lord Jesus Christ") counts the years since the conception or birth of Jesus. Those years before his birth are simply BC or "Before Christ".

This designation did not become widely used until after Venerable Bede, an eighth century monk, decided to gather all known calendar systems from the beginning to his time and synchronize them into one universal structure. After completing his book Ecclesiastical History of the _English People_ in AD 731, Western Europe embraced the new dating system and its usage became the common standard. Bebe also determined that Christ's birth was either 2 BC or 1 BC, which would make sense since there is no year 0.

The Julian calendar was amazingly close to the accurate yearly calculation but over centuries of just being just a few minutes too long each year, the calendar had drifted a full 10 days off course by the end of the 16th century. This resulted in the shifting of important religious days as well as times of year i.e. seasons. Due to this movement, the spring equinox was shifting seasons causing Easter to move as well.

Finally recognizing the problem, Pope Gregory XIII recalculated the length of the year finding the error. He modified the Julian calendar in 1582, accommodating for the 0.002% discrepancy in the 365.2425 day measurement. It took years to convert to the new Gregorian calendar with some historical events now showing two dates to denote the 10-day difference during the conversion years. The Gregorian calendar also continued the Anno Domini era.

Liberty, I have copies of several wills from our ancestors in the late 1800's which include the words, "In the year of Our Lord...." Over 1150 years after Dionysius established this dating method people still proudly recognized Christ's birth as the epoch for our yearly labeling.

As with everything, todays' atheists are attacking with full force by now labeling years as BCE (Before Current Era) and CE (Current Era) to try to remove Christ from the picture. This is an attempt to remove Christ from history as the monk Dionysius removed the Diocletian calendar from history. By removing Christ from the calendar, they are attempting to wipe away his existence. This, like other attempts, is a means to take people's focus off of God. However, God has written his plan on the stars and moon, on our days and nights, on our weeks and years, so that a sinful world will never forget a God who sacrificed himself for them.

So, Liberty, welcome to "The Year of Our Lord Jesus Christ" 2015. May she be full of peace, happiness, love, and grace.

That's my 2 cents.

Love,
Mom

January 6, 2015

Dear Liberty,

After Jesus was born in Bethlehem in Judea, during the time of King Herod, Magi from the east came to Jerusalem and asked, "Where is the one who has been born king of the Jews? We saw his star when it rose and have come to worship him."

When King Herod heard this he was disturbed, and all Jerusalem with him. When he had called together all the people's chief priests and teachers of the law, he asked them where the Messiah was to be born. "In Bethlehem in Judea," they replied, "for this is what the prophet has written:

"'But you, Bethlehem, in the land of Judah, are by no means least among the rulers of Judah; for out of you will come a ruler who will shepherd my people Israel.'"
(see *The Reason For The Season*-Vol.1)

Then Herod called the Magi secretly and found out from them the exact time the star had appeared. He sent them to Bethlehem and said, "Go and search carefully for the child. As soon as you find him, report to me, so that I too may go and worship him."

After they had heard the king, they went on their way, and the star they had seen when it rose went ahead of them until it stopped over the place where the child was. When they saw the star, they were overjoyed. On coming to the house, they saw the child with his mother Mary, and they bowed down and worshiped him. Then they opened their treasures and presented him with gifts of gold, frankincense and myrrh. And having been warned in a dream not to go back to Herod, they returned to their country by another route. *(Matt 2:1-12)*

Liberty, twelve days after Christ's birthday we celebrate the Magi's journey, or Epiphany. It is unknown exactly how many wise men actually made the trip, though Christians traditionally use three reflecting the three gifts brought for the baby Jesus. It is these gifts that witness to the truth about who Jesus really was. While such expensive gifts would not normally be given to a humble, "ordinary" baby, it is not their monetary value that is noteworthy.

Commonly a gift for kings, gold was a very precious offering. As

Christ is King, this gift honors his status as holy royalty. Frankincense, an incense, was often burned to please gods. By giving it to Jesus the wise men are acknowledging that Jesus is God. When bodies were prepared for burial, oils and other spices were used when wrapping the body. Bringing the burial oil myrrh to Jesus signified that He would die for our sins and become the Savior of the world.

May the saving grace of Our Lord and Savior Jesus Christ give you peace and comfort throughout the year and the rest of your days.

That's my 2 cents.

Love,
Mom

January 13, 2015

Dear Liberty,

Even on a short trip to the store, you are likely to see a bumper sticker that promotes peace and harmony, urging all religions and philosophies to learn to live and let live. The creator of the sticker took the word "COEXIST" and used the symbols of these different religions and philosophies to spell out each letter.

C = Islam
O = Peace/Pacifism
E = Male/Female or Gay Rights
X = Judaism
I = Pagan
S = Taoism/Confucianism
T = Christianity

It is a simple message of peace. Unfortunately, a horrific terrorist attack in Paris last week proves just how unrealistic this concept is.

Three Islamic extremists entered the Charlie Hebdo office, a French satirical magazine, and murdered ten employees, as well as two police officers, in cold blood. (see *I Am Garland*) The terrorists were heard yelling, "Allah Akbar," a common cry used by Islamists when doing such attacks meaning "God is great," during the massacre. They were also heard saying, "We have avenged the prophet" referring to cartoons the magazine published over the years depicting Mohammad.

To the Islamic extremist, the only way to COEXIST is for infidels, or non-Muslims, to convert or die. (see *A Crusade For The Truth*) There's not a lot of meeting someone in the middle, or accepting others for their beliefs. It's a "my way or death" mentality. The Islamic State (ISIS) has made this abundantly clear to Iraqi Christians after 4 young boys were beheaded for confessing to love Jesus. Christians all through Muslim countries are being kidnapped, raped, enslaved, and murdered for refusing to convert to Islam. (see *Holocaust: Then And Now*)

But it's not just Jews or Christians that Muslims have issues with. Every group on the COEXIST sticker would be wiped out if they had their way. Homosexuals are executed on site in Muslim countries. However, listening to gay rights activists, one would think Christians are the most suppressive group towards homosexuals simply *because we do not agree with gay marriage. (see We Reserve The Right To Refuse Service-Vol.1 and What Is Love?) Christians are called hateful, bigoted, and intolerant for defending their beliefs but Muslims are protected when they murder. When a massacre like Paris happens in the name of Mohammad, liberals race to the microphone to again proclaim Islam is a religion of peace. (see Washington, Adams & Mohammad-Our Founding Fathers, and To The Shores Of Tripoli-Vol.3) Muslims use these pacifists to degrade Jews and Christians but have no issue slitting their throats once their usefulness is over. Anyone of any other religion such as a pagan, Taoist, or Confucianist falls under the conviction of an infidel and is sentenced to conversion or death. It literally is them against the world, and they are determined to win.*

Liberals and the media argue that Muslims are misunderstood. They have been harassed and bombed, justifying the attacks on civilians. They desperately try to claim these terrorist strikes have nothing to do with a particular religion. To do this they completely ignore the shouts of "Allah Akbar", the demands of "Convert or die" and the praises to Mohammad during these attacks. Major newspapers even scrubbed articles that originally reported one terrorist telling a female employee at Charlie Hebdo that she would not be killed, but she should convert to Islam, read the Qur'an and cover herself. Why would that quote be removed from an article? The only reason is to hide the truth of the religious basis behind these terrorist attacks.

Two days after the Charlie Hebdo attack, while two of the terrorists tried to flee authorities, another extremist took several hostages in a Kosher deli near Paris. He demanded police let his "brothers" go or all the hostages would be shot. He assassinated four Jews before the incident was over. This terrorist proudly proclaimed his allegiance as a "soldier of the Islamic State" in a video filmed prior to his deli attack. (see The Ottoman Empire Strikes Back-Vol.4) While some question whether a Jewish shop was specifically targeted, others are proving the unmistakable growth of anti-Semitism in Europe in just the past few years. While American toddlers learn their A,B,C's, Al Jazeera, an Islamic controlled television station, uses children's programming to instill hatred and distain for the Jewish people in the hearts and minds of young Muslims. Hostility is ingrained in their souls from the earliest of ages. Until this stops, how will these two religions ever coexist?

The truth is they won't.

To be fair, not every Muslim subscribes to the hatred and violence of the terrorists. One Muslim employee at the Kosher deli did take action, leading several hostages to a freezer and hiding them inside until the ordeal was over. She should be commended and applauded for her bravery. However, within the Muslim world, she will be seen as an infidel as other Muslims are not immune to the utter savagery of the terrorists if they do not support the extremist view. As the Charlie Hebdo massacre occurred, an officer outside the building was filmed begging for his life before being mercilessly executed with a bullet in the head. He was a Muslim yet the terrorists had no sympathy, no connection, no humanity for someone who was a fellow believer. If they would do this to another Muslim, how can any non-Muslim coexist with them?

Most Muslims, even those who don't support these attacks, live under Sharia Law and believe all peoples should be beholden to it. Sharia Law allows males to kill any female relative who disgraces the family for wearing the wrong clothes, being in public alone or being too Western. They refer to this act as an "Honor Killing". Husbands are commanded to hit their wives if they disobey. Anyone with the audacity to leave the Muslim faith is ordered to be put to death and it is Sharia Law that calls for the execution of homosexuals. These rules apply for even the most moderate Muslim.

Like militant Islamists, many atheists show a similar hostility towards Christians. At every turn atheist groups are demanding Christians remove their faith and values from every aspect of their lives. Yet, no matter how many crucifixes people urinate on, how many pictures of Mother Mary have elephant dung smeared on them, or how many times Christ is degraded in our movies and TV shows, not one Christian has ever responded by massacring the perpetrators. However, there is very much an attitude amongst many atheists that Christians should convert to unfaithfulness or die in the public eye. It is political correctness in full swing and at its most destruction. Anytime you have any group of people trying to suppress and control another group, there is no chance of coexistence.

Liberty, we are Christians. Our prayer is that everyone would receive the gift of eternal life through faith in Jesus Christ, but we will not force that belief on others. We will not kill them if they choose to be Jewish, Buddhist, Hindu, atheist or even Muslim. But there are groups out there who insist their way is the only way. We must fight their grab for ultimate control but realize it will never go away. God has given Satan dominion over this world and because of that he will use every means possible to corrupt God's children any way he can.

So arm yourself with His Word, wrap yourself in His grace, and march forward in faith that Christ has already won the war. He has secured victory and one day He will return to take us home to live in that perfect world of peace and harmony.

That's my 2 cents. Love, Mom

January 19, 2015

Dear Liberty,

As a result of the Emancipation Proclamation signed by Abraham Lincoln on September 22, 1862, decades of slavery was abolished in all Confederate States. *(see Freedom Day-Vol.5)* In 1865 the 13th Amendment was adopted abolishing slavery in all states. *(see Founding Documents-Vol.7)* Policies were then written and implemented by the recently formed and empowered anti-slavery Republican Party ensuring the God-given rights and freedoms to the Negro. *(see America's Voting Record-Vol.3)* The path to pure liberation and equality for all Americans began its march.

After the Civil War, Congress adopted the 14th Amendment securing equal protection to all citizens. *(see Founding Documents-Vol.7)* Towards the end of the Republican run Reconstruction Era, southern Democrats regained power in their state legislatures. Racially discrimination laws against Blacks were implemented in these state, known as Jim Crow laws, touting the phrase "separate but equal" to bypass the 14th Amendment. *(see Separate But Equal?-Vol.6)* If they could not enslave the Negros with chains, they would enslave them with regulations.

With full support of blacks, the 1912 election, which brought the first southern president since the Civil War, deemed promising for minorities. Democrat Woodrow Wilson vowed equality, rights and compassion. What he delivered instead was federal workplace and military segregation, a rise in southern power, and a national suppression of minority rights. Wilson actively campaigned for black votes promising the rights due to them. Once in office, he not only reneged on his pledges, he allowed and pushed for policies doing the complete opposite. Jim Crow laws were now being implemented at a national level. Federal black workers all throughout the South were dismissed and replaced with white employees while Wilson turned a blind eye. Decades of advancement for the Negro was wiped out in just a few short years. The South was on the rise again. The battle for freedom was not over. It was just getting started. *(see Birth Of A Nation)*

A hundred years after the Emancipation Proclamation, blacks were having to fight for their liberty once again. Tensions from race relations were at an all-time high. Two leaders rose to oppose the inequality and discrimination. Both were sons of preachers but as young adults each questioned their family's religion and entertained other options. Malcolm, while in prison, converted to the teachings of the Nation of Islam. Michael returned to his Christian foundation. Malcolm professed violence, division, and separate nations for the races. Michael preached for peace, unity, and coexistence. By the 1950's Malcolm was a minister in the Nation of Islam Temple and Michael was a preacher in the Baptist Church. Both changed their names to support their beliefs. Malcolm Little, renouncing his "slave" name, replaced Little with "X" in honor of the "unknown name of his African ancestors." Michael King, Jr., following his father's lead, changed his name to Martin Luther King, Jr., in honor of the German church reformer. (see *The Knock Heard 'Round The World*-Vol.1)

Malcolm was greatly influenced by Nation of Islam leader Elijah Muhammad, winning over thousands of people to his idea of a bloody revolution. With Jesus Christ as his spiritual leader, Martin met with and was also greatly influenced by Gandhi. It was Gandhi's example of nonviolence that affected Martin's approach to the cause. Each of these men played a role in the Civil Rights Movement of the 1960's but with different results. One method ended the same way it began, violently. The other method led to change. One leader is mentioned in history. The other leader made history.

As with Woodrow Wilson, fellow southern Democrat Lyndon Johnson realized that the Civil Rights Movement would empower a people that he believed were inferior. Since he could no longer control blacks as slaves to a plantation owner, he'd control them instead as slaves to a government. He had to find a way to restrain the Negro or they would destroy him and his party. As Senate Majority Leader during the Eisenhower administration, Johnson, along with the majority of the Democratic Party, fought the Republican president's Civil Rights Acts. Johnson refused to make the Negro his equal, blocking every civil rights bill he could, only allowing a watered down Civil Rights Act, the first since Reconstruction, to be passed in 1957 with another in 1960. As President he recognized a political advantage in supporting Civil Rights Acts. Signing the bills as a Democrat allowed his party to add this accomplishment to their resume, ignoring their role in suppressing the exact same legislation that Republicans had supported for decades.

However, there were risks in passing such laws. Johnson needed to do something to make sure the Negros did not get too powerful. "These Negroes, they're getting pretty uppity these days and that's a problem for us since they've got something now they never had before, the political pull to back up their uppityness. Now we've got to do something about this, we've got to give them a little something, just enough to quiet them down, not enough to make a difference." With that Johnson declared a War on Poverty and developed multiple domestic programs referred to as the "Great Society." Johnson proudly proclaimed, "I'll have those niggers voting Democratic for the next 200 years." Like the slave owners, Johnson gave Negros food, housing, and clothing and only required a vote for the Democratic Party in return. He succeeded in promoting and causing the breakdown of the black family, forcing unwed mothers to find financial support in the government, taking responsibility and purpose away from black males. To fill that void, many young black men turned to drugs, violence and gangs. Martin Luther King, Jr., and Malcolm X did not fight for equal rights so over 34% of black babies could be aborted, becoming the leading cause of black deaths. They did not go to jail so the number of black babies born out of wedlock would go from less than 30% before the "Great Society" to over 70% after. They did not give their lives so that 93% of black homicides could be caused by other young black men. A fact that is completely ignored even today by some of the same Civil Rights leaders that stood with Martin and Malcolm 50 years ago.

The Civil Rights Acts removed the shackles of discrimination from the wrists of Negros, but Johnson replaced them with a yolk of dependency around their necks. The Democratic Party undoubtedly reveals this when someone of color has the audacity to endorse the Republican Party. They are attacked and verbally beaten, called stupid, ignorant, and an Uncle Tom because they dared to run off the government plantation. As in Roots, Democrats have whipped the black voter into submission until he believes his name is Toby. They support the freedom of blacks to vote, but only if it is a vote for them.

The beast of racial tensions is once again rearing its ugly head. Protests were sparked by the recent deaths of two black men at the hands of white police officers. (see Just The Facts, Ma'am-Vol.1) Protesters took to the streets to express their frustration. While many are following Martin Luther King, Jr.'s, example, others have decided Malcolm X's violent model is more effective. Unfortunately some used the occasions to loot, cause destruction and viciously attack innocent business owners and civilians. Many even called for the death of cops all over the country. One individual answered the challenge, executing two New York officers in their squad car. US Attorney General Eric Holder interjected himself in the civilian death cases calling for additional autopsies and federal investigations even though grand juries cleared the officers of wrongdoing. He completely ignored the illegal activity of the black suspects and automatically judged the white cops guilty because of the color of their skin. Americans hoped that the first black president and the first black Attorney General would have brought Martin Luther King, Jr.'s, dream to life.

"I have a dream that my four little children will one day live in a nation *where they will not be judged by the color of their skin but by the content of their character."*

Instead race relations in America over the past 6 years have regressed to 1960 levels. Judgments in the media and the administration seem to be simply black and white, ignoring facts as well as people's integrity.

Liberty, we must follow Christ's teachings of love for our neighbor and learn from the examples of Martin Luther King, Jr., and Gandhi. The world is on fire. America has its political and racial divisions, which have turned violent. Radical Islam is purposely causing chaos, believing it hastens the 12th Imam who will end the struggle between good and evil. Christians and Jews throughout the Middle East and now Europe are being targeted for persecution and death.

Last week 40 leaders from all over the world converged in Paris to march in support of the recent massacre at the Charlie Hebdo office. (see COEXIST) These leaders, even those specifically asked not to come, such as Benjamin Netanyahu of Israel, realized the importance of showing support and unity in face of the despicable, cowardly terrorist acts by the Islamic extremists. It was a peaceful, non-violent demonstration to send a message to the terrorists that they will not be intimidated.

Noticeably absent from the powerful march in Paris was America. After attending a meeting right along the march route, Eric Holder decided to leave Paris rather than participate with America's allies. While the rest of the world followed Martin Luther King Jr.'s example, showing love, peace and compassion to our neighbors while uniting and fighting for what is right and true, America turned its back in silence. While Holder can't get involved fast enough when race can be exploited, he ran from an opportunity to display true character by standing up against violence.

Today we remember and honor the Christ-centered message of Martin Luther King, Jr. May we continue to strive to unite as a country and bring his dream to reality.

"And when this happens, and when we allow freedom to ring, when we let it ring from every village and every hamlet, from every state and every city, we will be able to speed up that day when all of God's children, black men and white men, Jews and Gentiles, Protestants and Catholics, will be able to join hands and sing in the words of the old Negro spiritual:
Free at last! Free at last! Thank God Almighty, we are free at last!"

That's my 2 cents. Love, Mom

January 28, 2015

Dear Liberty,

In the recent State of the Union address, Pres. Barack Obama once again planted the seeds of disunity, watering disdain in one group of Americans for another group of Americans. He pitted blacks against whites, rich against poor, everyone against conservatives. This sort of division is in direct contrast to God's will for us. The 10 Commandments, or the Law, are well summed up by the two directives from Jesus Christ; "Love the Lord your God with all your heart and with all your soul and with all your strength and with all your mind" and "Love your neighbor as yourself." Luke 10:27

The 10 Commandments tell us how to do that. For example, do not steal, do not commit adultery, do not covet. God tells us in these commandments that we should not be envious or want what others have. It is wrong to desire someone's wealth, property, or spouse. It is equally wrong to then take those items because you feel entitled. Someone who promotes such thoughts are playing upon immoral desires. They are actively convincing people to sin. When this sort of rhetoric is being used we must not only condemn it, we must expose its dangers to the world.

When Barack Obama proposes more taxes on the rich, he is condoning people to covet what others earned. He intends to steal from the "haves" to give to the "have nots". He does this all in the name of social justice, which claims to make things equal for everyone. God made it perfectly clear that it is His job to administer justice the way He sees fit, not the government's. When anyone, regardless the political party, tries to tell you it is their responsibility to make things fair and equal and that they will give you something for free, it is Satan in the garden telling Eve to eat of the forbidden fruit and you will be as wise as God. (see *Fruit Of The Forbidden Tree*-Vol. 1)

It is obvious politicians wish to be God, a concept you must vehemently reject. We lost the privilege of the world being fair and equal when Adam first brought sin into it. You cannot fall into the envious and covetous belief that someone is evil or has done something wrong if they have more money or possessions than you. To do so would be to believe the false witness that is being presented to you, especially since many of those in government who profess the rich stole their wealth from you, are in fact, the wealthiest in America.

Many politicians use the story of Robin Hood to support their desire for redistribution of wealth, or socialism. They champion anyone who professes to make things "fair". Unfortunately, just like their view of fairness, their view of Robin Hood is completely false.

The story of Robin Hood begins while he was away at war with King Richard. During that time, the king's brother, John, declared himself King of England. King John, with the help of the Sheriff of Nottingham, took Robin's family property and declared it and all the animals on it as the king's. When Robin Hood returned to England and killed a deer on his family land, the sheriff branded him an outlaw for violating the king's laws. As the story goes Robin Hood gathers with others who were also oppressed by the king in Sherwood Forest. He begins robbing and giving the bounty to the poor.

What Barack Obama wants you to believe is that he is the good-natured Robin, robbing from the evil rich. The truth is, Robin robbed from the false king, returning to the poor what the corrupt government stole from the people. Barack Obama and other politicians are not Robin Hood in this story. They are the sheriff. They use the power of government to take from hard-working people, claiming they are making things equal. In truth, they line their own pockets and their rich donors with middle-class tax money.

For Obama to present himself as Robin Hood is outright deceitful. The government uses legislation to create laws to steal from everyone who works and produces to give to those who don't work and some who aren't even here legally! This is the most egregious fairy tale of all.

The truth is that tax increases never hurt the top 1% as claimed. These taxes are imposed on those who earn a wage. The top 1% are not employees working for a wage, instead they're businesses and investments, earning royalties, interest, and dividends. The taxes on such income is significantly less than the income of working Americans. So, where does Obama's money come from? Simple: the middle class.

Furthermore, Republicans claim to be against big government while Democrats profess to be against big business. But both parties have grown government to bail out banks, car companies and other businesses, taking tax money from the working class to pay the bill. For their efforts the government takes a little more control over the saved industry, thus killing capitalism one business at a time.

Throughout history, this little socialist charade has been played by every powerful dictator. The result is always the same, the wealthy and powerful shut the door for success behind them and decrease the opportunity for others to excel. This ultimately leads to a reduction or elimination of the middle class. As we have seen under Obama's watch the rich continue to get richer while the lower class continues to become more dependent on the workingman. This only causes the middle class to fall further into the pit of poverty thus shrinking the tax pool supporting the government.

Margaret Thatcher summed it up best when she said, "Socialism works only until you run out of other people's money." Obama boldly claims to represent the middle class in the fight against the wealthy. In reality, he has proven to do just the opposite.

For generations people flocked to America because it was the only place where people had a chance to pull their way out of the lower class. We use to have one of the largest and strongest middle classes. Thanks to a rapidly growing government by both Democrats and Republicans, we are quickly loosing that distinction.

God tells us that we as Christians will be persecuted. We will have tough times but to want what somebody has is a sin. To support the government in taking from individuals or a business, so either you can have it or just so they can't, is again a sin. The cornerstone of America is not taking from the rich to give to the poor, that is socialism. America was born on a strong foundation that allows everyone the opportunity to achieve their desires and dreams by their own effort. It is then through your faith and trust in Jesus Christ that you willing help those less fortunate.

Jesus told a parable of the workers wages in Matthew 20:1-16. While Jesus used the parable to demonstrate God's mercy in the Kingdom of Heaven, the real life story is also pertinent. Jesus describes how throughout the day a landowner hires workers to work in his vineyard. They all agree to do so for the wage offered. At the end of the day, whether they worked from early morning or were there for just an hour, the landowner paid each person the same. The first workers then complained, feeling they should be paid more than the ones there for just a short time. The landowner points out that he paid them what they agreed to. They have no grievance. This lesson holds true even today.

Politicians are provoking people into demanding higher minimum wages. Fast food employees agreed to work for the wage they were offered and now picket the restaurant because they feel they are not paid enough. The claim is the minimum wage needs to be a living wage. The truth is that less than 2% of minimum wage earners are the primary breadwinners. They have been convinced flipping burgers is a career, extinguishing any desire to actually make something of themselves. This is again a false argument used by politicians, which inevitably results in sin for anyone who falls for the scam.

Liberty, there are periods when everyone needs a helping hand. But it should only be for a short time until they are back on their feet. We now have people who are generational welfare recipients because they have been enslaved by the government's social programs. The chains of dependency have confined them to a life of no direction, no productivity and no self-respect.

The system has structured itself that anyone who tries to free themselves from the bonds of dependency and make it on their own lose so many benefits that they are at an even lower poverty level than if they remained in the government care. This is in no uncertain terms slavery. It not only robs individuals of their freedoms and liberties, it eventually eradicates their dignity and self-esteem. Instead of working hard, being productive, and becoming independent, they are forced to stay reliant on the government with no hope of rising out of their economic status. The same forces of government are used to push down on working Americans, making them work ever harder for less pay.

The government is not our Savior. It is not the government's responsibility to pick the winners and losers. And it is not the government's job to steal from the rich to give to the poor. This is a myth and a legend as much as Robin Hood is. You, Liberty, are charged by God to be compassionate and charitable as a result of the love and grace we received from Him. To be forced by government, that cannot monitor its own morality, to be moral is insanity. It is a false theology that God has warned us about again and again. It must be rejected and defeated.

That's my 2 cents.

Love,
Mom

February 3, 2015

Dear Liberty,

Antonio was one of the first individuals to arrive in the newly formed Colony of Virginia in 1620. Like many of the early Europeans that came to the new land, he worked as an indentured servant. Workers earned their freedom after working an agreed number of years. Not having the funds to travel to America themselves, thousands of Europeans agreed to pay for their travel, room and food expenses by working it off under contract to a farmer or some other skilled businessman in the Virginia Colonies. After their agreed time was up, they were often given some food and supplies. Many got to keep a portion of the land that they worked. Most importantly, they were free and had a skill to begin a new life for themselves.

The first settlers arrived in Jamestown, Virginia, in 1607. (see *Jamestown: A City Upon A Hill*) For a long time the majority of indentured servants were white Europeans. While it started out as a voluntary venture, it did not take long until an industry grew around kidnapping poor children and young adults who were then sold into indentured labor. This included Antonio.

His new life began after he was captured and sold to Arab slave traders. Like others in his situation, although he was brought here against his will, he was still contracted as indentured servant. In 1620, the English colonies did not allow any form of slavery. A merchant brought Antonio to Virginia where he was bought by a tobacco farmer named Johnson.

Although the majority of indentured servants in the colonies at that time were Europeans, the first African servants arrived in the English colony of Jamestown in 1619. Being baptized by their original Spanish captures, per English law, they could not be slaves. They were contracted under the same standards as the 1,000 white English indentured servants already here when they were sold to the colonists by the Dutch for food and supplies. For much of the early life of the new colonies, indentured servants were a simple fact of survival.

The indentured trade system was not only economically driven, but also used for political purposes. King James II used it to rid Britain of its Irish political enemies. Thousands of Irishmen and women were sent to the New World as servants, including the British colonies in the

Caribbean. In the beginning African servants were more expensive than the Irish servants. Owners were more harsh and more brutal to the inexpensive white servant than to the expensive black ones. For monetary reasons, some settlers decided it would be cheaper to begin breeding their white female slaves with their black African slaves, producing the mixed "mulatto" individuals seen in the Caribbean today.

While much of the new land welcomed the cheap labor, the Christian Pilgrim and Puritan Colony of Plymouth, Massachusetts did not. Because of their Biblical beliefs, these settlers had a much different view of servants and slavery. (see Thanks Be To God-Vol.1) When an African slave ship landed in their colony they immediately arrested and imprisoned the ship's officers. They then returned the slaves to their home in Africa at the colonist's own expense. However, the rest of Massachusetts did not have this same view of servitude and slavery as the early Christian settlers. Like the South, the majority sought the cheap labor provided by indentured servants. By the late 1600's, the need for cheap labor began paving the way towards slavery in every New World territory.

Twenty years after Antonio arrived in Virginia, John Punch, a Negro, attempted to escape his contract along with two white servants. A Virginia judge extended John's contract for the rest of his life, but did not legally call it slavery. The other two servants were sentenced to only four additional years along with 30 lashes with a whip. This decision by a single judge marked the beginning of a legal distinction between European and African servants.

Over the next few decades the views of slavery continued to evolve in the eyes of the colonists. (see America's Forgotten Rebellion-Vol.5) Laws were passed refusing Negros the right to own arms and ammunition, declaring children's free or slave status dependent on the mother's status, and removing baptism as a means of denying enslavement. Of course, not every state agreed with the practice. Many anti-slave laws were passed before the American Revolution, but they were all vetoed by Great Britain, forcing the continuation of the slave trade in the colonies. It was only after America broke from the ruling hand of King George a hundred years later that citizens were free to start the discussion of ending the practice of slavery in the new world.

Antonio watched all these changes around him. During his contracted time as a servant, Antonio met and fell in love with another servant, Mary. After working 14 years on the tobacco farm, he was granted his freedom in 1635. He was given some land and the essentials to start his own farm. Antonio changed his name to Anthony and adopted his master's name of Johnson. Anthony and his wife Mary began a life for themselves and had several children.

Anthony and Mary worked hard on their little farm but realized they needed more help and more land. King James I had established an incentive program awarding 50 acres to anyone willing to venture to the New World. These 50 acres were also promised to anyone willing to undertake the expense and responsibility of an indentured servant. Anthony purchased five servants, granting him 250 acres of land. With the acreage and the help of his own servants, his farm became very successful.

In 1654, one of his servants, John Casor, had fulfilled his contract and was demanding his freedom. Anthony refused to release him. Robert Parker, a neighbor, intervened placing pressure on Anthony to do the right thing. Anthony eventually agreed and released John. Unfortunately, the newly freed John chose to work for the neighbor. Anthony then filed a lawsuit against Robert, claiming that he stole John from him. Despite two other servants of Anthony's testifying that John had served his contract term, the court ruled that he was in fact the property of Anthony. This ruling declared Anthony the first legal slave owner in the British colonies. A single legal decision began the 7-year transformation from indentured servants to lawful slavery in the colonies.

As the acceptance of enslavement grew, so did the ownership of slaves by other blacks. In 1830, over 3,700 black families in the South owned black slaves. According to the 1860 Census, New Orleans alone about 3,000 slaves that were owned by black households. (see The Forgotten Representative-Vol.5)

Slavery is an ugly thing. If you listen to today's Civil Rights Activists, or the Democratic Party, you would think that America was the only country to ever suffer from the curse of slavery. Professors shoving White Privilege down our throats force students to believe that only white people owned black people. But slavery is not limited to one specific race enslaving another. Slavery has been used by every race and every race has been enslaved. The harsh truth is that slavery has been infecting our world since the fall of man. 3,000 years before Anthony was given legal right to own John, the Israelites were enslaved by the Egyptians in Northern Africa. It is common belief that the pyramids in Egypt are the result of slave labor. Rome was built on the backs of slaves and could not function without them. Slavery existed within African tribes long before the Portuguese started the African slave trade in the 15th century. Even Christopher Columbus witnessed slavery amongst Native American tribes when he landed in 1492, long before the first white settlers in the new world. (see What Is Columbus Day?-Vol.1)

As horrible and disgusting as the sin of slavery is, it is just a taste of the slavery of sin we are all under. We are doomed to a life of *tyranny with eternal death as our only ending. But God, our merciful Master, has taken compassion on us. He sent His son, His perfect heir, to pay our ransom and free us from sin, death and the power of the devil. As a result, anyone who believes will inherit the Kingdom of Heaven. We are no longer slaves, but the brothers and sisters of the King of Kings.*

God tells us how slaves are suppose to act towards their masters. They should do their job faithfully and reliably, with joy and gratitude. He also instructs masters in their duties. They should be honorable and treat their servants with kindness and respect. While His directions apply for our human relationship with others, more importantly it teaches us of our relationship to Him. We are no longer slaves to sin, but we should be grateful servants of Christ. As Jesus washed the feet of his disciples at the Last Supper, we too must be humble and meek. Not because it will earn us sanctification but because we are representatives of our Master. The love and mercy that God has shown for us should be reflected in our actions towards others.

That's what Anthony forgot. He forgot that he was freed as an indentured servant. Rather than sharing that with his own servant, he decided he had the legal right to own another. In the 1654 court ruling that set the stage for legal slavery, Anthony Johnson and his wife were declared, "inhabitants in Virginia (above thirty years) [and respected for] hard labor and known service." However, because of the changing views on slavery and the African, when Anthony died in 1670 he was declared a non-citizen of the colony. That's because Anthony Johnson was a Negro. Instead of going to his children, his vast estate was awarded to a white settler. In less than 20 years, the first man, a black man, who went to court to claim legal rights over another human being was striped of all his rights as a citizen of the colony. His actions not only brought slavery, but his own downfall.

Liberty, to be free you must be humble. We get so caught up in our own pride, our own self-worth that we disregard others and how we have been freed from the power of sin. You must be faithful, forgiving and you must remain a servant of the Lord.

That's my 2 cents.

Love,
Mom

February 10, 2015

Dear Liberty,

On Jan. 22, feminists across the country sang praises on the anniversary of Roe V. Wade, granting the "right" to kill their unborn baby. It is their most sacred sacrament given to them by their apostle Margaret Sanger.

Margaret was born shortly after the Civil War during the time of Reconstruction. Her father was an outspoken political radical whom many claim encouraged Margaret to always speak her mind, which she did. She called him a lazy drunk who forced her mother to have too many children, which Margaret blamed for her early death.

From here the myth of Margaret Sanger begins. PBS praises her saying she "devoted her life to legalizing birth control and making it universally available for women." Wikipedia touts her as "an American birth control activist, sex educator, and nurse...[who] popularized the term birth control." Biography.com states, "Sanger fought for women's rights her entire life," calling her an "activist" and a "social reformer".

Feminists worship Sanger for giving them freedom to control their reproductive lives. The truth is Sanger and her socialist friends were the ones seeking control.

While still a nurse, Margaret married William Sanger in 1902. Moving to Greenwich Village in Manhattan in 1910, their social circle consisted of the likes of Upton Sinclair, writer and Socialist/Democrat politician, and anarchist Emma Goldman. Sanger joined the Liberal Club, the Women's Committee of the New York Socialist Party and sent her son to Ferrer school founded by anarchists.

Margaret contributed articles on health to the socialist paper *New York Call*. By 1914 she quit nursing and started her own feminist publication, *The Woman Rebel*, with the slogan "No Gods, No Masters". She sent contraceptive information through the mail, which violated the The Comstock Act of 1873, landing Margaret in legal trouble. Estranged from her husband, she fled to England where she continued her work. Margaret had affairs with psychologist and eugenics supporter Havelock Ellis as well as writer and socialist H.G. Wells.

When she returned to the US she opened the first birth control clinic in America in 1916. She created <u>Birth Control Review</u> in 1917 and founded the American Birth Control League in 1921, later renamed Planned Parenthood Federation. She is championed for bringing safe and effective birth control to the states. What supporters so conveniently deny is her underlying purpose.

While in Europe, Margaret learned the art of persuasion. Her socialist and eugenic friends instructed her on using "family compassion and planning" as propaganda for their cause. It deceived people into thinking that free, inconsequential love and small families were the modern, feminist way to control their bodies. It allowed the real agenda of controlled breeding for human perfection and population management to be accomplished with wide support and participation. She used her mother's hardship of 18 pregnancies that included seven miscarriages to gain credibility. In reality Margaret's progressive ideology was the predecessor that gave birth to Hitler's "perfect race" campaign. (see <u>Finishing The Master Race</u>-Vol.4) As Margaret instructed teenagers in a 1915 handbook, "Stop bringing to birth children whose inheritance cannot be one of health or intelligence."

Sanger continued her crusade against inferior races with an article in <u>Birth Control Review</u> in 1921, sounding remarkably like Nazi propaganda produced by Joseph Goebbels. "The undeniably feebleminded should indeed, not only be discouraged but prevented from propagating their kind." Birth control was intended "to create a race of thoroughbreds" and "must lead ultimately to a cleaner race." She referred to blacks, immigrants and the poor as "human weed" and "reckless breeders", insisting, "we are failing to segregate morons who are increasing and multiplying... a dead weight of human waste... an ever-increasing spawning class of human beings who never should have been born at all." As a good socialist, she contended the state should control who would have the right to bear children.

A quick examination of some of her closest friends, supporters, allies and co-workers, her true goals are unquestionable. Author of <u>The Rising Tide of Color against White Supremacy</u>, colleague Lothrop Stoddard admired how the Nazis were "weeding out the worst strains in the Germanic stock in a scientific and truly humanitarian way." His writings were used in Nazi textbooks. Margaret rewarded him with a seat on the Board of her American Birth Control League. Another Board member, Dr. Harry Laughlin, spoke adamantly of purifying the American breed. He advocated cleansing the gene pool of "bad strains."

In 1939 the regional director of the South of her newly formed Birth Control Federation of America group, Dr. Clarence J. Gamble, of the Procter and Gamble company, proposed the Negro Project which Margaret embraced wholeheartedly. Fearing Negros might reject their cleansing ritual, Gamble suggested seeking out black religious leaders who would rally for their cause. In a letter to Gamble on Dec. 10, 1939, Margaret wrote, "We should hire three or four colored ministers, preferably with social-service backgrounds, and with engaging personalities. The most successful educational approach to the Negro is through a religious appeal. We don't want the word to go out that we want to exterminate the Negro population, and the minister is the man who can straighten out that idea if it ever occurs to any of their more rebellious members."

Supporters claim she wanted to extend birth control to poor blacks and was concerned some might wrongfully conclude they desired to eliminate the race. It's a reasonable argument if she had not stated that she "accepted an invitation to talk to the women's branch of the Ku Klux Klan," boasting "In the end, through simple illustrations I believed I had accomplished my purpose. A dozen invitations to speak to similar groups were proffered." I wonder what message got the KKK so excited they extended 12 more engagements to her on the spot. Her efforts have been successful as black women, who make up only 12.6% of the population, are 3 times more likely to abort their unborn baby that a white woman. In 2009, 35.4% of all abortions were of black babies while 36% were non-Hispanic white, which make up 63.7% of the population.

Probably Margaret's most famous supporter and a contributor to her Birth Control Review was playwright George Bernard Shaw. He stated, "I don't want to punish anybody, but there are an extraordinary number of people who I might want to kill...I think it would be a good thing to make everybody come before a properly appointed board just as he might come before the income tax commissioner and say every 5 years or every 7 years...just put them there and say, 'Sir or madam will you be kind enough to justify your existence...if you're not producing as much as you consume or perhaps a little bit more then clearly we cannot use the big organization of our society for the purpose of keeping you alive. Because your life does not benefit us and it can't be of very much use to yourself.'"

Shaw, sounding remarkably like Nazi Propaganda Minister Goebbels, "...appeal(ed) to the chemists to discover a humane gas that will kill instantly and painlessly. In short- a gentlemanly gas deadly by all means, but humane, not cruel." It is no wonder Shaw admired National Socialist leader Adolf Hitler in his efforts to produce the perfect Aryan race in Germany. They shared a common view of other inferior races and people.

Many abhor Hitler for what he did to the Jews, but few know that he started his cleansing of the German race with the eradication of mentally and physically handicapped people. (see Finishing The Master Race-Vol.4) It did not take long for the Nazis to use Shaw's arguments *to justify the elimination of the weak to the benefit of the 'master race'.*

As much as we detest Hitler's actions, he was merely carrying out the beliefs of Margaret Sanger, George Bernard Shaw, Woodrow Wilson, and Teddy Roosevelt before him. *(see The Birth Of A Nation)* In fact, Hitler acquired the idea of forced sterilization of the mentally handicapped from American laws supported by the Supreme Court. *(see Finishing The Master Race-Vol.4)* Hitler wasn't a lone mad man. He built his foundation of wiping out inferior people through the works and writings of American socialist eugenicists and existing American laws to support his actions in Germany.

Hitler slaughtered 6 million Jews and is considered the most vile man of the 20th Century. Margaret Sanger's efforts have led to 58 million babies being slaughtered since Roe v. Wade and she's hailed as a champion of women's rights. *(see Suffering In Utopia-Vol.6)*

As socialist herself, Margaret's beliefs nurtured Hitler's National Socialists of Germany. *"Eugenic sterilization is an urgent need...We must prevent multiplication of this bad stock."* In an article titled *The Eugenic Value of Birth Control Propaganda*, she wrote, *"Eugenics is...the most adequate and thorough avenue to the solution of racial, political and social problems."*

Margaret was never about a woman's right to control her own reproduction. It was a convenient cover. In an April 1932 *Birth Control Review* piece, Margaret laid out her *"Plan for Peace,"* including:

- to keep the doors of immigration closed to the entrance of certain aliens whose condition is known to be detrimental to the stamina of the race, such as feebleminded, idiots, morons, insane, syphilitic, epileptic, criminal, professional prostitutes, and others in this class barred by the immigration laws of 1924. *(see Coming To America-Vol.7)*

- to apply a stern and rigid policy of sterilization and segregation to that grade of population whose progeny is tainted, or whose inheritance is such that objectionable traits may be transmitted to offspring. *(see Finishing The Master Race-Vol.4)*

- to insure the country against future burdens of maintenance for numerous offspring as may be born of feebleminded parents, by pensioning all persons with transmissible disease who voluntarily consent to sterilization. *(see Finishing The Master Race-Vol.4)*

- to give certain dysgenic groups in our population their choice of segregation or sterilization. *(see Finishing The Master Race-Vol.4)*

- to apportion farm lands and homesteads for these segregated persons where they would be taught to work under competent instructors for the period of their entire lives. (This is nothing less than the rebirth of legalized slavery.)

The last point is nothing less than the rebirth of legalized slavery.

In her March 27, 1934, article for <u>American Weekly</u>, she proclaimed in <u>America Needs a Code for Babies</u>, the following arguments.

Article 1: The purpose of the American Baby Code shall be to provide for a better distribution of babies... and to protect society against the propagation and increase of the unfit.

Article 4: No woman shall have the legal right to bear a child, and no man shall have the right to become a father, without a permit...

Article 6: No permit for parenthood shall be valid for more than one birth.

According to Margaret, "Funds that should be used to raise the standard of our civilization are diverted to the maintenance of those who should never have been born." In her eyes, "Non-Aryan people [of the United States are] a great biological menace to the future of civilization."

Despite Margaret's obvious disdain for blacks, some of the strongest supporters of Planned Parenthood are African-Americans. Her actions and words are excused with barely a consideration. Some forgive her positions on sterilization and eugenics as just common thinking of the time. If you accept this argument, then what did Hitler do that was all that wrong? His actions were nothing more than the perfection and expansion of the popular arguments coming from the brilliant American progressive and socialist thinkers of the time, including Sanger.

Liberty, I am not saying that I am against being responsible in our reproductive habits. God told us to "be fruitful and multiply", but he also demands leadership and faithfulness within the family unit. We were married 19 years before you were born which wasn't by accident. My problem with Margaret Sanger was her desire for "control" to rid the world of "undesirables", striving for the perfect, healthy, intellectual race. Well, we lost that when Adam and Eve sinned.

Every family has members who Margaret would not consider worthy of life. Someone with Downs Syndrome, dwarfism, blindness, deafness, autism, cancer, low IQ, non-Caucasian ancestry, or small government values would be dangers to social evolution. But that *doesn't mean they don't have a purpose.*

Margaret, while believing she was bettering society, was making government a god with the right to decide who was worthy of life and liberty and who wasn't. Now millions of babies are being killed every year because socialist progressives actually took responsibility away from the individual, giving them a quick means of not being held accountable for their actions.

Many are convinced Margaret's motivation was purely for the advancement of women's rights. From her own words and those of her closest friends, I show clear evidence that she believed some people, basically minorities and the poor, were lesser people. That is always the common believe among progressive and socialist elites. However, in God's eyes, we are all the same. We are all sinners, we are all His children, and we are all worthy of life and his forgiveness through His Son Jesus Christ.

That's my 2 cents.

Love,
Mom

February 16, 2015

Dear Liberty,

As a lawyer, he argued a case in front of the Supreme Court and lost. He had already been defeated in five political elections. What in the world could the tall, linky backwoods attorney from Illinois with only a year of formal education be thinking running for President of the United States?

Abraham Lincoln came of age in a country that was increasingly divided over the controversial issues of slavery and state's rights. Acts of Congress and the Supreme Court only poured gasoline on the fire. The Missouri Compromise of 1820 prohibited slavery in the northern land of the Louisiana Territory, except within the Missouri boarders. This bill held things at bay until the Kansas-Nebraska Act of 1854 negated the terms of the Compromise. (see <u>Deal Of A Lifetime</u>-Vol.3, <u>Charting A New Course</u>-Vol.6, and <u>Abolishing Mistakes</u>-Vol.6) The act of Congress resulted in a violent and bloody struggle between pro- and anti-slavery settlers and gave birth to the Republican Party. Composed of both Democrats and Whigs, the new party attracted people who were tired of politicians promising to end slavery but never actually doing anything about it. (see <u>The Birth Of A Movement</u>-Vol. 1)

One such person was Abraham Lincoln. Before 1854 his views on slavery were not overly strong. But like his new fellow Republican Party members, the 1854 legislation forced people to take a hard stand as to what this country would tolerate.

The final blow came in the 1857 Supreme Court ruling of Scott vs. Sandford. (see <u>Dreadful Scott Decision</u>-Vol.4) Chief Justice Roger B. Taney delivered an opinion that put the country on the threshold of war. He claimed that because Dred Scott was a Negro, he could not file a federal lawsuit. Taney declared that Negros, whether free or slave, would never be citizens of the United States. Taney, who served in the Andrew Jackson administration, declared the Missouri Compromise as well as the Kansas-Nebraska Act unconstitutional. In one fell swoop Justice Taney removed all ability from the anti-slavery movement to even limit, let alone stop, the spread of slavery across the entire country. Southerners claimed victory, touting Taney had made the Jacksonian Democratic conduct of the South national policy. Abolitionists charged Taney of furthering "Slave Power", which allowed wealthy slave owners to use political power to obtain slavery in free states.

Justice Taney argued that the Founders never intended for Negros, regardless of slave status, to be citizens. He decided they were excluded from the inalienable rights granted by God as stated in the Declaration of Independence and the Constitution. *(see Inalienable Rights-Vol.5, Happy Independence Day-Vol.1, Constitution Day and Founding Documents-Vol.7)* In rebuttal, Justice Benjamin Curtis from Massachusetts was quick to point out that from the time of the Founders there were free Negros in Northern states. These Negros were not only citizens of those states, but voters as well. As state citizens, they were automatically national citizens.

In June of 1858, the Republican Party chose Abraham Lincoln as their candidate to run against Democrat Stephen A. Douglas for U.S. Senate in Illinois. Douglas was co-author of the Kansas-Nebraska Act, which Republicans saw as a pro-slavery abduction of power. Political tensions were obvious and quickly moving towards war. Lincoln was passionate and direct about the reality of the country's future in his "House Divided" Speech at the Republican Convention. He firmly believed "this government cannot endure, permanently half slave and half free." He promptly provided evidence that Democrats were using the national government to force slavery in every state.

While the speech may have cost him the Senate race, it was likely the beginning of his 1860 Presidential win. Regardless, it was a brave and courageous speech. Lincoln outlined the argument that Justice Taney, Senator Douglas, President Buchanan and Former President Franklin Pierce delayed and misguided the American people regarding the upcoming Dred Scott decision so as to win the Presidency. *(see Dreadful Scott Decision-Vol.4)* He pointed out the reluctance of these Democrat politicians to make any concrete statements regarding the Dred Scott decision before the election. After the election, both Pierce and Buchanan implored citizens to accept the ruling, whatever it may be. Furthermore, it was not only endorsed by Douglas, he also "vehemently denounc(ed) all opposition to it." In his speech, Lincoln had made a sound case that these pro-slavery Democrats were working in concert to make slavery legal everywhere.

Lincoln argued that Douglas' Kansas-Nebraska bill allowed for a situation where, "if any one man, choose to enslave another, no third man shall be allowed to object." With the Democratic bill in place, Lincoln warned the Dred Scott ruling would put the country at a tipping point. It was now not a question of state's rights, but if the Supreme Court would force free states to become slave ones.

Even though Senators were chosen by State Legislatures, Lincoln challenged Douglas to a series of seven public debates, known as the Lincoln-Douglas debates. *(see The New Trinity-Vol.3)* The two main topics would be the pressure points of the Civil War: slavery and state's rights. Lincoln repeatedly returned to his convention theme of "A house divided against itself cannot stand" while Douglas held firm to "popular sovereignty." Also debated was the contentious opinion revealed in the Dred Scott ruling of the Founders intent for Negros.

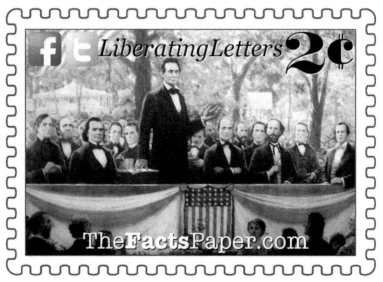

Douglas agreed with Taney's argument, while Lincoln insisted the God-given rights identified in the Declaration of Independence, including "life, liberty, and the pursuit of happiness" equally applied to Negros. (see <u>Happy Independence Day</u>-Vol.1 and <u>Founding Documents</u>-Vol.7) Douglas used Lincoln's friendship with outspoken Negro activist Frederick Douglass to paint his Republican opponent not only as an abolitionist, but as one who desired "negro equality and negro citizenship." (see <u>Reading, Writing, and Redemption</u>-Vol.3)

As Lincoln had warned, the Dred Scott decision put states in direct opposition with the federal government. Despite the federal ruling the State Supreme Court of Ohio decreed that any non-runaway slave who crossed their state boarder would be declared free and would keep that freedom even if they returned to a slave state. This decision was mirrored by a New York Court of Appeals. Soon the legislatures in other states began to echo Ohio's court decision. Maine's judges ruled Negros could vote in all elections, both federal and state.

Lincoln was clear in his views towards slavery, but lost his bid for the Senate. The citizens of Illinois elected Democrats to their state congress, which in turn sent Douglas back to Washington. Lincoln published the texts of the debate speeches between Douglas and himself. The debates were read by thousands and built a strong foundation of Lincoln's view towards freedom for all.

Two years later the country chose him over Douglas and two

other opponents, making him the 16th President of the United States. Lincoln won both the popular vote and the electoral votes despite not even being listed on the ballots of 10 Southern states. Fears of "Slave Power" also swept the new Republican Party into the majority of both Houses of Congress. Fearing Lincoln and the Republicans would remove all the political strength they had just grabbed with the Dred Scott decision, Southern Democrats resolved to separate from the Union. (see Sibling Rivalry-Vol.7 and Constituting Slavery-Vol.6)

Today, Lincoln remains one of the most significant Presidents to ever serve in office. He not only presided over a country at war, but a country at war with itself. After decades of contention and four years of a bloody, exhausting conflict, many Union Congressmen were angry, vengeful, and intent on punishing those who brought the country to its knees.

Furious over the deplorable treatment of Union soldiers captured in the South, several were resolved to insure that Confederate soldiers would be returned home in kind. Lincoln could not ignore the teachings of his most treasured book, the Bible. In his second Inaugural Address, just six weeks before his assassination by a Southern Democrat, he encouraged the citizens to move forward "With malice toward none, with charity for all, with firmness in the right as God gives us to see the right, let us strive on to finish the work we are in, to bind up the nation's wounds, to care for him who shall have borne the battle and for his widow and his orphan, to do all which may achieve and cherish a just and lasting peace among ourselves and with all nations." Lincoln recognized that for the country to survive it was imperative that everyone focus on forgiveness and reconciliation, embracing our brothers and sisters in love as prodigal children coming home. (see God's Divine Providence-Vol.3)

In his final public speech, just days before his murder, Lincoln again turned to our Heavenly Father in praise reminiscent of the pilgrims. "He, from Whom all blessings flow, must not be forgotten. A call for a national thanksgiving is being prepared, and will be duly promulgated." He again called for reconciliation, uniting with fellow citizens and not ostracizing them. "Let us all join in doing the acts necessary to restoring the proper practical relations between these states and the Union." (see Civility War Ends-Vol.5 and Conspiracy Theories-Vol.7)

Liberty, with a current president who said, "We're gonna punish our enemies and we're gonna reward our friends who stand with us on issues that are important to us," it is no wonder our country feels like it is again on the verge of another Civil War. Many are crying out for our generations' Abraham Lincoln. While politicians are dividing us into groups, pitting us against each other, we can find guidance in Lincoln's words. As he did, we must follow our Heavenly Father's plan for us of love towards our fellow man. We have all enslaved others with our words and actions and we are all slaves to our sinful nature.

Lincoln is considered one of our greatest presidents. Greatness is not a quality most people possess, it is a quality that is usually thrust upon a reluctant participant. It comes from humility, not arrogance. It comes from the desire to serve, not the lust to control. It comes from the craving to build up, not the hunger to tear down. It is a trait that when the times call for it, it shows itself in strength, reason, and courage. Abraham Lincoln was a great leader not because he won elections or fought on the battlefield, but because he submitted himself to God's will for us, calling for a uniting in our country in a time where division seemed the only solution.

Liberty, in a time where the country seems even more divided than it was in the mid-1800's, I pray the Lord blesses us with another great leader. I pray that my generation is able to pass a unified country on to you where we have learned to love our neighbor as ourselves.

That's my 2 cents.

Love,
Mom

February 25, 2015

Dear Liberty,

Barack Obama stated last week that, "Here in America, Islam has been woven into the fabric of our country since its founding."

He is correct. Islam is deeply woven into the tapestry of America. However, he conveniently left out how it is woven into our fabric. It is the root cause of slavery in America and led to our first foreign war, prompting the creation of the Department of Navy and the Marine Corps, or corpse as Obama likes to say.

At the turn of the 19th century when Thomas Jefferson became president, Muslims were terrorizing Western countries with piracy. Muslims cited their religion as their basis to torture and enslave infidels. Anyone outside of Islam was targeted as well as Muslims who were not Muslim enough. Jefferson tried to placate the extremists by paying exorbitant extortion fees along with ransoms for captured sailors and goods as his predecessors had before him. In fact, President Washington was paying up to 16% of the Federal Budget to the Barbary States when he left office.

Jefferson tried to understand the extreme behavior of Muslims by reading the Qur'an. After reading their holy book, he realized there was no satisfying the fanatics who were simply hell bent on killing. Rather than deny Islam or shield people from the truth, President Jefferson advised every American to read the Qur'an. He did not promote it for Americans to appreciate and accept Islam, but to understand its fanaticism and what America was fighting against. He even wrote in his copy of the introduction, "If you read this book, you will have nothing but contempt for Islamic law."

Years before, in a letter to John Jay in 1786, Jefferson wrote about what he and John Adams learned about Islam's motivation for the unprovoked attacks from the Ambassador of Tripoli: "The Ambassador answered us that it was founded on the Laws of their Prophet, that it was written in their Koran, that all nations who should not have acknowledged their authority were sinners, that it was their right and duty to make war upon them wherever they could be found, and to make slaves of all they could take as Prisoners, and that every Musselman [Muslim] who should be slain in battle was sure to go to

Paradise." George Washington's reply to the Ambassador's statement was, "Would to heaven we had a Navy able to reform those enemies of mankind (Muslims), or crush them into non-existence." In 1796 Washington called for Congress to form the Navy, which was created two years later under President John Adams.

After the Muslim terrorists captured, tortured and enslaved American sailors, President Jefferson decided to stop paying the Barbary States' bribes. Tripoli then declared war on America on May 10, 1801. Jefferson finally had to fund the US Navy and the Marines after years of opposing extensive military financing. In 1805 the Marines, also known as leathernecks, led a victorious campaign to free captured sailors in the Battle of Derna on "the shores of Tripoli" during the First Barbary War. (see To The Shores Of Tripoli-Vol.3) Marines earned the name "Leathernecks" due to the leather collars they wore to protect their necks against Islamic cutlasses meant to behead the enemy. Some things never change.

So yes, Obama was right. Islam is woven into America's fabric from its founding. Islamists have been terrorizing and torturing Americans from our inception and we have been fighting the extremist religion since Jefferson.

Unlike Jefferson, Obama is excusing radical Islam instead of desiring to defeat it. Obama even suggested we cannot condemn today's militant Islamist because Christians were violent against Muslims during the Crusades 1000 years ago. Again, he likes to leave out the full story. What he failed to mention was that the Crusades were the Christians' response to Muslim attacks on innocent travelers to the Holy Lands. Decades of unprovoked raids by Muslims on major Christian cities, overthrowing and overtaking them, also inspired Christian Crusaders. You simply have to question Obama's true knowledge of history and his motives as well. (see A Crusade For The Truth)

Last week Obama's State Department spokesman Marie Harf informed America that we cannot defeat the terrorists by killing them. We need to address the root problem, which she claims is poverty. We need to find them jobs. When asked a day later to clarify, she proceeded to degrade anyone critical of her strategy claiming they were just not sophisticated enough to really appreciate her brilliant plan for defeating ISIS. However, her statements aren't consistent with the facts. Osama bin Laden, the world's most wanted terrorist, came from a very wealthy family. Many, like bin Laden, convert to Islam to fight for the caliphate because of religious reasons, not socioeconomic causes.

Ms. Harf, like most progressives, believes that all the evil in the world stems from wealth disparity. It's been said that if the only tool you have is a hammer everything looks like a nail. In a similar fashion, with a socialist worldview it's reasonable to use poverty as the hammer and sickle as the cause of all the world's problems. But lack of jobs isn't the root of Islamic terrorism. The Islamic religion commands them to enslave others, kill infidels and bring about a caliphate, or one Islamic state.

In the recent letter, <u>The Color-Blindness Of Slavery</u>, I told you about the first legal slave owner, Anthony Johnson. He was originally captured in his native Angola and sold to Arab slave traders. The abductors were Muslims and were responsible for capturing Africans that eventually ended up at America's shores as slaves. Muslims were the backbone of the slave trade. Is this part of the amazing contribution that Islam made to this country that Obama so praised? If so, it would support Obama's claim that poverty leads to terror. After all, we destroyed the Muslims' economic foundation. We did it by eliminating slavery. We took away their jobs.

Our Administration is full of Ivy League scholars who have spent years developing their Utopian strategies for the world. All that has to happen is to level the playing field for everyone and everyone will be happy, or at least equally miserable. Social elitists are so wrapped up in their own brilliance and enlightenment that they are blinded to the reality of radical Islam, because it's outside their worldview.

Secretary of State John Kerry lectured ISIS saying, "This is the 21st century and we should not see nations step backwards to behave in 19th and 20th century fashion." That is great if we have risen above such barbaric means of warfare, but Kerry doesn't have the willingness to accept that these radical Muslims haven't. Radical Islamists prove it daily as they burn, behead, and crucify those that deny Allah in a manner reminiscent of Genghis Kahn.

If the leaders of our country don't wake up, we will actually fall because of our own arrogance. A few days before Harf's comments, some "rogue, isolated" ISIS members beheaded 21 Coptic Christians from Egypt on the shores of Tripoli. (see <u>To The Shores Of Tripoli-Vol.3</u>) Liberal elitists have been preaching to the unwashed masses that we should not fight the terrorists that hate us. We need to befriend them and understand them. (see <u>D-Day vs. Today: How Far We've Come-Vol.1</u>) Perhaps we should send in a wave of Peace Corps volunteers rather than Thomas Jefferson's barbaric response to terrorists two centuries ago of using Marines.

The simple fact is, only our response has changed, not their tactics. Radical Islamists want to kill us because their leader, the prophet Mohammad, demands that infidels be slaughtered. These beheadings are not isolated incidences for ISIS, they are the norm for

Islamists throughout history.

By conducting the beheadings on the Tripoli shores, ISIS is telling the world they want a Third Barbary War. They laid down the gauntlet to America telling the Marines "Come and get us." In response, Obama went golfing.

This administration refuses to look this evil in the face. Instead it fights nonsense battles against global warming, even as the country suffers under record breaking cold and snow. By not acknowledging evil and truly opposing ISIS, this administration, along with other European countries, is permitting ISIS to continue its killing spree. Unless we wake up and turn back to God, we are allowing ISIS to get stronger and more powerful to the world's detriment.

That's my 2 cents.

Love,
Mom

March 5, 2015

Dear Liberty,

On February 26, 2015, the FCC captured our last real frontier of freedom while the majority of Americans cheered and celebrated its surrender. They supported a non-

elected panel of five people accept 302 pages of regulations, which they refused to let the American people see until after the vote.

Utopian promises and glowing claims of cheaper costs, better service and less restrictions captivated many unsuspecting followers like Michael Moore to a jelly donut. Unfortunately people didn't hear the similar rhythm of another song and dance performed regarding another bill that needed to pass before we could see what was in it. "If you like your doctor, you can keep your doctor." "If you like your plan, you can keep your plan." "Healthcare costs will go down, saving families $2500." "Services will be much better." Well, we found out what was in it and it was even worse than was warned about.

Government regulation rarely if ever saves money. That's just economics 101. Proponents claimed it would allow less regulation on the Internet. However, the Internet was already an open platform without regulation. The Internet was the freest market America had seen since Woodrow Wilson began to chip away at freedom. Anyone who has an idea and the motivation can start a web business. That will all end quickly when the FCC requires applications and licenses for each new business. Along with fees, other FCC requirements, and application denials by bureaucrats, small businesses will be squashed all over the country.

But that's just the beginning. Opponents warning of content freedom being suppressed were mocked and ridiculed by supporters. It took only the weekend after it passed for the truth to start coming out. The details of the FCC package were finally reviewed and revealed to the American public. Those demanding and cheering this power grab are now becoming worried that the freedom they professed would remain is in fact eroding. Google confirmed content control warnings as they already try to get search results regulated. They want the most factual sites to come up first instead of the most popular. But who decides that? My letters are extensively researched for authenticity. I have spoken out strongly against evolution (see <u>Sleeping Beauty</u>-Vol.1, <u>The Science Is Settled</u>, <u>Is There Any Intelligent Life Out There?</u>, <u>Leap Of</u>

Faith-Vol.3, and *Evolution Explodes-Vol.4), global warming (see The Science Is Settled, Part II,* and *Actions Speak Louder Than Words-Vol.1), gay marriage (see We Reserve The Right To Refuse Service-Vol.1, What Is Love?,* and *Separation Of Church And State*), liberalism, Obama (see *Glass Houses-Vol.1, Robbin' Hood: The Prince Of Thieves* and *Wolves In Sheep's Clothing*), government overreach and Islamic radicalism (see *Family Feud-Vol.1, COEXIST, Washington, Adams, And Mohammad: Our Founding Fathers, Holocaust: Then & Now, I Am Garland, A Crusade For The Truth, To The Shores Of Tripoli-Vol.3*). Since all these stances go against the government, will my opposition be enough for my letters be considered less factual than the "accepted" view to the powers that be? Google already does such things for the Chinese government. How long until it is labeled "hate speech?"

As they said in *All the President's Men*, "Follow the Money". Who is behind the scenes pushing and funding this FCC control? The list is a who's who of socialist organizations and people: Media Matters, Open Society Foundations (George Soros), Ford Foundation, Center for American Progress, Free Press, Mark Lloyd, formerly of the FCC, and the White House, to name just a few. Together Soros and the Ford Foundation gave $196 million to groups supporting the measure. Most of the driving force can be traced back to extreme Liberal groups, many who follow Saul Alinsky's Socialist and Communist teachings, pushing for "public" control of the media. It sounds good. Yet when socialists use the word "public" it means "government", as in public sector vs private sector. To urge public ownership sounds like citizens are allowed to control it. However, that is the very definition of free private markets. Public means the government controls it and the people lose their rights to it. Socialists constantly pervert the language to mislead. As Hitler said, "By the skillful and sustained use of propaganda, one can make a people see even heaven as hell or an extremely wretched life as paradise."

One of the supporters of Net Neutrality is Free Press founder and former editor of *Monthly Review, An Independent Socialist Magazine*, Robert McChesney. McChesney's tactics mimic Lenin who used the Russian paper, *Pravda*, ironically meaning "truth", to push his Communist agenda. Lenin exerted editorial control over the paper using it as an indoctrination tool for the communist revolution. (see *Communism's Rise-Vol.5*) Robert also uses his publications for propaganda. The erroneously named Free Press was a main driving force of Net Neutrality. Proclaiming capitalism killed journalism due to the industrialization of the media, he believes owners of papers controlled the information released. He believes that information belongs to the public. What is his definition of public? He wants the government managing the news instead of free citizens, just like Lenin. This is why he has no problem with the intimidation, threats and even jailing of journalists by this administration. Socialists can never allow *journalists to report honestly on their actions. Only the free and private Internet reporters have been able to openly reveal and warn the American people of the true actions of our government.*

Mark Lloyd, a former Center for American Progress employee, was appointed FCC Chief Diversity Officer in 2009. Completely open about his advocacy for public media, he reveled in the position created just for him at the FCC. After Venezuelan President Hugo Chavez began financially choking groups critical of his regime and revoking over 200 radio licenses, Lloyd praised Chavez's success in taking control of news outlets critical of his policies. Lloyd has been intimately involved in championing Net Neutrality for the FCC, claiming individual Internet freedom for the people while praising dictatorial government domination.

Sharyl Attkisson, former CBS News reporter, exposed that major, damning stories were ignored by CBS news executives. Her reports were buried, including a highly incriminating Benghazi investigation. She watched as her computer was hacked and valuable research was targeted and erased. The President of CBS News, who is conveniently the brother of a top Obama Official, repeatedly covered up damaging reports by Sharyl and others. Now Sharyl is a free private reporter and is exposing the truth of our government. Thanks to McChesney and Lloyd, Net Neutrality just gave government the power to discredit, shut down and silence those "unofficial" private journalists like Attkisson.

The future of Net Neutrality can be plainly seen by looking at the history of the FCC, radio and television broadcasting. Until the creation of the Federal Radio Commission (FRC) in 1926, people could transmit private radio programs from their own home on the AM band. Anything could be aired. When the FRC was created it was given the authority to regulate and assign frequency levels and approve or reject broadcaster's licenses. This power gave bureaucrats control over content. Groups claiming commercial media dominated programing insisted that there must be equality in programming through regulation, overriding free market demand. Quality and advancement was stifled as the government implemented more and more regulations, allowing politics to dictate the media's behavior. The Radio Act of 1927 mandated stations give equal opportunities for all political candidates, suppressing political freedom. To avoid the problem, AM radio was eventually reduced to cooking, repair and other unpopular shows. Even today the FCC continues to flex its muscles by threatening broadcasting licenses over programming choices.

The FCC is comprised of five members, each representing a geographical radio zone. The 1928 David Amendment to the Radio Act required each of these zones to have the same number of licenses, operation times, station power, and wavelength. As a result, qualified applicants were denied licenses because it would violate the zone's quota. Heavily populated areas were forced to tolerate the same number of stations as the sparsely populated regions. Instead of letting free market demand dictate station supply, "fairness" and "equality" was enforced.

In 1934, the FRC was replaced by the Federal Communications Commission (FCC), which instituted the Fairness Doctrine for both radio and television in 1949. It required both mediums to offer opposing views without insisting on equal time for those presentations. What's to stop the FCC from implementing the same "fairness" and "equality" requirements with individual Internet sites? As the media outlets became more and more liberal, whole segments would be devoted to their agenda with only a simple statement of contrast given as the counter, usually in the last paragraph. Due to government control there were no options for conservative or libertarian alternatives.

This policy remained intact until its dismantling by the 1987 FCC panel. The Democratic controlled Congress passed a law to keep the Fairness Doctrine in place but President Reagan vetoed it. With a freer market back in play, consumers thirsting for their voices to be represented sent Rush Limbaugh to the top of the ratings charts. FoxNews was overwhelming received by citizens, filling a much neglected void for the American people.

As the Internet became an impactful information vehicle in the mid-1990's, the Clinton White House wrote a memo warning of the influence and damage this unregulated medium could pose to their news monopoly. Once Matt Drudge exposed President Clinton's sexual relationship with an intern in 1998, all their fears became a reality. The strictly controlled media monopoly was in serious jeopardy. Washington elitists, both Democrats and some Republicans, secretly desired to limit the Internet. Mainstream media and liberals began their attack on unlicensed, unrestricted and uninhibited writers and still claims Fox News is not really news. Sarah Palin said it best, "The real reason they feared him (Drudge) was because he wasn't beholden to the old media's machine and the Thought Police. Unshackled, he was free."

Furious that radio personalities such as Rush, Sean Hannity, Glenn Beck and others dominated talk radio, Nancy Pelosi tried again in 2009 to revive the Fairness Doctrine. After the liberal Air America failed to gain any sort of following, Nancy insisted on government regulation to ensure "fairness" over the airwaves. Apparently forcing you to consume their viewpoint would "level the playing field." Net Neutrality is just the Fairness Doctrine for the Internet.

By giving the government the power to pick winners and losers, people like William Randolph Hearst are chosen to control the information that actually reaches the masses. Practicing a type of reporting dubbed "yellow journalism", Hearst used sensational headlines and fabricated stories to manipulate public opinion and sell his newspaper. He became so powerful, he was able to boldly tell his artist, "You furnish the pictures and I'll furnish the war." (see Yellow Journalism: The Birth Of Fake News-Vol.6)

In 1968, because there was no accountability through alternative media due to the Fairness Doctrine, Walter Cronkite reported that the Tet Offensive in the Vietnam War was a defeat for South Vietnam and America. With no one willing or able to contradict Cronkite, the most respected man in television news, the lie flourished becoming a turning point for American support for the war. Some say he single-handedly lost a war America had already won. The power of such propaganda is so strong that to this day most people still believe we lost the Tet Offensive. The truth was it was a complete disaster for North Vietnam. Cronkite's reporting turned an overwhelming American victory into an embarrassing defeat. Hitler maintained, "If you tell a big enough lie and tell it frequently enough, it will be believed." This can only be achieved with government control of the media as Lenin, Alinsky, McChesney, Lloyd, and Obama believe.

Knowing that regulation of content would be impossible to garner wide support by the people, those like McChesney and Lloyd argued that if we got rid of the Net Neutrality concept, the Internet would fall apart. Net Neutrality was critical to the future of the Internet and government regulation was the only fix. At the forefront was the Comcast-Netflix argument. Netflix, a favorite online streaming service, *began dominating Comcast's available bandwidth forcing other Comcast customers to suffer. To keep production up Comcast decided Netflix should pay their fair share, which was why Netflix started pushing for regulation. They didn't want to pay their fair share for a product they are using. People adamant in ensuring nothing would interrupt their video streaming of* <u>The Walking Dead</u>*, jumped on board Netflix's cause. However, the free market allowed Netflix to negotiate with Comcast and the two companies came to an agreement resolving the issue without government interference. Having the government force Comcast to provide a service for a fixed cost regardless of client usage, which this regulation promises to do, is hardly free market. The truth is nothing was in danger until the FCC bill was passed.*

Another Net Neutrality argument was it would prevent monopolies, keeping big businesses from demanding higher prices and reducing service to the consumer. Unfortunately, big businesses like Netflix and Comcast are already in bed with the government. Many of them even had input in the Net Neutrality package. If this was truly about preventing monopolies, then why is the FCC still likely to pass several impactful mergers including Comcast and Time Warner, allowing them to become one major monopoly?

That's my 2 cents.

Love,
Mom

March 12, 2015

Dear Liberty,

It's a familiar refrain used by those who want to control what you think - The science is settled.

The science is settled!! The world is flat. Thankfully Christopher Columbus did not agree. (see <u>What Is Columbus Day?</u>-Vol.1)

The science is settled!! The universe revolves around the Earth. Galileo was kept under house arrest for 8 years for suggesting the Sun was the center of the universe. (see <u>The Science Is Settled, Part II</u>)

The science is settled!! Pluto is a planet. A simple fact taught to every grade school child. However, it was the willingness to challenge accepted ideas that led scientists to conclude Pluto is not a planet, but actually just an icy object in the Kuiper Belt.

The science is settled!! The atom is the smallest particle in existence. Once scientists had the equipment to look inside, our world exploded with electrons, neutrons, and protons.

The science is settled!! Life began through spontaneous generation. Louis Pasteur scientifically debunked this scientific theory in 1859. Through experimentation he disproved that maggots formed spontaneously out of raw meat, yet spontaneous generation continues to be the basis of evolution. (see <u>Sleeping Beauty</u>-Vol.1)

The science is settled!! The Brontosaurus existed millions of years ago. Scientists discovered in 1903 that the dinosaur was actually the Apatosaurus with the wrong head placed on it. However, museums continued to display the inaccurate dinosaur until 1979. The Brontosaurus was taught to children in textbooks even later than that.

The science is settled!! The Big Bang Theory is the only scientific explanation for the formation of the universe. Anyone denying it is not a true scientist. It was only after scientists were willing to challenge that belief that scientific discovery could be made. Last month scientists revealed that they couldn't explain matter developing out of nothing or why there was an explosion at all. Critics have always questioned the legitimacy of the theory for this very reason only to be mocked, discredited, and charged with hating science. Since they can't explain it, *scientists now accept that the universe has always existed. (see Keeping The Faith-Vol.3)*

The science is settled!! The globe is warming because of humans. Even though the temperature has not increased in 16 years, global warming is supposedly the most dangerous issue humans are facing. Liberty, this is nothing more than a power grab from the elites. If they were really concerned about it, they would practice what they preached. They don't. They regulate our cars and gas mileage, oil production, and corporate emissions while they take their private jets on vacations, to campaign rallies and to Global Warming Conferences during snowstorms of Biblical proportions. (see Actions Speak Lauder Than Words-Vol.1 and The Science Is Settled, Part II)

The science is settled!! Everything evolved from a single-celled organism. Even though there are hundreds of "missing links" that science conveniently fills in with their speculations of what happened, supporters cling to the theory as truth. The Cambrian Explosion, where all forms of life appeared in a single stratum without transitions, was known by science prior to Darwin's writing on evolution. He acknowledged that it was the single greatest threat to his theory, but hoped that future scientific discovery would prove him right. However, as scientific knowledge grew, it only went to disprove his theory all the more. The Cambrian Explosion, along with other scientific evidence disproving evolution are presented by scientists in the book and movie Icons of Evolution. Despite overwhelming scientific evidence contradicting evolution, the theory remains forced on children in schools and those that have an open mind to ask if life may have been created are treated with disdain. (see Is There Any Intelligent Life Out There? and Inherit The Truth-Vol.3)

When proponents declare that the science is settled, scientific discovery is exterminated. Science proves theories by actually trying to disprove them. Examples are actively searched for that negate a concept. Using the Scientific Method, experiments are conducted with the specific purpose to refute an hypothesis. Data is collected and examined. If these experiments fail, then the theory has actually been validated. Pseudoscience does just the opposite by looking only for confirmations of a theory and avoiding challenges. Welcome to the world of global warming and evolution.

Global warming activists have already declared their hypothesis as truth, only accepting data that supports their conclusion. This is quite frankly not only back-asswards, it's anything but science. After it was revealed that data was manipulated and falsified, the global warming theory has begun to unravel among the majority of people. It is those with an agenda that keep pushing the ideology along with irrelevant solutions. The proof is so overwhelming that the theory is false, activists had to relabel it as climate change as massive snow storms strike every single one of their global warming conferences. Here's an idea, schedule your meetings during the summer. If you really understood weather it would be easier to convince people it's getting warmer during July. That is, if they can't remember last July.

In fact, the mask has completely fallen off of the movement to the point that the activists are now open about their intentions. Christiana Figueres, the U.N.'s Executive Secretary on Climate Change, admitted that the objective of pushing global warming is not to save the planet, but to tear down capitalism. She stated, "This is the first time in the history of mankind that we are setting ourselves the task of intentionally, within a defined period of time, to change the economic development model that has been reigning for at least 150 years, since the Industrial Revolution." Global warming is not about science, it's about attacking freedom. (see One World Disorder-Vol.5)

There are only two so-called sciences today that required a "settled science" label: global warming and evolution. Contrary evidence and data is considered criminal. Activists undermine anyone who exposes proof and facts debunking these theories, claiming they are deniers who hate science. Yet it is they who are shutting out true analysis and rejecting scientific discovery.

Why? Why would scientists oppose science? Why aren't they interested the truth? In reality it is not all scientists who are claiming consensus. If that were true Pluto would still be a planet and the Big Bang Theory would still be considered valid. It's radicals pushing an agenda who are trying to silence the opposition. As global warming is meant to destroy capitalism, evolution is meant to destroy God. This is evident in the quotes I cited in the letter Sleeping Beauty (Vol.1).

"There are only two possibilities as to how life arose; one is spontaneous generation arising to evolution, the other is a supernatural creative act of God, there is no third possibility. Spontaneous generation that life arose from non-living matter was scientifically disproved 120 years ago by Louis Pasteur and others. That leaves us with only one possible conclusion, that life arose as a creative act of God. I will not accept that philosophically because I do not want to believe in God, therefore I choose to believe in that which I know is scientifically impossible, spontaneous generation arising to evolution." "One has only to contemplate the magnitude of this task to concede that the spontaneous generation of a living organism is impossible. Yet we are here—as a result, I believe, of spontaneous generation." Dr. George Wald, a Professor of Biology at the University of Harvard, Nobel Prize winner in medicine and stanch evolutionist.

Militant anti-Christian physical anthropologist Sir Arthur Keith declared, "Evolution is unproved and improvable, we believe it because the only alternative is special creation, which is unthinkable."

Satan is not pulling any punches, Liberty. He will use anything he can to get everyone, especially believers, to deny God. There are churches that claim the Bible is the Word of God yet promote evolution. They believe they are supporting science. Most don't know that scientists stating otherwise loose their grants, positions, tenure, and jobs. When money controls the outcome, true science cannot exist.

As Ken Hamm told Bill Nye the Science Guy though, "There is a book." It is not a science book, per se, but true science can never go against it. It is impossible for the secular world to allow even the possibility of a Biblical explanation being true, as that would open the door that God is actually real. All Satan needs to do is put enough doubt in the minds of believers on something as simple as creation and then he can get the believer to second guess everything in the Bible, including the life of Jesus Christ.

The Big Bang Theory has been the accepted science for decades. We were told there was a consensus. It is taught in school as fact and will be for years to come. Just because science hasn't found a reason for the phenomenon yet doesn't mean there isn't one. There is an answer. Matter did in fact form out of nothing as soon as God said, "Let there be..."

Liberty, I have given you repeated examples of settled scientific theories that have been proven otherwise. Never stop searching for the truth. Don't stand with the majority because it is easy. It is those that take a hard stance that change the world. It was Columbus who challenged conventional thought and discovered America. It was Galileo who was imprisoned for his beliefs who led us to the moon. It was Louis Pasteur who not only scientifically disproved the heart of evolution, his scientific discoveries lead to the principles of vaccination, germ theory of disease, and the pasteurization of food that allowed for massive economic development. Stand strong on your beliefs even if you are in the minority because it is not this world to which you need to conform.

That's my 2 cents.

Love,
Mom

March 18, 2015

Dear Liberty,

When Democrat Woodrow Wilson walked into the White House in March of 1913, his supporters believed the South was going to rise again. So did he. The first Southern President to be elected since 1848, Wilson was determined to return the country to pre-Civil War days of Southern Glory. With the loss of the Civil War, slave states lost most of their influence and power, as they were no longer able to count slaves for House representation without actually representing Negros. (see *The New Trinity*-Vol.3) For Wilson and the Democrats, it was time to put things right again.

Even though states where given the freedom to determine their own segregation laws, the federal government had made amazing strides during the Reconstruction Era as the Republicans fought for racial equality. (see *America's Voting Record*-Vol.3 and *Civil Rights...And Wrongs*-Vol.5) Negros worked side by side with White counterparts, receiving the same privileges, advancements, and titles. To gain Negro support, Wilson promised more equality and rights, hiding his true motives from the public. In actuality, his goal was to spread the Southern Jim Crow laws to the entire country.

Once in office, Wilson set the model for the progressive movement to this day, immediately appointing officials who destroyed the advancements made by the Negros and Republicans since the end of the war. Federal workplaces, restrooms, and cafeterias were again segregated in the offices of the Postmaster General, Treasury and Navy. A glass ceiling was put in place to kept high-level public positions well out of reach of Negros, unlike with previous Republican administrations. The highly intellectual Wilson professed that segregation reduced friction between the races, and he "sincerely believe(d) it to be in their interest". State governmental offices in the South freely banished Negro workers altogether with the blessing of the White House.

Two years into his presidency, Wilson had the honor of hosting the first motion picture screening at the White House on March 21, 1915. His movie of choice was *The Birth Of A Nation*, an adaptation of *The Clansman*, a book written by former classmate, friend, and political supporter Thomas Dixon. As a silent movie, dialog and other statements were written on the screen for viewers to read. It is no surprise Wilson chose this movie as it included quotes from his own book, *History of the American People*:

"...Adventurers swarmed out of the North, as much the enemies of the one race as of the other, to cozen, beguile, and use the negroes...In the villages the negroes were the office holders, men who knew none of the use of authority, except its insolences."

"The white men were roused by a mere instinct of self-preservation...until at last there had sprung into existence a great Ku Klux Klan, a veritable empire of the South, to protect the Southern country."

Also included was the statement: "The result. The Ku Klux Klan, the organization that saved the South from the anarchy of black rule, but not without the shedding of more blood than at Gettysburg, according to Judge Tourgee of the carpet-baggers."

Director D.W. Griffith glorified <u>The Clansman</u> with his movie adaptation, portraying Negros as violent and uncivilized. The defeated white Southerners were depicted as being defenseless against the freed Negros who searched out white women for sexual brutality. Whites were terrified until the honorable and upright Ku Klux Klan rode in to save the day. If you were going to make a movie that showed the complete

antithesis of reality, The Birth Of A Nation would be it. Wilson, in his excitement after the screening, proclaimed, "It is like writing history with lightning, and my only regret is that it is all so terribly true."

Upon the movie's release, Dixon stated, "The real purpose of my film was to revolutionize Northern audiences that would transform every man into a Southern partisan for life." He succeeded. The movie sparked protests and riots across the country. Believing Dixon's abominable lies, white mobs left the movie theaters in search for innocent Negros they could take revenge on. There was even at least one murder as a result.

The KKK, which had been virtually dead for over 40 years, was reborn because of the movie. The hate group and muscle of the Southern Democrats grew from basically nothing to 6 million members within 10 years. Thank you, Mr. Wilson, for your Progressive Democrat mindset. It's alive and well today and marching through the streets of Ferguson, Missouri. (see Just The Facts, Ma'am-Vol.1)

The same pathetic, dangerous, and deadly racial deception is happening today and is being perpetrated once again by a Progressive Democrat President. After 3 autopsies and an extensive investigation by the DOJ under the direction of Eric Holder, Officer Darren Wilson was exonerated of any wrongdoing in the shooting of Michael Brown. He was completely justified in using deadly force for self-defense. It was also confirmed without a doubt that Michael Brown did not hold up his hands and he did not say, "Don't shoot." However, facts don't matter to those who claim to embrace science, but deny evidence. (see Just the Facts, Ma'am-Vol.1)

Hundreds of African-Americans are protesting in Ferguson, still claiming that Brown was an innocent black man shot unnecessarily by a white officer while surrendering. On March 11th, two officers were shot outside the Ferguson Police Department in what is believed to be a targeted ambush. Both escaped with their lives, one despite being shot in the face. Many of the protesters don't care about the officers. They don't want to hear the truth, believing the racial charges the DOJ has been making for months. It's no different from the propaganda of Dixon's, The Clansman. Not much has changed in 100 years and it's just as wrong now as it was then.

As Dixon tried to rewrite the Southern post-Civil War history, MSNBC/Al Sharpton, George Soros, SEIU, the New Black Panthers and the Obama Administration are purposely lying to unsuspecting supporters, manipulating them into unjustified violence and racism. It is unfortunate our administration sees America the way Wilson did 100 years ago. If they can't control the black man with slavery they will simply use them as pawns, exploiting them into enslaving everyone under the Progressive/Liberal chains of tyranny.

Liberty, since the invention of the motion picture, moviemakers use the medium to distort and rewrite history. The movies <u>JFK</u>, <u>Noah</u>, and <u>Exodus: Gods and Kings</u>, are examples of fictional accounts that are told so dramatically that they become the accepted truth. <u>An Inconvenient Truth</u> (see <u>The Science Is Settled, Part II</u>), <u>Fahrenheit 9/11</u>, and <u>Gasland</u> are examples of movies claiming to be fact filled documentaries when, in fact, they are filled with proven distortions. However, these distortions are repeated often enough that many people buy into the lie.

Do not be manipulated and deceived by false narratives. Do your own homework. Search out the real truth. As Thomas Jefferson said, "Question with boldness even the existence of a God; because, if there be one, he must more approve of the homage of reason, than that of blindfolded fear." (see <u>Question With Boldness-Vol.4</u>)

So, let's celebrate the 100th Anniversary of the showing of <u>The Birth Of A Nation</u> at the White House by rejecting the racism put forth by Wilson, the Democratic Party and its thugs the KKK. We also reject the racism put forth in Ferguson by the same old Democrats and it's thugs from SEIU, the New Black Panthers, and funded to the tune of $33 million by Fabian Socialist George Soros. Racism is alive and well in the United States and like a hundred years ago, it's fed by the Progressive Democratic Party.

That's my 2 cents.

Love,
Mom

March 25, 2015

Dear Liberty,

A few days after Secretary of State John Kerry proclaimed to the world "The Science is Settled" regarding global warming, Al Gore declared that "we need to put a price on denial in politics." In essence, punish those who dare to question man-made global warming, aka climate change. This directly contradicts St. Paul, "For why should my liberty be determined by someone else's conscience?" (1 Cor 10:29b)

It doesn't matter that every single claim in Gore's movie, The Inconvenient Truth, has since been completely debunked. It's irrelevant that he has made over $100 million dollars selling the global warming lie. No one cares his home uses 20 times more energy than the average family home while he preaches to the common folk that sacrifices must be made with our energy use. Liberals cheered when he sold his TV network, Current TV, a widely unsuccessful liberal propaganda channel, to someone other then Glenn Beck. It was completely glossed over that the buyer, Arab based Al Jazeera, paid for it with money received from oil production. Those pushing this agenda are so full of their own self-superiority that they freely contradict their own supposed principles if it furthers their objective. (see Actions Speak Louder Than Words-Vol.1) If Gore believes man-made emissions cause climate change, why would he sell his network to an oil-producing company? As one spokesman said, it was because he had "more in common" with Al Jazeera than Glenn Beck. That says it all.

About the same time liberal late night talk show host, Seth Meyers, posed a "gotcha" global warming question to Senator Ted Cruz. Cruz affirmed that he followed science, noting that satellite data shows no increase in temperatures over the last 17 years. Meyers tried to deflect this fact by making an off-handed joke, asking Cruz if he trusted satellites over computers. Seth claimed more confidence in computer models over actual empirical evidence. Computer models are at the mercy of the information entered. This is called garbage in, garbage out. It's known that the original data entered was incorrect, completely negating anything that was produced. Computer models present projections, a theory. When this theory is tested by empirical evidence, or observable, provable data collected by satellites, the theory falls apart and is proven to be false. This is why the argument has to be shut down. Empirical evidence is the basis of science. If it can be establish scientifically that climate change is not happening, the left's power grab *is crushed. Therefore, they must claim, "The science is settled."*

PolitiFact, a supposed fact-checking site, agrees with Cruz that temperatures have not increased in the past 17 years. They then go on to claim that the computer models that have been incorrect for the past two decades are still accurate and authentic. They argue that the only reason their models are off from reality is because of natural phenomenons such as El Nino and volcanoes. Well, that's the point. These models do not account for such radical natural events, yet they are the gospel for activists. This idea is known as uniformitarianism. It fails to take into account the dramatic changes to the environment that come about due to volcanoes, tornados, Sunspots, hurricanes or other natural events. (see Leap Of Faith-Vol.3, Evolution Explodes-Vol.4, and Weather The Storm-Vol.4) These are the natural events that cause the majority of climate change. So, PolitiFact concludes, that even though Cruz's statement was in fact correct, he was mostly wrong. I must conclude the people of PolitiFact are the very people Gene Wilder was referring to in Blazing Saddles, "You've got to remember that these are just simple farmers. These are people of the land. The common clay of the new West. You know... morons." They trust in theory, over empirical, proven evidence. This is not science.

To force his unbelievable moneymaking lie down America's throat, Al Gore is demanding that political opponents pay a price for their freedom to not buy into his lie. California Governor Jerry Brown, on cue, degraded Ted Cruz for having a different point of view. He claimed Cruz is unfit for office, let alone the Presidency. Brown went about demonizing the opposition, taking a page straight out of Saul Alinsky's Rules for Radicals. This is the same approach used daily against Conservatives, to degrade them rather than disprove their evidence.

Brown continued to state, "Over 90% of the scientists who deal with climate are absolutely convinced that the humans' activity, industrial activity...are building up in the atmosphere, they're heat trapping, and they're causing not just one drought in California but severe storms and cold on the East Coast." First, what Brown doesn't say here is because of radical, leftist policies, farmers have been denied access to many rivers and waterways because of a tiny endangered fish. It is in fact these liberal policies that are causing much of the drought problem in California, not global warming.

Second, if heat is being trapped then the whole world would be warming in unison. How can a place that is warming have record cold? How can trapping in heat make it snow more?

Third, Brown claims over 90% of scientists believe this theory. This is the perfect example of using false statistics. If a survey says, "I believe man has an impact on the weather," what are the odds someone would agree with that? The question isn't worded, "I believe man is the primary reason for climate change." The wording of a question totally changes the results. This, like a computer model, shows how easily data can be manipulated and skewed. What radical leftists want to do is exactly what the Catholic Church did to Galileo for his view that the Earth revolves around the Sun. The Catholic Church wanted to silence and punish Galileo for going against what they deemed Biblical doctrine. They put him under house arrest for 8 years. Galileo was not going against the Bible, he was going against the church. (see The Science Is Settled)

Even Martin Luther, along with the Catholic Church, was against Copernicus' theory years earlier of the Earth going around the Sun, citing Joshua's command that the Sun stand still and not the Earth. Kepler reprised the scientific theory a half century later gaining a little more support. At the time of the invention of the telescope in 1608, Galileo threw his theories into the arena of ideas, disproving many scientifically accepted concepts originally theorized by Aristotle. The Catholic Church tried desperately to squash these scientists, claiming the "Science is Settled." Much like today, though, the powerful majority was proven wrong. (see The Science Is Settled)

Our Founding Fathers saw how the Catholic Church and the Church of England in Europe influenced the leaders to control the people. They wisely designed America so the church would not command the government and the government would not command the church. But they in no way intended for the two entities to be separate. (see Separation Of Church And State) In fact, they found it imperative that citizens remain faithful, religious people if they wished to keep a republic. As Thomas Jefferson said, "That government is best which governs least, because its people discipline themselves." (see The United Church And States Of America-Vol.6)

Americans have turned from God and the tyrants are moving in for the kill. We allowed them to curse our churches, remove prayer and God from our schools, our culture, and everyday life. Now they are replacing it with their own religion. Mother Earth is their god, evolution is their genesis, and computer models are their Bible. They worship creation and spit on the Creator. Trees, animals, and air are all more important than humanity. Nature is so important that their most honorable sacrament is abortion as the sacrifice of another evil human that would otherwise consume Mother Earth's precious resources. We were long ago warned about these people, "For they exchanged the truth of God for a lie, and worshiped and served the creation rather than the Creator, who is blessed forever. Amen." (Romans 1:25)

The same people who criticize the Catholic Church for suppressing Galileo over his views are proudly using the same techniques of the Catholic elite to silence their critics as well as free thought. Liberty, this is not freedom, this is pure fascism. Fascism is defined as totalitarian, right-wing governmental control. I must emphasis here that this is the European definition of right-wing, which consists of nationalist or socialist regimes which demand complete subservience to the government. American right-wingers are Constitutionalists who believe in as little government involvement as possible with emphasis on personal freedom and responsibility. The Europeans have no such term for our right-wing. They have never argued for individual liberty. (see Hear No Evil, Speak No Evil?-Vol.1)

Liberty, as I stated before, science is never settled. As you go through life you will receive pressure from family, friends, teachers, and politicians to "follow the crowd". Those who reject such pressures are the ones who change the world. The most common argument is "Everybody's doing it." Please don't use this argument with me because then I'll be forced to respond, "If everyone jumped off a cliff, would you?" and no one needs that. When you need strength, turn to the Lord. Jesus never followed the crowd. He never told the people what they wanted to hear just to make friends. The truth was always more important. Keep this as your guidance and hold firm to your beliefs and principles.

That's my 2 cents.

Love,
Mom

April 3, 2015

Dear Liberty,

"Rejoice greatly, O Daughter of Zion! Shout, Daughter of Jerusalem! See, your king comes to you, righteous and having salvation, gentle and riding on a donkey, on a colt, the foal of a donkey." Zechariah 9:9

Last Sunday we remembered our Lord and Savior entering Jerusalem under praises and songs of "Hosanna! Blessed is he who comes in the name of the Lord!" By the week's end that same man would be hanging on a cross, dying an innocent death.

It should have come as no shock to anyone when we search the Old Testament. The Lord's birth and death were plainly told for generations.

"Therefore the Lord himself will give you a sign: The virgin will be with child and will give birth to a son, and will call him Immanuel." Isaiah 7:14

"For to us a child is born, to us a son is given, and the government will be on his shoulders. And he will be called Wonderful Counselor, Mighty God, Everlasting Father, Prince of Peace." Isaiah 9:6

When the angels appeared to the shepherds and told them to go find the Christ child, they said, "And this will be a sign for you: you will find a babe wrapped in swaddling cloths and lying in a manger." (see *The Reason For The Season-Vol.1*) This was more than just a sign of his birth. It was a prediction of his death.

To swaddle a baby, strips of cloth were used to tightly wrap the newborn, keeping it warm and secure. Strips of cloth were also used to wrap a body after its death in preparation for burial. For the angels to specifically point out that the Christ would be in swaddling clothes, it was a sign to us that He was born to die for our sins.

On the Friday after entering Jerusalem, Jesus would fulfill all the words prophesied about Him. Accepting that it was God's Will, He endured the punishment for the world's sins and silently suffered the beatings we were told He would.

"I gave my back to those who strike, and my cheeks to those who pull out the beard; I hid not my face from disgrace and spitting." Isaiah 50:6

Then he withstood the pain and suffering of having his hands and feet nailed to the cross and the humiliation of a public and disgraceful death.

"Dogs have surrounded me; a band of evil men has encircled me, they have pierced my hands and my feet. I can count all my bones; people stare and gloat over me. They divide my garments among them and cast lots for my clothing."
Psalm 22:16-18

"He was despised and rejected by men, a man of sorrows, and familiar with suffering. Like one from whom men hide their faces he was despised, and we esteemed him not. Surely he took up our infirmities and carried our sorrows, yet we considered him stricken by God, smitten by him, and afflicted. But he was pierced for our transgressions, he was crushed for our iniquities; the punishment that brought us peace was upon him, and by his wounds we are healed. We all, like sheep, have gone astray, each of us has turned to his own way; and the LORD has laid on him the iniquity of us all. He was oppressed and afflicted, yet he did not open his mouth; he was led like a lamb to the slaughter, and as a sheep before her shearers is silent, so he did not open his mouth." Isaiah 53:3-7

This is a horrible, gruesome way to die. So why, Liberty, do we celebrate it? Because this is by far not the end of the story. At the moment of Christ's death, He conquered Satan. (see <u>The Serpent And The Tree</u>-Vol.3) As Christ said, "It is finished." All the suffering and all the punishment that is rightfully ours because of our sins, Jesus took upon himself and bore for us. He was innocent. He was sinless, yet he lovingly allowed himself to be our substitute. This is not only a good Friday, this is the best Friday ever.

His victory, or should I say our victory, was made known to all when his burial clothes were found folded neatly in the empty tomb on Sunday morning. This is significant as well because if he had been stolen as many want to believe, the thieves would not have had the time to unwrap Jesus, let alone stop and fold the strips of cloth.

So, Liberty, this is a very, very Good Friday as our relationship with God was restored and renewed through the blood of His Son. As the temple curtain ripped at the moment of Jesus' death, the barriers between God and humanity were torn down with Christ becoming our mediator. We are now free from the power of sin, liberated from the power of death and the power of the devil.

Many want to forget and ignore Good Friday. They don't go to church or even acknowledge the day. But to truly understand the amazing importance of the Resurrection on Easter Sunday, you much recognize and appreciate His death on Good Friday.

That's my 2 cents.

Love,
Mom

April 9, 2015

Dear Liberty,

Mark Twain is often quoted as saying, "History doesn't repeat itself, but it does rhyme." As we celebrate Easter, the similarities to Christ's time and ours appear to be carrying a similar tune.

John chapter 11 shows the Pharisees scheming against Jesus. "But some of them (Jews) went to the Pharisees and told them the things which Jesus had done. Therefore the chief priests and the Pharisees convened a council, and were saying, 'What are we doing? For this man is performing many signs. If we let Him go on like this, all men will believe in Him, and the Romans will come and take away both our place and our nation.'"

Jesus was teaching the people and performing many miracles. He was gathering believers wherever he went. Instead of rejoicing that God's promised Savior was here, the Sadducees feared that the Romans would take their authority over the people away from them. The Sadducees were driven by political motivation to remain in power, while the Pharisees manipulated them for their own ideology.

Although they both had opposing views, they worked together, plotting against Jesus. They did this despite knowing the scriptures. They knew the prophecies of the Messiah and they knew Jesus was fulfilling them. But if this itinerant rabbi grew in power and respect, both the Sadducees and Pharisees would only lose their control over the people. The people in power over the political and religious life of the Jewish nation were obsessed with maintaining control rather than confessing God's Word. As a result the Jewish leaders choose to eliminate one of their own rather than risk losing their authority. As John writes, "So from that day on they planned together to kill Him."

The deceitful Sadducees that plotted against Jesus for their own political motives have their modern day counterparts in John Boehner, Mitch McConnell, Karl Rove, John McCain, Peter King, and Lindsey Graham. These men, and others in the establishment GOP, have seen the strength and effectiveness of the conservative movement. (see Tyrants And Tea Parties-Vol.4) Fearing the loss of their own power, they have chosen again and again to attack, demean, and destroy anyone in their own party who dares threaten their political power, often siding with the ideological Pharisees of our day, the progressive democrats.

Let me make it perfectly clear that I am in no way saying a Ted Cruz, Rand Paul, Mike Lee, or Ben Carson is our "savior". They are certainly no Barack Obama. That being said they could very well save the Republican Party and bring the nation together rather than divide it. However, instead of embracing the Constitution (see Founding Documents-Vol.7), the establishment GOP have hardened their hearts, circled their wagons and begun plotting the political deaths of their own. They have abandoned their principles and sold out their consciences in exchange for the influence and privileges that comes with high government office. This goes for both Republicans and Democrats alike.

The political leaders on both sides of the aisle have deserted the law and the Constitution of the United States for their own gain. They are scared to death when they see an honest, God-fearing person gaining the trust and respect of the people. They have no concern for protecting and serving the people. They only have the desire for debilitating control. The establishment in both parties is drunk with the concept of a big government that gives them the keys to people's lives. Those promoting a small government, pro-private sector atmosphere threaten the chokehold both parties have on the American people.

Many politicians have the mindset of the high priest Caiaphas. He said, "You know nothing at all, nor do you take into account that it is expedient for you that one man die for the people, and that the whole nation not perish." In Jesus' case, this was true. Jesus had to die so that "whoever believes in Him shall not perish, but have eternal life." As John continues, "Now (Caiaphas) did not say this on his own initiative, but being high priest that year, he prophesied that Jesus was going to die for the nation, and not for the nation only, but in order that He might also gather together into one the children of God who are scattered abroad."

Jesus' mission was not of this world. His intention was and is unity. His one death was the saving grace for all humanity. Washington elites are more in line with Caiaphas' earthly meaning of his statement. Seeing only division and disunity, they use this as justification to politically eliminate not only conservative opponents but any person who threatens their authority. But, if God wills, He will use Caiaphas' mindset and actions for His benefit regardless of the Sadducees', or Washington's, objectives.

Liberty, as I write you this letter, know that your father and I are fighting every day to open people's eyes to the lies and deceit of American politics. I pray every night that it is God's will that He raise up honest, trustworthy, God-fearing Americans to lead this country back into His loving arms. I pray that we have not forsaken him so much that He has forgotten us.

When you read this letter, our future will have been cemented in your past. I pray with all my heart, my dear Liberty, that we also give you a unified, productive, and hopeful future.

That's my 2 cents.

Love,
Mom

April 16, 2015

Dear Liberty,

German Lutheran minister Dietrich Bonhoeffer was killed 70 years ago on April 9, 1945, for sounding the alarm against the evils of Nazism. Bonhoeffer had been arrested two years before for his resistance to the Nazi regime. While he was in prison, Hitler survived an assassination attempt, which Bonhoeffer helped organize. Once this was discovered by the Nazis, Bonhoeffer's days were numbered. He was executed just one month before Germany's formal surrender to the allies.

From the beginning of Hitler's reign, Bonhoeffer was trumpeting the warnings against the Nazis. Hitler used the state to take control of the German Evangelical Churches so he could extend his power. Ludwig Muller was elected imperial bishop of the new state church where he used his authority to impose acceptance of the Nazi agenda of racial supremacy. At the time, churches that rejected the political propaganda of the Nazis gathered together to form the Confessing Church synod of which Bonhoeffer was a member and leader. These churches fought to not only save the converted Jewish Christians, but they fought for the rights of practicing Jews. Even after being forced underground, the Confessing Church remained politically active protesting the euthanasia and persecution of the Jews.

After Adolph Hitler assumed power in 1933, he vigorously used persecution, torture and murder as his means of punishing and controlling his opponents. At first he started with his political enemies. However, Hitler was consumed by dreams of an Aryan Utopia, leading quickly to the oppression of the Jewish race. His goal was not only a racial cleansing, but to unite the German people by giving them a common enemy. (see <u>Finishing The Master Race</u>-Vol.4) The Nuremberg Laws of 1935 defined a person with three or four Jewish grandparents a Jew, while those with just two Jewish grandparents were regarded as Mischlinge, or half-breeds. This allowed for even Christians with Jewish ancestry to be abused.

Germany's anti-semitism exploded in November 1938 during the "night of broken glass", or Kristallnacht, in which windows were smashed in synagogues and Jewish shops set on fire. (see <u>Veterans Day</u>-Vol.1) Most of the Jews that remained in Germany, instead of fleeing like hundreds of thousands did, were gathered up, imprisoned in camps and killed by execution or gas chambers. When it was all over, Hitler had slaughtered 6 million Jews.

Seventy years after of the end of the Second World War, Nazi concentration camps are sacred ground. They hold the memories of the atrocities committed there as silent reminders of the evil that man can inflict on his fellow man. We cry at the pictures of the people who were little more than walking skeletons and gasp at the horrendous experiments the Nazis performed on Jewish women and twins in the name of science. (See Evil Is As Evil Does) We become nauseous at the images of hundreds of dead bodies stacked upon each other. We speak the familiar refrain, "Never again!"

Liberty, my response is, "You hypocrites."

Right now President Obama is trying desperately to negotiate a nuclear deal with Iran, the single largest supporter of Islamic Terror. Obama and John Kerry are trying to pen a peace accord while Iran's Ayatollah Khomeini declares that Israel should be annihilated. It astounds me the amount of anti-Semitic rhetoric I hear these days from people all across the globe. Do they not know history? Have they learned nothing? Even our administration can't admit a Jewish French deli was specifically singled out by a Muslim for a terrorist attack. (See COEXIST)

As wicked as the Nazis were, there is an evil out there even greater, more vile, more dangerous. It is led by Islamic extremist groups such as ISIS and Boko Haram. While these groups are targeting Jews, their current more aggressive goal is massacring Christians, which they are doing by the thousands. Parents are being murdered in front of their children. Women are being raped and tortured in the name of Allah. Christian boys are being beheaded in the streets. Christian girls as young as 9 are being sold as sex slaves. Where is the anger? Where is the outrage? This is a Christian Holocaust occurring right now and almost no one is talking about it, certainly not our government and more frightening, not our churches.

This ambivalence can have staggering results. At the time of Mohammad, 90% of Egypt was Christian. Since that time, Muslims have forced the conversion of those Christians or slaughtered them to the point that only 10% of Egypt is Christian. Today militants are quickly massacring them. The Coptic Christian church, one started by an apostle, is in grave danger of being destroyed.

Boko Haram, a militant Islamic terrorist group, is targeting 200,000 Christians in Nigeria forcing them to convert or die. So far, 200 churches have been lost and 15,000 Nigerians have died since the group increased its efforts in 2009. Another 1.5 million have fled their homes to escape the horror. Boko Haram abducted over 200 girls, sparking a fierce response by first lady Michele Obama. She tweeted #BringBackOurGirls. To date, this is the most aggressive policy action taken by the Obama administration towards radical Islam. At least the U.N. human rights chief is truthful about the extremism we are facing. (see One World Disorder-Vol.5) Just this month he warned the world that Boko Haram was using children as "expendable cannon fodder" and "human bombs."

In February, Islamic extremist militants in Libya beheaded 21 Coptic Egyptian Christians on the shores of Tripoli. As I explained in my letter Washington, Adams, and Mohammad - Our Founding Fathers, this location was no accident. Islamic extremists have been fighting for the final caliphate since our country was founded. Tripoli was where Jefferson's Marines defeated the Muslim pirates during the First Barbary Wars over 200 years ago. (see To The Shores Of Tripoli-Vol.3) The extremists desperately want a rematch and to usher in the Apocalypse.

Less than two weeks ago, four Islamic extremists stormed Garissa University College in Kenya. They separated the students into Christians and Muslims. After releasing the Muslims, the four terrorists preceded to open fire, massacring 148 Christians. Somalia's al-Shabab militant group took responsibility for the slaughter, claiming it was retaliation for Kenyan troops sent to Somalia to fight the extremists. Why then, were Christians singled out and everyone not killed? Obama would not acknowledge that religion played any part of the slaughter, only stating that some "folks" were killed. Even worse, Obama won't acknowledge that ISIS is even an Islamic group. It's this blindness to evil that has allowed an ISIS training camp to be created just 10 miles into Mexico on America's southern boarder.

While these violent acts are occurring, a soft tyranny of thought is happening at the same time. Christian storeowners in America are being singled out and forced out of business by compassionate members of the secular community. The sensitivity of the secular left could only be enhanced by adding a Star of David to the store window to warn others of the evil people inside. Radical violence and separating people into groups is a clear goose step down the same road of Germany 1939.

Today is Holocaust Remembrance Day. (see Remember The Holocaust-Vol.3) As we contemplate what we consider to be one of the most disgusting moments of recent history, I pray to God, Liberty, that you don't look back on my generation and ask, "How could they have been so blind? Why didn't they do anything?"

Churches today do not like to be political. They don't feel it is their job. But as Bonhoeffer charged in 1940, "the Church was silent *when it should have cried out because the blood of the innocent was crying aloud to heaven. She is guilty of the deaths of the weakest and most defenseless brothers of Jesus Christ."*

May we wake up before our fate is sealed like that of Bonhoeffer's. As he also said, "Silence in the face of evil is itself evil: God will not hold us guiltless. Not to speak is to speak. Not to act is to act." Liberty, this is me speaking. This is me acting. Dear God, have mercy on us all.

That's my 2 cents.

Love,
Mom

April 22, 2015

Dear Liberty,

Feminists and liberals pride themselves on promoting that women are strong and resourceful. Since the 60's we have been informed that women can stand on their own two feet, are as strong as men, and can do everything on their own. This has been such a significant issue with Liberals that many feminists are convinced that men are irrelevant. I guess that is unless you interview Rand Paul.

In a recent interview, NBC's Savannah Guthrie tried to distort and mischaracterize Rand Paul's political views. She also spoke over him in efforts to push her agenda. Rand Paul stopped her bloviating, called her on her misrepresentation and proceeded to set the record straight. Judging by the Liberal media's response you would have thought he beat her with a stick on live TV. They were outraged a man dare verbally attack a woman. Fellow Liberal journalist Chuck Todd felt the need to defend Savannah and criticize Rand for his behavior. In all their criticism of Rand, though, they failed to realize they were arguing that a woman was not strong enough to be intellectually challenged by a man. It boggles the mind how feminists have absolutely no comprehension of the contradiction of their principals. Could it be because they don't care?

Liberty, it's time to expose this propaganda for what it is. If Savannah had been a man, this would not have been a issue. Since she is a woman, Rand Paul was accused of being mean and rude to a woman. However, this event has nothing to do with her sex. It's all about political opportunity.

After eight successful years of shutting up the competition by charging racism against any Obama critic, the media is setting the stage to play the gender card for Hillary. They are recalibrating their guns to go from a race war to a gender war.

Liberals know they can't win in the arena of ideas. They have to change the subject to demean and degrade their opponent because they know most Americans will flat out reject their ideas. As they were able to do with Obama, Liberals want to force the Republican candidates to soften their attacks against Hillary Clinton. It's not that Hillary can't handle herself because she's a woman. It's that Hillary can't handle herself because she's not likable. (see Above The Law*-Vol.3)*

It is one thing to say Obama was attacked just because he was black, but in this instance Rand was accused of being mean to a woman. The claim actually makes women look weak, rather than empowering them. If women, including Hillary Clinton, are going to be so fragile that they have to be handled with kid gloves by Republicans running for President, how is a woman going to be able to stand up to world leaders like those in Iran who think women are property? Are Liberal journalists going to tell Iran's Supreme Leader Ayatollah Ali Khamenei that he can't be tough with Hillary Clinton because she's a woman? First, he would laugh in their face. Then he would agree, and say, "Yes, women are weak. Women should be controlled by men and kept in their place. Welcome to Islam!"

Hillary Clinton, a supposed champion of women's issues, has been taking millions of dollars for her Clinton Foundation from countries like Saudi Arabia and Yemen which stone women for walking outside without a male escort. The truth is Liberals only care about women's issues when it can be used for political advantage. (see <u>Suffering In Utopia</u>-Vol.6) It's about the money, it's about the power, and it's about destroying what they believe to be the ultimate enemy, conservatism and capitalism.

Hillary and N.O.W. undeniably proved this in the 1990's when Bill Clinton was accused of sexual abuse. Feminists went after the accusers like wolves to red meat. Meanwhile, Liberals trumpeted Bill for being able to get a little on the side, ignoring that he was cheating on his wife. The 2008 campaign reignited this Liberal indignation when they attacked and degraded Sarah Palin, calling her stupid and a backwoods hick. Michelle Bachman got the exact same treatment in 2012 during her presidential run. Not one Women's Rights group came to either of their defense. Why? It's because it's never about women's rights. It's about Liberal, socialist ideology and only women who subscribe to it are protected. Conservative women be damned.

While liberals play this pathetic propaganda game using women as their pawns, they are completely ignoring the true "War on Women" by Muslims. Feminists and Liberals show their true colors when they embrace Islam and eviscerate Republicans who dare to talk back to a woman. Islamists rape, torture and enslave girls as young as 9 years old and Liberals believe Republicans are evil because they don't want to pay for someone else's birth control. It's insane. Muslim women are forced to cover themselves from head to toe, denied driving privileges, have to obtain permission to travel, are married off before they hit puberty, are never given a "choice" regarding birth control let alone abortion, and Liberals continue to support these countries while demanding "gender equality" from Republicans.

Do feminists even know, or care, that a Muslim man can only be convicted of rape if there are four male witnesses (that are willing to testify to the rape) or the accused actually confesses to it? Otherwise, if a woman accuses a man of rape without either of those elements, she is confessing to having sex. If either are married then she has admitted to adultery for which she can be stoned. All the man has to do is say the sex was consensual. How about writing THAT rape story, _Rolling Stone Magazine_? They never will because it would expose who they really are, lying hypocrites driven by ideology and politics over principles.

I'm quite frankly sick and tired of this mantra that more women should be on school boards, Senators, Representatives, and now, "it's time for a woman President". I could care less what gender our leaders are. The paramount concern for our politicians should be who they are. They need to be guided by principles, values, ethics, and morals, not by what they are. Our electorate has gotten lazy, brainwashed and frankly stupid. In a recent poll of college students regarding their decision to vote for Hillary Clinton, the most popular answer for their support was, "She's a woman." If that's all they really cared about then Sarah Palin would have been Vice President and maybe President now.

We were told it was "time" for an African-American President eight years ago. Millions voted for Barack Obama to show they weren't racist, which in and of itself was the most racist thing they could do. Well how well is that working out for us? I'm perfectly fine with a black President. Let's see those that tout they want a black President vote for Allen West, Ben Carson, Allen Keys or Condoleezza Rice. They won't because race is actually a propaganda tool, not a character trait.

I believe we should strive for Dr. Martin Luther King's dream. As he said, "I have a dream that my four little children will one day live in a nation where they will not be judged by the color of their skin, but by the content of their character." (see _Free At Last?-Vol.2_) America elected a man simply because of the pigment in his skin with absolutely no regard to his character. The Liberals are beginning the identical game with gender. Let's be clear, voting for a woman just because she is a woman is the epitome of sexism.

The great news is Rand Paul and Ted Cruz are not playing the game. They are not kowtowing to the media's gotcha questions. When Rand was asked an abortion question, he instructed the interviewer to ask the DNC first and then get back to him. When Ted was asked about gay marriage, his response outlined the constitutionality of the issue. He argued that the 10th amendment clearly directs states to decide the issue, not the federal government or unelected federal judges. (see _Founding Documents-Vol.7_)

Liberty, be vigilant and reject those who try to intimidate or bully you into abandoning your principles and beliefs. Evaluate people on how their actions compare to the principles they profess. Protect the rights of the individual and also judge people individually, not based on what group they are assigned to by a politician. People are not labels. If you vote for or against someone simply based on their race, gender, or religion without any regard to who they are personally, you have committed the greatest sin, acting like a racist, sexist, bigot. You know....a Progressive Liberal.

That's my 2 cents.

Love,
Mom

April 29, 2015

Dear Liberty,

From the beginning of time, as populations grew and expanded across the globe, distinct traditions, practices and even physical traits emerged in various regions from the North Pole to the South Pole. Divergent cultures mixed and mingled because one country conquered and enveloped another. The defeated kingdom would often lose much of their own identity as they were forced to adopt another. Then in 1776, America was born.

When the colonists broke from England, they made sure to define America as having a "government of the people, by the people, and for the people." This concept united individuals, making them a strong unit and giving them the power to govern themselves. Immigrants blended in with those already here, forming a national bond that became unbreakable. As a nation, we cared about and supported our neighbors. As a nation, we welcomed our similarities. As a nation, we strove to be the best we could be.

Immigrants didn't completely abandon their native heritage nor were they forced to. Likewise, they didn't force their traditions on others. They did come with one common desire, though, to be an American. Ultimately different customs and traditions from all over the globe were brought here and added to the ingredients of the Great American Melting Pot, producing one of the most diverse and encompassing cultures in the entire world.

"You simply melt right in, It doesn't matter what your skin, It doesn't matter where you're from, Or your religion, you jump right in, To the great American melting pot, Oh, what a stew, red, white, and blue." (The Great American Melting Pot, School House Rock.)

The only way to remove the people's power is to "divide and conquer" them. It's being done and as Lincoln warned, it's not being done by an outside enemy. Lincoln predicted, "America will never be destroyed from the outside. If we falter and lose our freedoms, it will be because we destroyed ourselves."

America had been trying to dig up the deep roots of racism since she broke from England. The English slave trade imported a racial divide that Liberals will not let die. After the Civil War, even though

Southern Democrats passed Jim Crow laws to keep black people separated and virtually enslaved, Americans realized the injustice and made tremendous strides in race relations. Meanwhile Progressive Liberals starting with Woodrow Wilson, have been keeping racial tensions alive and well for their own benefit. (See <u>The Birth Of A Nation</u>)

Over the past 8 years, these tensions have been cultivated and magnified. As Lincoln said, "A house divided cannot stand," and Americans are being driven apart at every turn. (see <u>Disunity Of The Union</u>) Progressives are directing and capitalizing on the current atmosphere to separate young and old, female and male, gay and straight, Christian and atheist, Republican and Democrat, rich and poor, pro-life and pro-choice, police and citizen. Every issue that can be spotlighted and exploited is being used as a wedge to segregate Americans. Progressives in America want to force us to see people as part of a particular group, not as Americans. Once this is achieved and citizens are not standing together anymore, tyrannical and dictatorial politicians will put the last nail in their oppressive governmental coffin. We're almost there.

Even when Liberals expose their own hypocrisy regarding their support for particular groups, most still can't see that these divisions are a manufactured lie. Last week's letter, <u>War On Women</u>, gave explicit examples how those touting women's rights are completely ignoring true female oppression because it does not fit their agenda. It recently happened again as pro-gay activists displayed their true rainbow colors in two separate instances. (see <u>The Rainbow Connection</u>)

During an interview with Diane Sawyer, 1976 Olympic Decathlon Gold Medalist Bruce Jenner revealed that he was not only a cross-dresser, he was a Christian and Conservative. Social Media went nuts. They loudly applauded him until Diane called him the "R" word. Those who pride themselves on embracing all sexual diversity were completely intolerant of Jenner for daring to actually have his own opinion.

Wealthy businessman and hotel owner, Ian Reisner, who happens to be gay, hosted a dinner at his home for Ted Cruz. His motivation was to learn more about the presidential candidate and his views. This is the most responsible thing one could do to educate themselves. The backlash from the gay community was overwhelming. Ian quickly apologized for not researching Ted's views before inviting him. So in essence, the gay community was furious Ian actually wanted to talk to the candidate himself instead of just accepting what the gay community claimed his views were.

The Progressive definition of tolerance is excoriating someone for choosing a different path than the one they want to force you into.

Americans are being trained to mix as well as oil and water. Unfortunately this is an agenda that is promoted by those as powerful as the White House. Feeling confident, the gloves are coming off. The true haters are revealing their distain for those who practice genuine liberty and freedom.

While the liberal gay community was vilifying Bruce Jenner, Log Cabin Republicans, a LGBT Republican group, was readily supporting him. Progressives love women, unless they are pro-life. They accept blacks unless they believe in the Constitution. (see Founding Documents-Vol.7) They stand-up for homosexuals unless they lean to the right. The Progressive agenda is always first and foremost. Liberals will champion those special interest groups if and only if they accept the roles that have been designed for them.

Liberty, we are always one generation away from giving away all our ancestors fought for. We must reject anyone whose focus is division and hostility between citizens. You have ancestors that came in the early 1600's through the mid-1800's. They voyaged the Atlantic Ocean for the opportunity to choose their own future. (see The Original Iron Man-Vol.4, Coming To America-Vol.7) Many came to spread the Gospel. (see What Is Columbus Day?-Vol.1, Jamestown: A City Upon A Hill, The Apostle Of Viginia-Vol.4, The Forgotten Founding Father, and 'Higher' Education-Vol.3) Others came fleeing religious persecution. (see Thanks Be To God-Vol.1) Some came as indentured servants. (see The Color-Blindness Of Slavery) One grandmother even came because her home city said she couldn't have turkeys anymore. They raised families, lost families, fought in wars, and built homes and cities. They left their tyrannical governments in the quest for independence and freedom. They were German, Scottish, Irish, English, French, Polish and more. Counties that have long histories of fighting and attacking each other. When they came here though, they became neighbors. They became family. They became Americans.

We cannot allow anyone to rebuild those barriers generations of our ancestors worked so hard to destroy. We must not let Lincoln's prophecy come true.

That's my 2 cents.

Love,
Mom

May 6, 2015

Dear Liberty,

After 11 years of religious persecution, William Bradford along with 49 other brave Separatists set out for the New World in search of religious freedom. More important than their possessions, their safety, and their lives was their desire to worship God freely. In their hearts they knew King James had no right or authority to tell them what they could believe.

After arriving in America in 1620, the first pilgrim colony in the New World was established on Christian principles. The very first governing document, the Mayflower Compact, states clearly that the new land was for "the glory of God and the advancement of the Christian faith." (see *Thanks Be To God-Vol.1, America's First Founding Document-Vol.3*, and *Founding Documents-Vol.7*) Over 150 years later our Founding Fathers followed the pilgrim's lead and structured the new country on Biblical principles. Patrick Henry himself said, "It cannot be emphasized too clearly and too often that this nation was founded, not by religionists, but by Christians; not on religion, but on the gospel of Jesus Christ." (see *If This Be Treason-Vol.6* and *Give Me Liberty-Vol.5*)

The Declaration of Independence states each man is entitled to "the separate and equal station to which the Laws of Nature and of Nature's God entitle them..." It is this understanding that God, and not man, gives an individual his or her freedom. (see *Happy Independence Day-Vol.1* and *Founding Documents-Vol.7*) This is so important that it became the First Amendment to the Bill of Rights; the freedom of speech and religion.

After years of suppression by the Kings of England, our forefathers wrote America's founding documents knowing the importance of limiting governmental control. When the government is not limited then it will claim unbridled power over the people. The government was designed specifically to never be able to dictate to the people what to believe, religiously or otherwise, for this was the very act that the Church of England demanded under the king. The colonists recognized the importance of both religious freedom and the crucial importance of having God-fearing, moral individuals serving in government positions. Political servants were actively encouraged to bring their faith to the table to guide their decisions, but restrained from *forcing their beliefs down other's throats. (see <u>The United Church And States Of America</u>-Vol.6)*

Fast forward to today. In a recent stump speech, Hillary Clinton informed her supporters that "deep-seated cultural codes, religious beliefs and structural biases have to be changed." Disguising it as "reproductive health care", Hillary wants to dictate that pro-lifers who view abortion as murder must change their beliefs because she demands it. (see <u>Suffering In Utopia</u>-Vol.6)

So the party that claims to champion a person's right to choose will allow choice, but only in the slaughter of children. The ideology that stipulates inclusiveness proudly excludes those with different opinions on all other subjects. The party that declares to be progressing and evolving towards the future just took America back to circa 1775. They want to replace our God-given inalienable rights with government-given entitlements, telling us what to do and how to think. (see <u>Inalienable Rights</u>-Vol.5)

At the Supreme Court, activists are insisting the judicial branch destroy the definition of marriage that has stood from the beginning of time. (see <u>We Reserve The Right To Refuse Service</u>-Vol.1) This is just one more arrow the Progressives are aiming towards Christian targets. Obama and Congressional Democrats started the aggressive governmental assault on Christians with the Affordable Health Care bill. They want to force Catholic organizations and other faith-based establishments to provide abortion-covered health care for their employees. After all, nuns are well known for their promiscuous lifestyles. Activists are pushing and shoving business owners, demanding they participate in gay weddings or risk loosing everything. Perhaps they should demand they put gold stars of David in the window. It worked so well for the Nazis. Liberal judges have been dutifully playing their part, ruling against the Christian business owners even when gay marriage is illegal in their particular state. Ironically, they are punishing people in those states for not participating in an unlawful event.

Many are insisting if the Supreme Court redefines marriage, making same-sex unions legal, then the church can't preach against homosexuality as a sin. (see <u>Keeping The Faith</u>-Vol.1 and <u>What Is Love?</u>) Making it legal does not make it any less a sin. Slavery was once legal too. Should Christians have left that issue alone as well? It's legal to live with someone without marriage. Does that negate the 7th commandment? It's lawful to drink until you pass out. Does that make it a good idea? Having a child out of wedlock is now socially acceptable. It is also the best indicator of poverty.

Activists self-righteously claim that Christians who continue to believe that homosexuality is a sin are clinging to a very old, very outdated doctrine. This attitude has even infected the church. According to evangelical Christian David Gushee, a Christian ethics teacher at Mercer University, "Human understanding of what is sinful has changed over time." Here is the key and linchpin to the errancy of his argument, "Human understanding." Satan rejoices when we decide what is and is not sinful. Liberty, it is not our decision to determine sin. Sinfulness is defined solely and exclusively by God. Since his Word does not change, to say that our understanding of what is sinful has changed only shows the human desire and eagerness to become gods ourselves. (see Fruit Of The Forbidden Tree-Vol.1)

Progressive politicians and activists are pushing to use the government to force Christians to abandon their beliefs. Apparently they truly have no clue about and no concern for the First Amendment of the Bill of Rights. (see Founding Documents-Vol.7) The Founding Fathers could not have been more clear that neither the government nor anyone else has the right, authority or power to dictate a person's religion or beliefs in any way.

Liberals demand separation of church and state if their ideology is threatened, such as abortion (see Suffering In Utopia-Vol.6), global warming (see Actions Speak Louder Than Words-Vol.1 and The Science Is Settled, Part II), or evolution (see Leap Of Faith-Vol.3 and Evolution Explodes-Vol.4). However, it is only the Progressive Liberals who consistently violate the separation of church and state as part of their political movement. They use the government to do precisely what Jefferson stated it would and could not do when he wrote about the "wall of separation between church and state" in his letter to the Danbury Baptist Association over 200 years ago. The Danbury Baptists feared the government would dictate their beliefs no different than King James did to the colonies. (see Keeping The Faith-Vol.1 and The United Church And States Of America-Vol.6) Thankfully, Hillary is here to bring the glory of King James back to life for the American people.

The "separation of church and state" is so often misquoted by Liberals that few people understand its true meaning and many believe the phrase is in the Constitution. It is not. (see Founding Documents-Vol.7) What is in the Constitution is the direction "Congress shall make no law respecting an establishment of religion, or prohibiting the free exercise thereof." Liberals are trying to package gay marriage as a civil right issue so they can use discrimination laws to force it on Americans. To further handcuff churches, they are threatening the tax-exempt status of religious organizations. By doing so they are in fact making laws prohibiting the free exercise of one's religion, knowing many churches will not survive without their tax-exempt status.

74

What is very clear is that Liberals are tolerant, but only if you agree with them. Liberals believe in free speech as long as you say what they want to hear. Liberals demand an individual's choice as long as you choose what they want you to, or they use the power of government to force on you.

Liberty, Jesus told us we would be persecuted in his name. "If the world hates you, keep in mind that it hated me first." John 15:18 It is our cross to bear. "Then they will deliver you to tribulation, and will kill you, and you will be hated by all nations because of My name. At that time many will fall away and will betray one another and hate one another. Many false prophets will arise and will mislead many. Because lawlessness is increased, most people's love will grow cold. But the one who endures to the end, he will be saved." Matt 24:9-12

So hold firm, Liberty. As much as it tears my heart to see this happening to my country and fellow countrymen, this is not our home. We are already free. We have already won. We must continue to spread the Gospel and share the Good News. That is the most liberating truth of all.

That's my 2 cents.

Love,
Mom

May 13, 2015

Dear Liberty,

A crucifix in urine is divine but a cartoon of Muhammad is distasteful. The Virgin Mary in elephant dung is praiseworthy but a political drawing for free speech is worthy of death. A musical mocking the Mormon religion receives Tony Awards while images of a religious leader are awarded gunfire and death threats. To the mainstream media and Liberal pundits this all makes perfect sense, unless it happens to them.

Just 4 months ago, two Islamic terrorists rushed the offices of Charlie Hebdo, a French satirical magazine, killing 12 people. (see COEXIST) The media elite, Hollywood elite, and the world, raised their voices in unity stating, "Je suis Charlie Hebdo" (I am Charlie Hebdo). People on all sides of the political spectrum marched arm in arm in the streets of Paris declaring the attack an abomination against humanity. Well, all except any member of the Obama administration. Even those who strongly disagree with the magazine and the sexual cartoons the artist's drew of Muhammad denounced the terrorists' actions. This was a spontaneous support for freedom of speech and a condemnation of violent extremism from all but one nation.

Apparently only Liberal publications are awarded this unbiased support from political opponents. On May 3, the American Freedom Defense Initiative hosted a freedom of speech conference in Garland, Texas. As part of the itinerary, coordinator Pamela Geller held a contest for the best cartoon depicting Muhammad. Unlike the Charlie Hebdo cartoons, which were all sexual in content, the conference contest winner was a pure and simple statement on free speech. Muhammad was drawn holding a sword, stating, "You can't draw me." The caption read, "That's why I draw you."

The very same commentators who denounced the massacre in France ripped into Pamela Geller for purposely offending Muslims. Even a Charlie Hebdo cartoonist was able to excuse and defend his magazine's cartoons while blaming Pamela for inciting the attack in Garland. He claimed his magazine is an equal opportunity offender of religions while accusing Pamela Geller of targeting only Islam. The flaw with that argument is that Pamela Geller was making a very specific point. Christians don't kill when their religion is attacked. Jews do not slaughter when their faith is assaulted. Rare indeed are the mass beheadings conducted by Mormans or Seventh Day Adventists. If you are trying to make a statement about free speech, it doesn't accomplish much to challenge those who believe you have a right to be offensive. You only prove that point by singling out the hypocrisy of the one group that refuses to be offended.

The fortunate difference in the Texas attack was officers who, unlike the French officers, were armed and quickly eliminated the threat in a matter of seconds. Protected with body armor, armed with AK-47s, the two ISIS terrorists intended to do significant carnage. However, an officer on a traffic post and nearby SWAT members ended the potential threat in less than 15 seconds. Armed good guys are always the best defense against armed bad guys. God bless Texas. The officers protected the convention goers, stopped the threat, and prevented a massacre like Charlie Hebdo.

It's not just how these events ended that's significantly different, but how the media reacted after it was over. If you are honest about your principles, your opinion should be consistent regardless the political position of the person presenting the event. If you are not, then you are just playing politics. The Charlie Hebdo massacre and the Garland attack were both senseless, horrific displays of intolerance by Islamic extremists. Regardless of whether you agree with any of the cartoons, you must defend the right for them to be drawn. This seems lost on most in the media.

Those claiming Pamela was purposely trying to offend Islamists are the same people who support and defend homosexuality. Do they not know that homosexuality is incredibly offensive to Muslims yet it is being forced into Western society in movies, television, and now by law? Islamists murder homosexuals throughout the Middle East, no questions asked. ISIS threw two off of a building in January, taking pictures and video to make sure everyone knows their beliefs on the matter.

So why are these sympathetic Liberals offended by Pamela Geller while they demand same-sex marriage? Shouldn't they be more sensitive to the Muslim's feelings on this subject? (see _Sex, Lies, & Marriage_) Why do they insist on insulting them? Actors and actresses will demonize Pamela Geller for offending Muslims while proudly participating in on-screen and often publicized off-screen love affairs. Adultery is punishable by death in Muslim society and is usually carried out without even a trial. An ISIS video shows a woman accused of adultery dragged across the ground while pleading and begging for her life, only to be pummeled with large rocks by those around her. Her covered lifeless body is the last image of the video. Hollywood, media, and political elite, are you still, "Je suis Charlie

Hebdo?" Or do you only stand when the barbarians are at your gate?

On the plus side, there are a few on the Left who are remaining consistent. Far Leftists Jon Stewart and Bill Maher have both criticized the Garland terrorist attack as strongly as they did the Charlie Hebdo attack, standing with many Conservative commentators. Maher very clearly pointed out the fringe Westboro Baptist Church, "Protest(s) me every week, and it never ends in a gun battle."

Those who say Pamela Geller had it coming could have said the same about the assassinations of Malcolm X, Martin Luther King, Jr., John F. Kennedy and Robert Kennedy. (see Free At Last?) All these men stood on principle, not politics. By doing so they offended specific groups of people, including the Nation of Islam. A fatwa, or call for death, has been issued against Pamela Geller and anyone who hosts her events. Many, including some Conservatives, are condemning the cartoon event even going as far as claiming they were in fact inciting a violent reaction for holding the cartoon contest. By doing this they are declaring victory for the terrorists. Islamic extremists use threats, fear and panic to control others. The critics are masking their fear by calling it respect. It is not respect if it is controlled by terror. It's only respectful when you know you can freely get away with the insult and you refrain anyway. By condemning Pamela Geller instead of the terrorists, critics are playing right into the hands of those organizing these attacks. Bullies win when you back down.

Discouraging anyone from producing images of Muhammad just gives more power to the extremists. Once they've won this battle and silenced their opponents, what will they go after next? Christianity? Jews? Women? Homosexuals? Adulterers? Already waging those wars. When will people start fighting back? When they finally come after those in America? They're already here and already in full battle. If you start cowering to the fanatics and attack Pamela Geller, or the Christians, or the Jews, who will be left to defend you when they come after you and your sin?

We can't back down and give in to the terrorists. If we stood together and all drew pictures of Muhammad, what could the terrorists do? They can defeat us 2 or 3 at a time, but if we all unite with a peaceful protest, we could overpower every last one of their weapons.

I am Garland!

That's my 2 cents.

Love,
Mom

May 21, 2015

Dear Liberty,

*Liberating Letters   The***Facts***Paper.com*

    "We cannot continue to rely only on our military in order to achieve the national security objectives that we've set. We've got to have a civilian national security force that's just as powerful, just as strong, just as well-funded," said Barack Obama in July of 2008. He made this comment in a speech while referencing increasing foreign service and expanding the role of the Peace Corps, both noble causes. But many on the Right heard those words as an indication of something somewhat more sinister. Perhaps because it has the rhyme of history.

    Following his response to the Ferguson riots and his administration's reactions to the death of a Baltimore teen in police custody, that sense of foreboding has returned. (see <u>Just The Facts, Ma'am</u>-Vol.1) Determined to follow the advice of Rahm Emanuel, Obama's former Chief-of-Staff, "You never let a serious crisis go to waste," Al Sharpton has stepped forward to help the cause. "We need the Justice Department to step in and take over policing in this country." Disguising it as a Civil Rights issue, Sharpton continued, "In the 20th century, they had to fight states' rights - to get the right to vote. We're going to have to fight states' rights in terms of closing down police cases."

    As with Ferguson, those with an agenda are exploiting the death of an African-American for their own benefit without any regard to the facts. Claiming racist police brutality, professional protest groups, many funded by George Soros, or other regular suspects like the Nation of Islam and the Black Panthers were aided by the violent street gangs the Bloods and the Crips to descend on Baltimore and organize violent, destructive riots destroying many of the essential businesses in the area. As facts are coming to light, the early reports we were told regarding the events are becoming more and more disturbing, but not because what was done, but what was allowed to happen.

    After a peaceful protest in Baltimore turned violent on Saturday, April 25, local high-schoolers planned a 3pm "purge", or time for unlawful behavior, on Monday at the Mondawmin Mall. Because the event was announced on social media, city officials were aware of the event well in advance. This warning allowed the police and political leaders to take preemptive action, to minimize the event. However, this never happened.

The purge was allowed to occur and the criminal conduct quickly spilled into the streets of Baltimore. Businesses were looted. Unoccupied police cars were destroyed and set on fire. A CVS was burned to the ground. One business owner called emergency dispatch 50 times with no response. Anticipating a Monday night riot, Mayor Stephanie Rawlings-Blake scheduled a city curfew. The curfew didn't take effect until Tuesday night. The Mayor even stated that her actions "gave those who wished to destroy space to do that as well." She backtracked her comment, but it was later confirmed by officers that she told the police to stand down and allow the destruction to happen.

But that's just the beginning of the questionable actions of local authorities. Hours after State's Attorney Marilyn Mosby received Freddie Grey's autopsy, she charged six officers with unlawful arrest and murder. This is highly unprecedented. Thorough investigations take weeks, not hours. Race-bater activists cheered the prosecutor's indictments not knowing she conveniently concealed the fact that three of the six officers charged were black, including the officer with the harshest charges. She also didn't divulge her personal and political relationship with the Grey family lawyer, Billy Murphy. He was not only a campaign donor, he was on her transition team and a "mentor" to her. Ethically she should have recused herself from this case, but ethics plays no part in social change. (see A Change Of Heart) How can she be impartial when she has close ties to the family's lawyer? She has given the defense a strong argument to have the case dismissed, possibly allowing guilty suspects to go free. This will only lead to more violence at a later time.

The racism accusation is easily dismantled with a simple look at the facts. Half of the officers charged are black. In fact, over half of the Baltimore Police Department are minorities. Four of the top six commanders as well as fifty-four percent of those ranked as captain or above are minorities. Just like all the other cities that Obama, Sharpton and Liberal Democrats label as disasters, Baltimore has been run by Democrats for decades. If they're still in ruin after 40 years of Democrat control, is it possible that Democratic policies are the problem? Or do they not want these problems fixed because they have another objective?

Baltimore receives millions in federal money. After the riots there was a call for federal oversight. Is there a connection between this and the cops being told to stand-down? Why were abandoned police cars in the streets when the rioting happened just waiting to be destroyed? Who made this decision to start the curfew on Tuesday night and not Monday? Why was the destruction allowed to happen when it could have been avoided or at least minimized?

When events like this happen, its important to look back to history *for guidance. History provides us with both insight and warning. In Baltimore, rival gangs were brought together to fight the police. They are simply falling prey to political propagandists to become what Lenin termed, "Useful Idiots." They can be manipulated, angered and led to demand, riot, destroy and even kill for what they believe to be a noble cause. During the rise of the Nazi Party in the 1920's, a paramilitary group formed known as Sturmabteilung, or the SA. They earned the nickname "Brownshirts" due to their uniforms. Strong advocates of socialism, these revolutionaries, consisting of a large number of youths, used threats and violence to destroy political opponents. Hitler willingly allowed these soldiers to bring him and his Nazi Party to power in 1933 as they effectively ruined anyone who opposed him.*

A year later, Hitler realized the Brownshirt's mobster-like mentality was too threatening and radical to those he needed to rebuild Germany. Regular Army leaders, leaders of industry and ordinary citizens had to support him if he intended on conquering more territory for Germany. The Brownshirts were threatening Hitler's plans as they terrified the average German citizen.

Hitler thought he brokered a compromise between the SA and the regular Army, but SA leader Ernst Rohm continued his efforts, declaring, "The SA is the National Socialist Revolution!!" Heinrich Himmler led a subgroup of the SA known as the Shutzstaffel, or SS. They became Hitler's personal bodyguards. Hoping to oust Rohm and benefit from his downfall, Himmler stirred the pot, exploiting the already growing tensions. He lied to Hitler claiming the SA was planning to overthrow him and convinced him to take action against the SA.

Many SA leaders, including Rohm, were homosexuals. Hitler ignored this, even though he was actively targeting homosexuals at the time, because the SA was too useful to his rise in power. Once their services became a hindrance instead of a help, Hitler used their unlawful homosexuality as an excuse for their execution. They had merely become another group of Lenin's useful idiots. He ordered the SS to "purge" the Brownshirt's top leaders on June 30, 1934. That night they were arrested, imprisoned and eventually killed by the SS.

After the top officials were in custody, the next day Hitler commanded the execution of other SA leaders along with other undesirables, some of whom helped put Hitler into power. SS troops followed the Reich List of Unwanted Persons, murdering upwards of 1000 Germans in one weekend with less than half actually being SA officers. In a speech two weeks later, Hitler declared, "In this hour I was responsible for the fate of the German people, and thereby I became the supreme judge of the German people. It was no secret that this time the revolution would have to be bloody; when we spoke of it we called it

'The Night of the Long Knives.' Everyone must know for all future time that if he raises his hand to strike the State, then certain death is his lot." Getting his wish, SS leader Himmler, along with Reinhard Heydrich, rose to great power and were instrumental in carrying out Hitler's violent and murderous reign over the next decade.

Seeing this history, why would Al Sharpton demand a federal police force that gives this president, or any future president, the power Hitler had? When the police are under local control, the people have the power to protest, vote and fix problems in the department. This was seen very clearly in the massive changes made in Cincinnati's police force following that city's 2001 riots.

On the other hand, who do you vote out or protest with a federal police force? The police force would be run by a political appointee who was not elected. If a president wishes to use the police force as a political tool instead of law enforcement, what recourse do citizens have? Could the Jews resist when they were thrown in concentration camps? What happened to German citizens who disagreed with what was happening or chose to hide or help a Jew? Who refused when the Nazis religiously and racially persecuted the Jews, forcing them to wear a yellow Star of David inscribed with the word Jude (Jew)?

Barack Obama shrouded his call for a civilian army behind a stronger national security. Al Sharpton changed the narrative to include racism. In the end, the goal is the same - federal control of police. A federal police force is not only completely unconstitutional, it is a threat and danger to both the freedoms and the lives of the American people. There are those that support Obama no matter what he does. But they should at least take an honest look at his behavior and see how it mirrors behavior of the past. When the demand for a federal police force is combined with the Obama administration's demand for strict gun control, the pattern of history becomes all too clear. Hitler enforced gun control before unleashing his civilian military on the people. That is part of the reason the citizens, both Jews and non-Jews, had no ability to fight back. (see Gun Control: The First Steps Of Tyranny-Vol.3)

The 99 percenters, Soros funded groups, the New Black Panthers, Crips, Bloods and other anarchists stirring up trouble in Ferguson and Baltimore are going the way of the Brownshirts if America does not wake up. Terrified citizens will eventually call for an end to the violence, rioting and destruction. The Administration will become judge and jury, just as Hitler did, and those carrying the Revolutionary banner will be the first to be sacrificed. Each of these groups are merely the next stanza in the rhythms and rhymes of Lenin's ode to useful idiots.

Progressive soldiers don't have to be violent, though. Despite the fact that just a few years ago Obama and Hillary Clinton were adamantly against gay marriage, they seem to have radically changed their views and embraced the cause. Some Progressive politicians are cheering the religious assault radical homosexuals are waging against Christian businesses. (see <u>We Reserve The Right To Refuse Service-</u> Vol.1) It destroys their opponents, causing Christians to remain silent as more and more rights are taken not only from them, but everyone. How long until these useful idiots are no longer beneficial? Are these homosexuals just being exploited like Ernst Rohm until they too become a liability?

Liberty, you must always study and learn from the past as it is doomed to be repeated. The good news is if enough of us are paying attention, we can change the path we are on. I will do my best to make this a better outcome for you.

That's my 2 cents.

Love,
Mom

May 28, 2015

Dear Liberty,

    Liberals and Progressives like to promote themselves as the enlightened people of choice while painting Conservatives as the political movement of control. They pridefully insist a woman has a right to choose what she does with her body. But are they really that open to allowing women that freedom? As a conservative woman, here's what I choose to do with mine.

Pro-Choice should apply to more than just murder.
LiberatingLetters
The**Facts**Paper.com

    When I found out I was pregnant with you four years ago this week, concerned about a pregnancy over age 40, I had one major choice to make, whether or not to have an epidural. Really not a tough decision if you think about it for more than a minute. We also had to choose a name for you, but again, not a really tough decision. We chose a middle name, Grace, which glorified and honored God. After you were born, your father and I chose to have you baptized. Every Sunday I choose to get up and take you to church. I then choose to stay after for Bible Study while you are in Sunday School. To be fair, these are not so much choices I make, as they are actions the Holy Spirit leads me to do. My sinful nature would much rather stay in bed asleep.

    I have chosen to homeschool you. In preparation, I chose to start doing my own homework and preparing myself to be able to teach you about history, science, both creation and evolution, social issues, current events, our founding, and more. I choose to spend hours researching topics and then I choose to spend more time writing a letter to you about what I learned.

    I also choose whether we go out for dinner or eat at home as well as what the meal will be. Some nights it's baked chicken at home, sometimes it's pizza at CiCi's. Fast food restaurants have been under attack for years by people who insist on a woman's right to choose. They'll let it slide if I decide to not to kill you in the womb, but I'm not smart enough to decide if you should have chicken nuggets. They must determine that for me.

    Healthcare, education and food are some of the choices I have the freedom and liberty to make. Progressive and Liberal "pro-choicers", on the other had, are very adamant that they need to be made for me. Yet I am supposedly the close-minded, enslaving one. They are content if I would have chosen to murder you in the womb but they go berserk if I let you eat McDonald's fries, claiming they are not healthy for you.

When your quad screen test came back with an increased possibility of you having downs syndrome, many "pro-choicers" would have argued the responsible thing would be for us to abort you. In fact, a mandatory abortion bill in this circumstance would be widely supported by those who otherwise insist on the woman's right to choose. As Progressives always eventually reveal, they are happy with your right to choose as long as you select their choice.

If it were up to "pro-choice" Progressives, I wouldn't have to worry about whether to homeschool you or send you to the church because nothing but state run public schools would be allowed to provide education. Many also agree with Bill Nye "The Science Guy" that creationism is "not appropriate" for children and want to remove that choice from me as well. They want to follow the German model that allows authorities to take children if their parents do not send them to the state run schools.

I choose to hug and kiss you as much as I can and I choose to discipline you when needed. I choose to give you treats when you are good and take away your scooter when you aren't listening. Many believe their way of discipline is best while others disagree with any form of punishment at all. Their children are often called bullies, divas, thieves, drug addicts, and murderers. They have every right to have their opinion but too many have decided it's their right to force me to follow their ways.

The federal social worker program has grown into such an enormous strong-arm for the government, some citizens are actually scared to say anything negative to their child in public in fear of having their children taken from them. Some government bureaucrats even believe they have the right to decide what the appropriate medical choice for their child is.

Fourteen year old Justine Pelletier was held captive at Boston Children's Hospital for 16 months because an emergency room doctor claimed the parents were "too aggressive" in caring for their daughter's illness. After being successfully treated for years for mitochondrial disease, a quick exam led an ER doctor to change her diagnosis to mental illness basically because he doesn't believe mitochondrial disease is real. He called the Department of Children and Families (DCF) and escorted the parents out of the hospital without their daughter.

Four days later the DCF took custody of Justine. She was denied her medication, her siblings, her parents and her freedom while her health quickly deteriorated. As her family fought for her release, the government dug in their heals. Finally after over a year of captivity,

Justine was given back to her parents in June of 2014 but at an amazing price to her health.

Two months after Justine was confined to Boston Children's, a five month old was taken by Children's Protective Services (CPS) from a young Russian couple in Sacramento. Sammy had some flu-like symptoms so the parents took him to Sutter Memorial Hospital. After he was given unprescribed antibiotics from a nurse and then told their son needed immediate open-heart surgery, the couple gathered their child and quickly rushed him to another hospital for a second opinion. Kaiser Parmanente Medical Center concluded he was fine to go home.

Sutter called CPS because the parents took Sammy without being discharged, which they had every legal right to do. CPS came and took the child the next day. A week later a judge moved him from protective custody to Stanford Medical Center for a second opinion but required the CPS visit the house and monitor the situation.

With these two examples, loving, caring parents only wanting the best for their children were denied their choice in the child's care. As it turned out in both cases, the parents were absolutely right and the government entities were absolutely wrong.

Liberty, you will find that you will never agree 100% with anyone. Many times you can't find even one thing to agree upon with someone. We are all allowed our opinions and the freedom to try to persuade others to our point of view. Where the danger lies, and hypocrisy rears it's ugly head, is with those who demand I view the world exactly the way they do.

The majority of "pro-choicers" are happy to champion a "woman's right to choose" but only when it comes to killing my baby. Other choices like food, education, religion, and medical treatment are too important for me to make. I'm free to snip your spinal cord while you are being born but I should be flogged and imprisoned if I give you a Twinkie or, heaven forbid, teach you that God created the universe.

Liberty, I am a staunch conservative and I am overwhelming pro-choice. I believe all people have the right to determine the direction their life takes, even if it means they might get hurt. I am vehemently opposed to abortion, but that's because I oppose murder. I believe in trying to educate people and let them make an informed decision.

The reason this is important is that over 90% of women wanting an abortion decide to keep their baby after seeing the ultra-sound. That's why abortion activists reject any effort to make it a prerequisite for abortion. Instinctively a woman knows that image is not only a human life, but their child. A woman, whether Liberal or Conservative,

86

would do anything to defend her child. However, they are told it is not a life and won't feel anything. You must change hearts and minds, Liberty, not laws.

Liberals like to control the argument by controlling the language. It is time to take that advantage away. When the issues are looked at one by one, facts reveal that Conservatives are far more "pro-choice" then Progressives could even dream of being.

That's my 2 cents.

Love,
Mom

June 3, 2015

Dear Liberty,

 Every culture in the world has marriage and always has. This includes both Eastern and Western nations as well as civilized and uncivilized communities. Whether you believe the Bible is the word of God or just a book written by men, it is one of the oldest records of history. It predates dominant cultures such as Rome or Greece, where many start their history of marriage. In doing so they choose to ignore cultures such as Native Americans, who we know practiced marriage long before either society came into existence.

 The Bible also establishes traditions including a bridal price, parental blessing, and the importance of faithfulness, which are core marriage rituals found in cultures all over the world. Many who want to redefine marriage disregard the first marriage recorded in Genesis. Rejecting God's establishment of marriage doesn't mean it doesn't exist, it just means one refuses to see it.

"The Lord God said, 'It is not good for the man to be alone. I will make a helper suitable for him.' So the Lord God caused the man to fall into a deep sleep; and while he was sleeping, he took one of the man's ribs and then closed up the place with flesh. Then the Lord God made a woman from the rib he had taken out of the man, and he brought her to the man. The man said, 'This is now bone of my bones, and flesh of my flesh; she shall be called 'woman,' for she was taken out of man.'

That is why a man leaves his father and mother and is united to his wife, and they become one flesh." Gen. 2:18, 21-24

 The unity of a man and a woman has been foundational to developing a society from the beginning because the family is the smallest societal group. As with everything else, after sin came into the world the understanding of marriage and relationships became corrupt and unhealthy. (see Fruit Of The Forbidden Tree-Vol.1) By God's own definition, matrimony was never intended for multiple wives, extramarital relationships, cohabitation, promiscuity, abusive partners, same-sex couples, or divorce. (see What Is Love?, The Rainbow Connection, and We Reserve The Right To Refuse Service-Vol.1)

 In many cultures, a wedding ceremony isn't even required. Up until the 1500's, the Christian church would declare a marriage valid, even without witnesses, as long as the couple affirmed they had exchanged marital vows. Marriages were private agreements between two families, sometimes for love but sometimes for royal lineage, financial, social, or simply procreational reasons. The union was recorded in the Family Bible and with that, it was official. The church was out of it unless asked to participate but more importantly, the government was not involved. Primarily to prevent invalid marriages, the church eventually called for couples to post their upcoming nuptials in the town to confirm that both persons were available for wedlock. This is why some claim the church was not associated with marriage until the 16th century, thus denying any religious history of marriage.

So why did the government start requiring a marriage license to participate in a custom that existed freely for thousands of years?

It was during the pre-Civil War years that states began restricting marriages by outlawing unions between blacks and whites. Massachusetts began requiring licenses as early as 1639. Other states followed suit over the years. People were free to marry within their race as they desired as long as consent was given by the bride's parents. It was still the parent's responsibility to grant approval, not the state's. This is why when the minister asks, "Who gives this woman to be married to this man?" the answer is, "Her mother and I," not "The State of Ohio."

Slaves were allowed to wed, even those at different households, if they obtained permission from their owners first. This is just like citizens must do today from their state. Regardless, slave owners still had the right to sell either spouse or the children as they saw fit. After the war, several states began allowing interracial marriages but only after obtaining approval from the government. In other words, states said, "We will let you perform an illegal act if you ask permission to do it first and pay a fee." Thus begins the governmental overreach and intrusion into the institution of marriage and the license became a political tool. Pay the government and they'll allow you to participate in a legitimate act they deemed illegal. In other words, bribery.

States quickly expanded their authoritative power by requiring all people to apply for a license before getting married. The Federal Government passed the Uniform Marriage and Marriage License Act in 1923, followed by the Marriage and Divorce Act of 1970. With these laws the Federal Government interjected themselves into the process, granting states the permission to permit not only marriages but divorces. In 1969, California started granting no-fault divorces where either party could file for divorce under the guise of "irreconcilable differences." You could discard your marriage as easily as discarding an unwanted pet, even if your partner didn't want to separate. That's why a long "Hollywood Marriage" is anything over 13 weeks.

By requiring people to obtain a license, the government forced themselves into the marriage contract itself. Liberty, when your father and I got married, our pastor made it clear there were three people in this union; your father, me and God. The government agrees marriage contains three entities. According to the State of Ohio: "Marriage is a legal as well as a spiritual and personal relationship. When you repeat your marriage vows, you enter into a legal contract. There are three parties to that legal contract: you, your spouse, and the State of Ohio. The State is a party to the contract because under its laws, you have certain obligations and responsibilities to each other, to any children you may have, and to Ohio." They kicked God out and thrust themselves in His place, taking top billing in the contract. Once again, the government has declared itself Supreme Being making the couple obligated to it, but no responsibilities in the reverse.

The license grants Children's Services rights to your children under the guise of protecting the child. They gave themselves the authority to sue you on your child's behalf as well as the freedom to take your children at their leisure. So in reality, is the government's power over your marriage and family any different than that of the slave owner? This legal contract allows them to control your family unit and rip it apart as they so desire.

Marriage licenses were not limited to racial grounds, but included biological purposes as well. Many states required blood tests to get a license claiming health concerns, looking for signs of venereal diseases. This provision has since been abolished but not before denying many people the right to marry. With the advancements of DNA tests, how long until the government requires a DNA sample before allowing marriages to take place? Half of the states prohibit first cousins marrying, citing reproductive concerns. Another six only allow them if the parties are beyond childbearing years. What is to stop the government from using DNA to ensure healthy progeny from a union? They've already claimed the principle partnership in the marriage as well as authority over products of the union. What's to prevent them from insisting on oversight of the children's health before they are even conceived?

Government first replaced God in the marriage contract. They now want to make Him completely irrelevant to the issue. Because they granted themselves the power to issue marriage licenses, they wrongly concluded it also gives them the right to determine what marriage is. With all the accepted perversions to marriage throughout history, it has never been defined as a union between people of the same sex. A man may have had many wives, but each marriage was between a man and a woman.

It is important to note that even without governmental or church oversight, societies having freedom in wedlock still rejected homosexual unions. Even in Ancient Greece, where adult males were presumed to take a young boy as a student and lover, they were still expected to have a wife and children. Homosexuality was openly accepted, yet it was never recognized as marriage and never seen as the dominant or preferred relationship.

American's all over the country have overwhelmingly voted to reject same-sex marriage, understanding it's true definition of one man and one woman. Activist judges are usurping their authority, ignoring the will of the people, and changing thousands of years of history by issuing marriage licenses to same-sex couples anyway. They punished bakers, photographers, florists and caterers for not participating in same-sex ceremonies even if their religious beliefs oppose the union. Many of these cases occurred in states where same-sex marriage was still illegal at the time. So judges fined business owners hundreds of thousands of dollars for not participating in a ceremony that was illegal and rewarded the couple that willingly broke the law, thus making the government a co-conspirator in a crime. (see What Is Love?, The Rainbow Connection, and We Reserve The Right To Refuse Service-Vol.1)

As history shows us, humans and civilizations tend to tumble into more and more moral decline until they completely crumble. The deterioration of the traditional family and marriage are results of this decline in America, which now faces its own demise. According to British historian Arnold Toynbee, "Of the 22 civilizations that have appeared in history, 19 of them collapsed when they reached the moral state America is in today." Surprisingly, he made this statement long before the effects of the policies of the 1960's, such as rising divorce, unwed births, and astronomical abortions rates, truly took root.

Those trying to abolish marriage altogether are attempting to convince people that marriage is racist and oppressive. They twist, turn and combine the history of the marriage license with marriage itself. What they fail to reveal is that the racist and oppressive components did not enter the issue until the government took control. Marriage is not the problem, government involvement is. As they always do, the government took an institution that was working perfectly fine, legislated it until it was almost completely broken and now insist they are the ones to fix it.

Liberty, when the Federal Government has grown as big as Washington is now, the only way to cut it back down to size is for the states to reclaim their rights and freedoms. Alabama has taken a very good first step to reverse this intrusive and blatant overreach of the government. The State Senate passed a bill abolishing marriage licenses thus removing the ability of federal judges to illegally issue *them to same-sex couples. Alabama should be applauded and used as a model for other liberty-loving states. They should be replicating this action with issue after issue until the Federal Government is reduced to the manageable level it was intended to be.*

Instead of debating whether the government should allow gay marriage or not, we should be asking why the government is involved at all. If we follow Alabama's lead, they soon won't be.

That's my 2 cents.

Love,
Mom

June 11, 2015

Dear Liberty,

Starting in the 1960's and picking up steam in the 1990's, people began subscribing to the idea that it was unfair to have winners and losers. Youth baseball and soccer teams stopped keeping score and everyone was declared a winner by receiving a participation trophy. The ones with natural talent, or those that put in their best effort, feel slighted while those who know they aren't that good realize their trophy for just showing up is nothing more than a joke.

No one wants their feelings hurt or to feel bad about themselves. We should never purposely cause that. But if one doesn't experience a little disappointment and failure in their life, then what is there to push them to do better? If we are satisfied with the status quo, we are never motivated to strive for something better.

If America would have had this attitude at the beginning, we wouldn't have cars, planes, microwaves, computers, cell phones, iPads or even zippers or Velcro. We never would have won any wars. The Army rangers that climbed the jagged cliffs at Normandy while machine gun fire rained down on them would have given up before they reached the beach. (see Safe Spaces-Vol.6) Your grandfather would have surrendered when his squad was killed around him and allowed the Germans a free pass in World War I possibly changing the dynamics of the Cantigny campaign. (see A Hero's Story-Vol.1 and Big Red Won-Vol.5)

Liberty, you have reached a stage where you love to compete. Running up the stairs, getting to the car, buckling yourself in, everything is a race. Even while I'm driving, you always want to be in the lead telling me to "go faster, Mommy." You instinctively know how great it is to be victorious which you declare enthusiastically with, "I win! I win!" In fact, you get quite upset if you don't. I LOVE that. It is important to always give it your all and strive to be the best. In doing that you can inspire others to search for the very best in themselves.

However, there is a movement in America to eradicate our natural tendency to compete. While we shouldn't flaunt our success, we shouldn't be ashamed of it either. God gives each of us gifts and talents that we should use, not hide. We should find things that we are good at and practice, work hard, and strive to do our best at the task.

In Genesis 11, the people at Babel "said to each other, 'Come, let's make bricks and bake them thoroughly.' They used brick instead of stone, and tar for mortar." It is extremely significant that God's word points out that the people started building with bricks. When stones were used, each one was different and unique. The builder had to carefully turn and maneuver the stones, using them as they were, so they fit together into positions that built a strong wall. Bricks were definitely easier to use, because they were all made from the same mold. There was no uniqueness, no individuality, and no personality. They stacked neatly upon each other, no fuss, no concessions, no resistance.

At this point they then said, "Come, let us build ourselves a city, with a tower that reaches to the heavens, so that we may make a name for ourselves; otherwise we will be scattered over the face of the whole earth." (see The Rainbow Connection) So, after abandoning originality and distinctiveness, they were going to become their own god by constructing the Tower of Babel. Here they would build a monument to themselves, not God. This was the first example of socialism in the world. As Genesis accounts, it did not work out well for the people. God scattered them by confusing their language and the tower was abandoned. (see Putting Right What Once Went Wrong-Vol.3)

When we allow society to remove competition, forcing equality of outcome regardless of ability and effort, we are being forced into the brick mold. God did not create us to be identical replicas of each other. Paul explains that we all make up the body of Christ. One of us is a hand, one is an eye, and another is an ear. No one part is more important than another, and they work in concert making the body function as a whole. Each person is unique but important to the whole.

But bricks are what socialists want. They cast people as a black brick, or a white brick, or a union brick. You are not unique. You are simply a member of a group they have placed you in. Such thinking leads to the idea that cops target someone only because he is black. (see Just The Facts, Ma'am-Vol.1, Everything Free But Speech, There's Nothing Right About The Alt-Right-Vol.4, and Is God Dead?-Vol.7) But is that true, or is he a unique individual who made bad decisions to engage in crime and most likely violent crime?

America has gone from raising entrepreneurs and self-motivators to producing 30-year-old couch potatoes whose greatest accomplishment is living in their parent's basements surrounded by their participation trophies. By denying children the ability to fail, we are withholding a fundamental learning experience that they need to prepare for reality.

Young adults who have never been allowed to fail are entering the real world with no idea how to respond when they are rejected. Instead of picking themselves up, learning from the experience and moving forward, they lay around like bricks, inventing reasons why they aren't successful and searching for other people to blame. Perhaps the $100,000 student loan for a degree in English literature was not money as well spent as that on a degree in engineering. One allows you to build the future; the other allows you to supersize an order of fries.

Without failure people are led to believe in equal outcomes no matter the decisions they make or the effort put forth. Taken to it's extreme, this way of thinking leads to making horrible decision after horrible decision. They then claim the need to be bailed out, declaring they are too big to fail. Actually, failure was exactly what was needed. Rather than patting GM and Wells Fargo on the head and giving them billions of dollars of participation money to cover up their mistakes, they needed to know there are consequences for bad decisions. Instead, big banks and big business are convinced they can make any bad decision because the government will insure a proper outcome. At some point, reality will set in.

When everyone receives the same prize, there is no motivation to work harder than anyone else. We sit there in line with the other bricks, take our wages, and say nothing. While the intentions may be honorable, the consequences of an "everybody wins" attitude has led to the development of a generation that accepts socialism as a fair and reasonable idea. Unfortunately, they are never shown the enslaving and debilitating effects of a concept that makes everyone equal. It's not done by raising the standard, but by reducing it to the lowest common denominator, making everyone equally poor. The only ones who benefit from a socialist society are the ones that hold power, by grabbing your money and your freedom all in the name of the "common good." The easiest place to find the evil 1% is in the hallowed halls of a socialist government.

We must respectfully resist becoming bricks. Never be ashamed of your accomplishments. Never give up on doing your best. In your victories, humbly thank the Lord for your success and accept your award with grace. When you lose, thank the Lord for the opportunity to compete and continue to display gratitude. In either situation, show the love and forgiveness of Jesus so others may desire to have the peace you know through Christ.

In Romans, Paul specifically addressed the troubles we will encounter because of our faith in Christ. His words can also be expanded to all we do as everything should be done in the glory of God. "Not only that, but we rejoice in our sufferings, knowing that suffering produces endurance, and endurance produces character, and character produces hope, and hope does not put us to shame, because God's love has been poured into our hearts through the Holy Spirit who has been given to us." (Romans 5:3-5)

Liberty, never deny the desire to be your very best because hard work builds character. Failure inspires determination and endurance. Victory breeds more victory. Individuality ensures freedom and liberty.

That's my 2 cents.

Love,
Mom

June 18, 2015

Dear Liberty,

Because Christians preach that we should not sin, many unbelievers conclude that Christians then presume they don't sin. This is a complete misunderstanding of the Christian faith. Christians know that "all have sinned and fall short of the glory of God," which is why we need a Savior. What unfortunately happens is often Christians appear pious in their witness to the world, which results in many wrongfully assuming that Christians consider themselves better than others.

This was showcased again when it was recently revealed that Josh Duggar had sexually abused several of his sisters twelve years ago. The Duggar family, a Christian, conservative family, became famous through the reality TV show, "19 Kids and Counting." Always ready to pounce, social media and news outlets immediately accused hypocrisy among the Duggar family as soon as the news broke. Reporters were appalled by the past actions of a 14-year-old Josh Duggar while in the next news story vocally supporting the idea that we have gender-neutral restrooms in schools. Instead of questioning if Josh received the help he needed for his problem, public opinion promptly condemned him without even a cursory review of the facts.

As soon as the Duggar parents found out what Josh did, they put both him and his sisters into counseling. After Josh's treatment, his parents took him down to the police department to confess. Josh is not immune to sin just because he's a Christian and he knows it. When he did sin, he and his family took responsibility. He owned up to his sin, repented, and asked for God's forgiveness. This gives him spiritual blessings from God, but it does not eliminate the need to pay the price for doing something wrong. A contrite heart acknowledges that a wrong requires a proper punishment; it does not flee that punishment. The Duggar family claims that the circumstances of 2002 actually brought them closer to God.

Being a Christian is not a "Get Out Of Jail Free" card on this side of Heaven. It's not that you don't sin, it's that you repent. (see The Skinny On Fat Tuesday-Vol.4, The Serpent And The Tree-Vol.3, and Fruit Of The Forbidden Tree-Vol.1) It's not that you aren't held accountable, it's that you take responsibility. It's not that you don't have troubles, it's how you let your faith guide you through them. It is how we respond and react to events, both in and out of our control, that sets a Christian apart.

When the news broke, Josh resigned his position at the Family Research Center. TLC pulled all the current and future episodes of "19 Kids and Counting" until further notice. Many could rightfully argue Josh brought this upon himself. It's also a justified consequence of his sin. But what about those trials we experience that happen as no fault of our own?

Mrs. G, the pastor's wife, was in a debilitating car accident when she was a teenager. She sustained injuries that left her unable to use her legs. Physically confined to a wheelchair, her spirit is more active and more mobile that anyone else I know. Mrs. G never allows her physical limitations to restrict her love and concern for others.

Many who experience similar injuries or circumstances can fall prey to anger and hate. Anger at the person who caused them the injury, anger at the world and even anger at God. Though it took Mrs. G. several years to learn to emotionally cope with her new way of life, over time the Holy Spirit turned any anger, regret, and sadness into love and inspiration. She teaches at the church's school and daily demonstrates to her students that nothing should limit you. Through her attitude and actions, she also shows the children as well as the world, that everything can be turned into glory to God. The years that she journeyed through learning to accept her physical condition gave her a unique perspective and appreciation that she shares with others. With God's help, she took a tragedy and turned it into a gift, which she uses to serve and witness to His grace.

A few months ago doctors told her that she will need to have another surgery. Not only did she have to stop teaching the remainder of this year, she has to take a leave of absence for the following school year. It would be perfectly understandable if Mrs. G was disappointed and possibly depressed by this. Instead, Mrs. G has used her time off to do more studying, both of the Bible and as a teacher. She has written several of her own Bible Studies to help further the learning of others. Still wanting to help the kids, she has offered her assistance to the school to do other administrative duties they need. Focusing on serving others, rather than focusing on ourselves, is how we are to live as Christians.

We are told in church all the time that we should live our lives as a witness to Christ. Our attitudes should reflect God's love in a way that others will desire to learn about Jesus because of the peace He has given us. Pastor G. asked a very interesting question in church on Sunday, "Will people recognize the family resemblance between you and your brother Jesus?" That is a question we should ask ourselves everyday as we venture into this world as a child of God. Mrs. G. does an amazing job reflecting her branch on the Heavenly family tree. I would not be surprised if she is frequently asked how she can stay so positive despite her injury and ongoing surgeries. Her joy in the face of suffering gives a perfect opportunity to fulfill Peter's call to, "Always be prepared to give an answer to everyone who asks you to give the reason for the hope that you have. But do this with gentleness and respect, keeping a clear conscience, so that those who speak maliciously against your good behavior in Christ may be ashamed of their slander." Her joy comes from being a forgiven child of God.

The world does not want to be told we are sinners. It is a very difficult truth to admit about ourselves. That is why people are so eager to attack Christians when they are caught in a sin. It is an attempt to shame Christians into silence. If people aren't constantly reminded that they sin, then they think they can happily live their life without any guilt.

Christ told us, "If the world hates you, keep in mind that it hated me first." (John 15:18) But He encouraged us with, "You will be hated by all for my name's sake. But the one who endures to the end will be saved." (Matt 10:22)

We must strive to live our lives as evidence of God's love no matter what our trials, tribulations, successes and blessings in life. We must show God's love by acknowledging our own flaws and need for a savior. There will always be those who reject our message no matter how peacefully and lovingly we say it, but that should not stop you from constantly trying. Find comfort in the fact that it is the Holy Spirit's job to change hearts, not yours. You are merely a mirror that reflects the true grace of God. You do this by loving others, serving their needs, and by confessing your forgiveness through the Good News that Jesus Christ is risen. He is risen indeed.

That's my 2 cents.

Love,
Mom

June 25, 2015

Dear Liberty,

  As I was writing last week's letter about Christian response and attitude to hardships, an extremely troubled young man walked into a Bible Study in Charleston, South Carolina, opened fire, and killed 9 people. After being captured a day later, he confessed his goal was to start a race war.

  He purposely sought out an African-American church, which happened to be the oldest African-American church in the country. One victim's son believes the real target was Rev. Clementa Pinckney, the church's well-known minister and a state senator. Before completing his massacre, Dylann Roof entered Emanuel AME Church and joined the study for an hour. He excused himself, retrieved his weapons, re-entered the building and began shooting. After telling one survivor he allowed her to live so she could recount the events to the world, Dylan put his gun to his head and fired. To his dismay, the gun was empty.

  Dylan's disturbing and deep-rooted racism was not enough to satisfy the endless questions. Why did these good people have to be slaughtered? Why couldn't he have just killed himself too? What was God's purpose of this horrific massacre? The answers were quickly revealed.

  The day of the shooting, the children of Sharonda Coleman-Singleton stood bravely in front of cameras and proclaimed that even though they are deeply dismayed by the death of their mother, the love and faith in Jesus Christ that she passed on to them will see them through. A day later, as Dylann was being arraigned, one by one grieving family members stood up in court and addressed the 21-year-old suspect. One by one they said despite the tremendous pain he caused them, they forgave him. Some also urged Dylann to give his life over to Christ.

  If Dylann's gun had just had one more bullet, these family members would not have been able to share with him and the world their love and forgiveness through Christ. They would not have had the opportunity to invite Dylann to repent and turn to Christ himself. While being questioned by the police, Dylann admitted that he almost didn't go through with the massacre because the victims had been so nice to him. By continuing that display of Christ's love, family members heaped coals of compassion upon his head. Dylann may never seek the forgiveness of Christ or repent of his actions, but millions across the globe who heard the family members' words may take the opportunity to seek Christ's forgiveness in their own lives.

Here at home, hours before Dylann appeared in court, another very disturbed 21-year-old man wrote farewells to his friends through texts and on Facebook, grabbed his gun, and called the police to report "an erratic man armed with a firearm". He called 911 twice within a 10-minute window. Officer Sonny Kim, a 27-year veteran of the police department and good friend of your father's, responded to the call. Despite the young man's mother desperately trying to just get him home, Trepierre Hummons broke free from her hold and shot Officer Kim. He then rushed the injured policeman to struggle with and take his gun. After using the gun to shoot Officer Kim one more time, he turned it against another officer. At this point the other officer had no choice but to eliminate the threat by killing the suspect. Now it was our turn to decide how to respond to a horrible tragedy. Would we be able to forgive, or were we going to be bitter?

Several prayer vigils were held that night for Officer Kim, one of which your father and I attended. Prayers were said for his family and support was given to his fellow officers. I, along with others, prayed also for Trepierre's family, as they are hurting as well. In particular Trepierre's mother, who witnessed her son being shot and killed. She showed tremendous forgiveness as she opposed neighbors and family members wanting to attack the officers. She understood her son's behavior and actions resulted in his death. Trepierre's father was bitter at first, mostly because he at least wanted his son remembered as well. After an earlier tense exchange at a vigil that evening, he was able to return and make peace with the officers.

The community immediately opened its heart to the Kim family, raising over $130,000 through one fund alone. The University of Cincinnati extended free undergraduate tuition for any of the three Kim children who choose to go there. Over the next few weeks and months, other fundraising events are sure to occur that will only give more opportunity for the Tri-State area to express their gratitude, love and support for the Kim family.

Liberty, it is quite ironic to me that the same week I wrote to you about walking the Christian walk, two events happened where an amazing witness of love and forgiveness were displayed. (see Walking The Walk) One was also an extremely personal event for your father and me. The America that I know, the America that I love, was displayed and revealed on both a local and national stage.

Your dad reached out with concern and compassion for his

friends on the force only to have them return that sympathy to him. They helped him through an extremely difficult time. There was no hatred or vile towards the suspect or his family but empathy and kindness for each other as a family of their own. Even one of Officer Kim's sons wrote an extremely touching tribute to his father showing no disdain or contempt for Trepierre, but only love and thankfulness to his father.

I found hope in the actions of the victims' families and supporters in the events of last week. I was overwhelmed by the tenderness and humanity of people who experienced tremendous pain, but displayed immense mercy. With the help of Christ, Liberty, love and forgiveness will always win out over hatred and revenge.

May all the victims Rest In Peace. Their deaths, though horribly tragic, allowed an outpouring of Christ's love. I'm sure they are humbled and proud of the way their family and friends have expressed God's forgiveness and concern. Because of that, their deaths were not in vain.

Liberty, life is fragile. You may only have one chance to be a witness for Christ which is why you must be that witness every day in every way.

That's my 2 cents.

Love,
Mom

June 30, 2015

Dear Liberty,

As people are celebrating the Supreme Court ruling on same-sex marriage, social media is on fire proclaiming, "Love wins." I join with those embracing the hashtag of the day, gladly declaring, "Love wins," showing the example of true love.

The Bible clearly defines marriage as a union between a man and a woman while revealing that homosexuality is one of the sins that is reprehensible to God. (see We Reserve The Right To Refuse Service-Vol.1 and Marriage Is What Brings Us Together Today) By unrepentantly practicing what God has deemed damaging to one's soul, which is more loving, for Christians to express their views to protect individuals, or keep their mouths shut and willfully allow participants to potentially damn themselves to eternal darkness?

In a similar fashion, for those who support gay marriage, does it show love to allow those who disagree with them to continue to hold their religious beliefs, not bullying their churches or businesses? Or is it loving to force others to reject their own conscience by threatening them with lawsuits, loss of businesses and loss of freedom of speech?

It's fairly easy to explain this by looking at the word bigotry. Bigotry is defined as the intolerance of those who share different views than you. It does not mean people can't disagree with you, it means you are intolerant of that disagreement. Even if you don't believe one word of the Judeo-Christian-Islamic view of marriage, many people do. Please keep that in mind when bakers, florists, photographers, churches, synagogues and mosques say, "I'm sorry, but my beliefs prevent me from participating in your ceremony." If this offends one to the point of taking action against that person's beliefs, then who is the true bigot? No one should be forced to participate in a ceremony that goes against their religious doctrine. It is not discrimination; it is practicing their faith. They are not preventing gays from having a ceremony; they are just declining to be a part of it. If we follow the LGBT agenda of forcing compliance against one's beliefs, then naturally an atheist could be forced to have a Christian burial.

Marijuana is legal in Colorado but that doesn't mean I have to smoke it if I go to Denver.

Open-carry is legal in Texas but that doesn't mean I need to strap on a sidearm if I walk the streets of Dallas.

Abortion is legal countrywide but that doesn't mean I have to murder my unborn baby if I don't want to.

Same-sex marriage is now allowed in all 50 states but businesses and religious organizations do not have to participate in the ceremony if their conscience tells them otherwise. Likewise, they should not be forced to, no more than one should be forced to smoke pot, carry a gun, or kill their unborn baby. (see Separation Of Church And State)

The LGBT community should celebrate their victory. However, the ball is now in their court. They should enjoy the freedom to marry whomever they choose. On the other hand, if they decide to suppress and punish those who continue to uphold traditional marriage, they will become the very bigoted and intolerant group they claim persecuted them.

Why is it so outrageous if a church declines to marry a same-sex couple? Should we insist that every doctor perform an abortion on demand? There are churches and public officials that are happy to perform a same-sex marriage without question. The same applies to bakers, florists or any other wedding related business. (see We Reserve The Right To Refuse Service-Vol.1) What is the true motivation of suing that business if they decline to provide services to a same-sex wedding? Is it out of love? Or is it because they can't tolerate someone saying, "No?"

Those who feel suppressed eventually rise up, as the LGBT community did, and overpower those doing the suppressing. (see The Rainbow Connection) The LGBT group has a choice to make, tolerance and acceptance for those with differing opinions, or totalitarianism. Can we all now live and let live, or must we continue with divisive, anger-filled behavior?

Now that the 6,000-year-old definition of marriage has been eradicated, the door is open to anyone wanting to express their love to whomever or whatever they desire. It will not be long before polygamists and pedophiles will demand their day in court. They will be calling for the same dignity and equality that homosexuals just received. There will be no reason now to deny them their free expression of love. Priests can finally be celebrated for their special bond with altar boys instead of stigmatized and all pedophiles cheered for the strong physical attraction they have towards little children.

So, yes, I embrace the term, "Love wins," because love is an amazing and powerful force. But love is more than who you sleep with.

It is a simple acceptance of others that can change hearts, minds, and lives. It can unite people, overshadowing even the most intense hurt, anger, and disagreement. Love nearly stopped Dylann Roof from massacring nine wonderful Christians two weeks ago as they openly embraced him with no regard to the color of his skin. Unfortunately, for the families and himself, he allowed his bigotry to overpower his humanity. But love won out. Love gave the victim's families, still dealing with the ultimate pain of the murder of their loved ones, to face the killer and say, "I forgive you." (see Their Deaths Were Not In Vain) That is true love. And, yes, love wins.

If we want love to win, then allow me to express my love to the LGBT community. You don't ever have to agree with me, or my faith, nor will I force you to. But, as you argued, don't I have the right to express my love? I want everyone, EVERYONE, to share in the eternal blessings given to us by our Lord and Savior Jesus Christ. I desire this so much and love you so deeply that I plan to continue my commitment to spread the Gospel of salvation through Christ's sacrifice regardless of the persecution and discrimination that might come my way. In this manner I am very much like the LGBT community that has been fighting for this ruling for so long.

If love is a right, then I have the right to love whomever I choose. I love humanity. A humanity that lives in a fallen world, plagued by sinful desires and selfish ambition. Because of that love I have no choice but to expose everyone to the forgiveness, compassion and tremendous love of Jesus Christ. As He states in John 15, "Greater love has no one than this: to lay down one's life for one's friends." Yes, I want love to win. I want the amazing love of Christ's sacrifice, dying for the sins of the world so we may have eternal life, to touch everyone's heart.

"Three things will last forever--faith, hope, and love--and the greatest of these is love." 1 Corinthians 13:13

Love,
Mom

July 9, 2015

Dear Liberty,

As information emerged regarding Dylann Roof, the suspect in the recent Emanuel AME Church massacre, a Facebook photo surfaced of him with a Confederate flag in the background. (see *Their Deaths Were Not In Vain*) *Overnight the discussion turned from the actions of one radical racist to the destruction of every Confederate flag in the country. Demands cried out for Southern governors to remove "The Stars and Bars" from their state capitals. Flags that stood as silent sentinels at Confederate monuments for over 100 years are under fire to be removed. Walmart, obviously clueless about their customer base, promptly pulled all products with the image from their shelves; an act just short of slandering Dale Earnhardt. Companies immediately stopped production of the highly offensive flag, while continuing to manufacture and sell Nazi flags. Suddenly a flag became the target for Dylann's racism, giving people an insignificant object to attack and a feeling of effectiveness in the cause against racism.*

One of the most ridiculous moves happened at TVLand. The executives of the channel took The Dukes of Hazzard out of their lineup because the Dixie Flag rode prominently on the roof of the Duke boys' iconic Charger. Anyone who grew up in the late 1970s was glued to the TV every Friday night to see how "two good ol' boys" were going to escape from the corrupt dealings of Boss Hogg and Sheriff Coltrane. Bo and Luke Duke raced along the dirt roads of Hazzard County in an orange Dodge Charger nicknamed "The General Lee" with a big "01" on the doors and a Confederate flag on top. I was in love with Bo and every red blooded American boy was enamored with Daisy Duke and her famous cutoff jeans. A television show that was innocent and fun entertainment overnight turned into a supposed recruitment tool for racists. Even Warner Brothers began removing the flag on their toys of the famous General Lee car that had raked in money for the company thirty years after the show left the air.

People are acting like the flag is causing hate. Do they honestly think that removing it is going to solve racism? Not once did I watch Bo slide across the hood of the General Lee and think, "Man, that flag really makes me hate black people." I was too busy trying to figure out who sewed him into those tight blue jeans.

The simple fact is, this is a pathetic attempt for people to perceive they are doing something about racism, declaring to the world they themselves are not racist, when in fact they accomplish nothing. Such knee jerk reactions prevent society from addressing the real issue and cause of the problem. Instead it allows for the cover-up of the true story of the flag and the history behind it. Which, for those in power, is the goal.

To be honest, I personally am not that offended by the Confederate Flag. I've always seen it as a symbol of Southern pride, just like the majority of Americans recently polled, standing proudly as the backdrop to Lynyrd Skynyrd and their brand of Southern rock. I certainly don't associate it with racism. Perhaps that's because the public schools failed to indoctrinate me. You see, the reason the Flag of Dixie has to go is it reveals the history of the Democratic Party. Eliminate the flag and you remove the truth the Democrats want secret because they have been rewriting the truth about the Civil War ever since it ended.

Progressive Democrats began hiding their support for slavery by claiming the Civil War had nothing to do with slavery. They maintain Abraham Lincoln had no ambitions to free the slaves, even though his famous debates against Senator Stephen Douglas made it clear that his intention was to free the slaves. (see _Disunity Of The Union_) The rewriting of history claims Lincoln went to war with the South simply because those states seceded. The reason put forth is that the Union refused to let the tariffs and taxes they collected from the Southern states go. Articles and school textbooks argue that the Southern states believed they had the constitutional right to withdrawal from the Union over tariffs. These people that are rewriting history are the same ones demanding the removal of the Confederate flag. Some go as far as demanding the removal of war monuments, statues and memorials of Southern leaders. (see _There's Nothing Right About The Alt-Right_-Vol.4 and _Doing Our Duty_-Vol.7) If these things are so offensive and racist, then they are clearly admitting the Civil War was in fact about slavery and not about unfair taxes.

What they carefully sidestep around and ignore in their argument is WHY the South seceded. Liberty, you know from several of my letters that Lincoln was not only very passionate about ending slavery, the abolitionist movement was the entire basis for the formation of the Republican Party, which officially organized this week in 1854. (see _The Birth Of A Movement_-Vol.1) In their declarations to secede, Southern states make it very clear they believed in white supremacy and their right to have slaves. If Democrats hide the Dixie Flag and other Confederate memorabilia, there are many other truths they can hide as well.

Liberal Progressives are trying desperately to dump their sinful past on the GOP. If my party were responsible for the advancement of slavery, the persecution of Negros, the formation of the Ku Klux Klan, I would want to rewrite history too. They want people to believe that the Republican Party, the party that developed specifically and purely to end slavery, was responsible for Southern racism. Democrats can't let the truth out that it was the first Republican president that freed the slaves and that whites along side blacks in the North actually went to war to give slaves their freedom. The Democratic Party can't let today's youth know the true history of their party. Liberty, as the Bible says, "The truth shall set you free," so here we go.

The President of the Confederate States, Jefferson Davis, was a Democrat from Mississippi. While Republicans were championing the fight to end slavery, the Confederate States were governed by Democrats, who designed the very flag that is now being bashed. Davis, along with most other Democrats, continued to believe that Negros were inferior to whites till the day he died. (see Constituting Slavery-Vol.6) Now we begin to see why the Democrat's history must be rewritten.

After the war, Republicans gained control of Congress and went to work. The 13th Amendment banning slavery was passed in Congress with 100% Republican Party support and only 30% Democrat support. (see Founding Documents-Vol.7) Republicans moved forward pushing forth legislation such as the Civil Rights Act of 1866 that protected the rights of the newly freed slaves only to be blocked at every move by Democrat President Andrew Johnson. Despite his veto, Republicans were able to override his objection and made the bill giving citizenship rights to Negros law. Republicans continued by passing the 14th Amendment which guaranteed due process and equal protection of the law to all citizens despite 100% of Democrats voting no. That means Northern Democrats as well as Southern Democrats were against equal protection for blacks. (see America's Voting Record-Vol.3 and Founding Documents-Vol.7)

Johnson fought the Republican Reconstruction efforts at every turn, defying Congress and enacting policies that allowed former slave states to continue their suppression of Negros through "Black Code" laws. Johnson even declared, "This is a country for white men, and by God, as long as I am President, it shall be a government of white men." Having enough of Democrat Johnson's racism, House Republicans impeached Johnson in 1868. (see Views And Vetoes-Vol.5) His only salvation was the Senate narrowly failed to convict him. Later that year the Democratic Party pushed forward with a national campaign theme of "This is a white man's country: Let white men rule."

Blacks were elected to government offices exclusively as

Republicans but were often removed unconstitutionally in the South by Democrat controlled State governments. (see *The Forgotten Senator-Vol.3*, *The Forgotten Representative-Vol.5*, *Riots And Rights-Vol.6*, and *From House Slave To House Of Representatives-Vol.4*) In 1870, Republicans gave voting rights to all Americans regardless of race with almost no Democrat support, as well as passing the Civil Rights Act of 1875 with absolutely no Democrat votes. (see *America's Voting Records-Vol.3* and *The Rights Fight For Rights-Vol.3*) In 1909, black Republican and women's suffragists Ida Wells and Mary Terrell co-founded the NAACP on the 100th anniversary of Abraham Lincoln's birth. The organization is now nothing more than a mouthpiece for the Democrat agenda.

It's not just history over 100 years old that is being rewritten. History is even being lost on living generations that saw it happen. The Civil Rights legislation credited to Democrat President Lyndon Johnson was actually proposed by Republican President Dwight Eisenhower years before and blocked in the Senate by Lyndon Johnson himself. Democrats overwhelmingly opposed it and the legislation was only passed due to almost unanimous support of Republicans. Many Americans today who actually lived through the 50's and 60's believe the lie that Johnson and the Democrats were for Civil Rights. Johnson signed the law purely for political reasons as he proudly claimed, "I'll have those niggers voting Democratic for the next 200 years."

As I explained in the letter *The Birth Of A Nation*, the offensive and inaccurate movie of the same name described a South where the black man was portrayed as vicious and angry. They were depicted as attacking white men and terrorizing white women. The Ku Klux Klan, or KKK, were characterized as saving the whites in the South from the evils of the freed Negro slaves and were hailed as heroes. The movie quoted writings of then Democrat President Woodrow Wilson and he repaid the honor by making it the first movie ever shown at the White House. The film is credited for reviving the KKK movement, exploding membership in the racist organization that had almost completely dissolved before the movie. It also was a massive boost for the Democrats, as the KKK was well known as the strong-arm of the party. After 50 years of equal treatment for blacks, it was Woodrow Wilson who introduced segregation into the Federal Government offices, allowing for the firing of blacks due entirely to their race.

Up until this time the black population was as exclusively Republican as it is Democrat today. Because of Wilson and the effectiveness of this movie, the KKK grew in numbers to a group that affected real change. They persecuted and lynched not only black but white Republicans. The KKK intimidated voters, putting guns to their heads as they entered the voting booth with the threat to vote Democrat or pay with their life. The party has never strayed far from its bigoted roots. A similar tactic was used in Philadelphia during the 2008 election by the New Black Panthers, as they stood with clubs in front of polling stations as a form of intimidation.

Today's Democrats generally use a more subtle form of coercion. Blacks with the audacity to support the Republican Party, such as former Secretary of State Condoleeza Rice, are verbally flogged and lynched in the media. But Condoleeza's own words reveal the truth, "The first Republican I knew was my father, and he is still the Republican I most admire. He joined our party because the Democrats in Jim Crow Alabama of 1952 would not register him to vote. The Republicans did. My father has never forgotten that day, and neither have I." Black voters are still intimidated at the voting booth with threats of losing everything if they vote for the evil, racist Republicans. Yet Democratic Party leader Senator Robert Byrd, who was an officer in the KKK until he entered politics and repeatedly used the term "white niggers" on national TV in 2001, still held the respect and admiration of the Democratic Party and the NAACP until the day he died in 2010.

So, to continue their deception, Democrats are demanding the Confederate flag be removed from American history. It is just one more piece of reality they have to bury so they continue their fabrication of their past. Out of sight, out of mind. Republican Governor Nikki Haley took action to remove the Confederate flag from the state capital in South Carolina following the recent uproar. What's ignored is that Democrat Governor Fritz Hollings was the one who raised it there in the first place in 1962. Similarly, while Governor of Arkansas, former President Bill Clinton signed into law an act celebrating the Confederacy by placing a blue star on Arkansas' state flag. The Clintons proudly presided over Confederate Flag Day while in the Governor's Mansion. Today Hillary distances herself from the controversy. Democrat organizations are using the racism of the flag as a fund-raising tool, deceiving uninformed voters into believing that it is Republicans who support the supposed racist flag.

Liberty, know your history so this kind of harmful, dishonest propaganda will never influence you. They have whitewashed the facts hoping no one has the sense to verify the truth.

Since groups like the KKK and the neo-Nazis use the flag, it does have racist connotations. But the majority of Americans in fact see it as a symbol of Southern pride. Do people have the right to fly it? Absolutely. Should it be removed from state capitals? Probably. Do you have to like the flag? No. But this hysteria over a symbol in our nation's history is absurd. Canceling reruns of a 30-year-old TV show over it is ridiculous.

By hiding the flag you are denying its past, which in turn allows such hatreds to repeat. Focusing on a symbol solves nothing, allowing the real problem to continue. There were 82 shootings resulting in 16 fatalities in Chicago alone this past 4th of July weekend. Most of the bloodshed was directly related to gang and drug violence. I would bet a million dollars not one of the shooters was carrying a Confederate Flag in their hands. They were carrying hate in their hearts. (see It's Not What's In Your Hand, It's What's In Your Heart)

I'm sure all would be right with the world if all the Confederate flags were replaced with rainbow flags. People cheer a baker or store for refusing to make a cake with a Confederate flag on it, but sue the same person for not making a gay-wedding cake. (see We Reserve The Right To Refuse Service-Vol.1) That says way more about the people and the state of our society than about the baker.

So I propose this. TVLand produce a new Dukes of Hazzard. Bo and Luke are a proud Southern gay couple. They are the ones wearing Daisy Duke shorts and the General Lee is a Prius renamed Mr. Sulu with a Rainbow flag on top. (see The Rainbow Connection) In the first episode the boys' objective is getting a wedding cake with the Confederate flag on it. Let the hilarity ensue.

That's my 2 cents.

Love,
Mom

July 15, 2015

Dear Liberty,

    For many, the Crusades started in 1096 A.D. when the first Christian army began its march. This is equivalent to reducing World War II to America dropping Atomic bombs on Hiroshima and Nagasaki, Japan, disregarding the entire war up until that event, including the devastating attack on Pearl Harbor by the Japanese on December 7, 1941. (see <u>Notice To The Japanese People</u>-Vol.3 and <u>A Date Which Will Live In Infamy</u>-Vol.3) The complete record of events must be studied leading up to the bombings to understand the entire context of the attacks just as the Muslim history in the Middle East before 1096 must be examined to understand the Crusades.

    Even under persecution and threat of execution from the Roman Empire, Christianity spread throughout the known world in the first few centuries not by force, but by the simple teaching of the Gospel. As stated by Norman Geisler, President of Southern Evangelical Seminary, "While early Islam was spread by the sword, early Christianity spread by the spirit, even while Christians were being killed by Roman swords." By the end of the 2nd century, Christianity had reached Northern Africa where twelve natives of the Roman province of Scillium were executed on July 16th, 180 A.D. just for being Christians.

    Around 325 A.D. Emperor Constantine I, the first major Christian Roman ruler, made Christianity the state religion of Rome and ordered the building of a Christian Church in Jerusalem. (see <u>Yes, Liberty, There Is A Santa Claus</u>-Vol.1) In <u>Life Of Constantine</u>, Eusebius Pamphilius records that during the excavation for the church, a tomb exhibiting "a clear and visible proof" of Christ's burial place was discovered. The locations of Jesus' death and resurrection were drawn into the design of the church. The True Cross, believed to be Christ's cross, was also discovered and housed at the new church. After construction of the Church of the Holy Sepulchre, Christians from all over pilgrimaged to its site every year to worship and see the precious settings of their Savior's victory.

    The Christian church continued to grow and spread until the 7th century when Mohammad wrote the Quran. Many Christian cities and churches were conquered and destroyed by Muslims in their quest to convert the world to Islam by force. They attacked and overthrow Jerusalem in 637 A.D. The new Muslim ruler allowed the Church of the Holy Sepulchre to remain Christian and protected Christians as well as allowing Jews to return to the city after years of exile.

Over the next 700 years the church was damaged and eventually totally destroyed in 1009 along with other Christian churches in the city. After Caliph Ali az-Zahir came to power, he agreed to allow the rebuilding of the church, which was completed in 1048. Christians were again permitted free access to visit the site. After the Seljukian Turks, Sunni Muslims who were considered "zealous followers of Islam", gained control in 1071, they began persecuting the Christian Pilgrims and massacred 3000 of them in Jerusalem. The rebuilt churches were again destroyed or turned into items such as stables. Because of this and the threat to the church in Constantinople by the Turks, Pope Urban II delivered a sermon at the Council of Clermont in 1095 calling for a Crusade.

For a year, the Pope along with the notable preacher Peter the Hermit, delivered sermons building support for a Crusade. Their main goal was to reclaim the Church of the Holy Sepulchre. On August 15, 1096, a band of soldiers departed on their journey. The Crusades had begun.

It is at this point that most uninformed pundits, along with President Barack Obama, begin their history. Completely ignoring the invasions, attacks, destruction and bloodshed of Muslim empires, Christians are condemned for starting a war against Islam.

Over the course of three years, crusaders reclaimed Nicaea (1097), Dorylaeum a few days later, and Antioch (1098) from the Turks. On July 15, 1099, the crusaders obtained their goal by taking back Jerusalem and the Church of the Holy Sepulchre. On the 150th Anniversary of this event, the reconstructed church was consecrated in Jerusalem.

Crusades continued throughout the Holy Land for nearly two decades as Christians tried to reclaim territory lost during Muslim invasions. There were times throughout that period where the current Pope did choose to wage an unjust offensive. At these times Crusaders attacked anyone of non-Christian faith, including Jews and on at least one occasion, other Christians. Once the Christian church transformed due to the Reformation, the power and hold of the papacy diminished. (see The Knock Heard 'Round The World-Vol.1, Here I Stand-Vol.4, and All In Due Time) The authority of the Catholic Church was greatly reduced as Protestant churches gained followers.

As the Pope's grip over government leaders died, so did the call for crusades. So while the Christian church refreshed their commitment to Jesus Christ and peace in the 16th century, the Muslim faith continues its pursuit of domination throughout the Middle East and the world with terrorism and death. Furthermore, the Catholic Church is still rebuked for its Holy Wars of 1000 years ago while Muslim jihads happening right now are virtually ignored. (See *Washington, Adams and Mohammad – Our Founding Fathers*)

Many excuse the current radical brutality of ISIS on two fronts. First, they reference the Christian Crusades as if to give Muslims the right to their radical, savage behavior because of these Holy Wars that occurred almost a millennium ago. Second, they claim the Islamic extremists are not following the teachings of Mohammad while others believe Muslims are fighting in self-defense, which is approved by Mohammad.

With just a little natural curiosity and minimal research, one can easily discover a more accurate truth. Mohammad himself led attacks on cities claiming them for Islam. In the historic biography of Mohammad by Ibn Ishaq and edited by Ibn Hisham, they give proof that Mohammad waited to see if a town had a call to morning prayer before deciding to attack Khaybar. "When the apostle raided a people he waited until the morning. If he heard a call to prayer he held back; if he did not hear it he attacked. We came to Khaybar by night, and the apostle passed the night there; and when morning came he did not hear the call to prayer, so he rode and we rode with him." They continued, proving the townspeople were not prepared for battle. "We met the workers of Khaybar coming out in the morning with their spades and baskets. When they saw the apostle and the army they cried, "Muhammad with his force," and turned tail and fled... The apostle seized the property piece by piece..." (Ibn Ishaq/Hisham 757) This is not the action of a peaceful man responding in self-defense.

The 9th Sura of the Quran clearly spells out Mohammad's plan to convert. "Proclaim a woeful punishment to the unbelievers, except to those idolaters who have honoured their treaties with you in every detail and aided none against you. With these keep faith, until their treaties have run their term. God loves the righteous. When the sacred months are over slay the idolaters wherever you find them. Arrest them, besiege them, and lie in ambush everywhere for them. If they repent and take to prayer and render the alms levy, allow them to go their way. God is forgiving and merciful." (Quran 9:4-5) There is no self-defense angle in this passage either. Mohammad himself preached and practiced conversion by force.

It is with these precedents and directions that Muslims attacked and conquered major Christian cities, as well as vast territories of the area, destroying ancient churches and buildings.

When people dismiss ISIS and the Muslim uprising in the Middle East, excusing it because "Christians did the same thing in the Crusades," *they are showing their complete ignorance of history and the Quran. They are being manipulated as useful idiots. The Crusades did not happen because some Christians out for a walk one night decided to go kill some Muslims. They were responding to deadly attacks made on them by a zealous group of people, not unlike those of ISIS today who are invading people's homes, demanding they convert or die, and carrying out that threat in videos posted on the internet.*

Liberty, this is why knowing history is so incredibly important. ISIS is not a movement that just started in the last few years because President Bush went to war with Iraq after September 11th. (see Never Forget-Vol.1) September 11th happened because Muslim leader Osama Bin Laden was already at war with the United States for two decades. In fact, this war was waged when Mohammad declared himself a prophet of God. But before that, it's a war that begun the moment Satan convinced Eve and Adam to eat the forbidden fruit. (see Fruit of the Forbidden Tree-Vol.1)

Just this week, the Obama Administration announced a nuclear deal has finally been reached between the superpowers and Iran. The problem is Obama did not get any of his conditions he promised would be in the deal. In fact, he didn't even try to get four Christian American prisoners released that are detained in Iran and beaten repeatedly because they refuse to denounce their faith. Where the crusaders at least stood up to the tyrannical Muslims, Obama bowed down and complied to Iranian leaders while they chanted, "Death to Israel, Death to America."

Liberty, this letter is one for the history books as we are repeating the beginnings of another World War. The Obama Administration is claiming peace through diplomacy and honestly believes Iran, the leading supporter of state-sponsored terrorism, will soften and learn to live along side infidels without even one incentive to do so. It is the 1939 Neville Chamberlin Munich Agreement with Adolph Hitler all over again. (see The British Bulldog-Vol.3) Chamberlin declared it "Peace in our time." As history shows, Hitler signed the document and used the period of "peace" to build his army and destroy his German enemies. Within two years the World was at war.

Because Progressive ideologues refuse to understand history, they continue to believe that their intellect will affect and change those hearts and minds that seek death. (see A Change Of Heart) They excuse and pander to the terrorists while blaming and lecturing the victims, primarily Jews and Christians.

The actions and behavior of ISIS in the region is no different from that of the Seljukian Turks. Christians are being massacred, churches are being destroyed, women are raped and Christian girls are sold into sex slavery. But God is still in control. Many of these victims are peacefully facing their death because they choose it over denying Christ and converting to Islam. ISIS is going as far as throwing homosexuals from buildings and killing other Muslims because they are not radical enough.

Christ said we would suffer for His name. While my sinful self wants desperately to personally destroy those persecuting and killing my fellow brothers and sisters, they are providing a much stronger witness with their actions of peaceful resistance. Their families are comforted that their loved ones are in Heaven with Christ as they chose to cling to Him instead of cowering to the demands of the terrorists. Those that have complied with their captors' ultimatums should be held in our prayers as they are facing a daily decision I don't know I would be strong enough to withstand.

That being said it is the responsibility and duty of the government of this country and governments of all countries to stand up and confront this kind of radical ideology. It is here that action should be taken and Obama, along with the other superpowers, are stepping aside and allowing this abomination against humanity. Where the crusaders justly tried to end the barbaric actions of the Islamic terrorists, today's leaders are passively allowing it. Because of his refusal to see true history, Obama has convinced himself he doesn't need guns or force to defeat ISIS, he can do it with words and ideas. While he is busy talking though, thousands of Christians are being slaughtered and enslaved throughout the Middle East while hundreds of thousands are forced to flee for their lives.

As from the time of Christ, His followers have been targeted and persecuted by non-believers all over the world. Satan uses these people to try to force believers to abandon Christ through fear. There really is not much different now than at the time of the Crusades except Christians are not calling for a Holy War against their attackers. They are peacefully and proudly accepting the cross they must bear, including dying for their Lord. Non-believers are turning to the Christian church in the Middle East and converting even at the threat of death. The church is growing, just as it did in the first centuries under Roman persecution, because it offers something they can't find anywhere else; the Hope we have and Change of heart we receive through faith in Christ.

We must follow in the footsteps of the original church and continue the Great Commission of spreading the Gospel through love and peace.

That's my 2 cents. Love, Mom

July 23, 2015

Dear Liberty,

Obama touted at a recent Prayer Meeting that slave owners used Christianity to defend slavery. What he conveniently left out was many of those churches were infected with the doctrine of evolution which preached that the Negro was not as evolved and therefore lesser than the white man. It is the philosophy of evolution that Southerns gravitated to rather than the teachings of Christ, which the abolitionists preached. Margaret Sanger, founder of Planned Parenthood, capitalized on this ideology when she spoke to KKK members about the organization she wanted to build. She believed Negros were inferior and "undesirable" and her goal was to eliminate them. The KKK of the Confederate South was eager to help.

Many Christians today have convinced themselves that God is perfectly fine with abortion and gay marriage even though the Bible is quite explicit about the sinfulness of both murder and homosexuality. (see Suffering In Utopia-Vol.6 and We Reserve The Right To Refuse Service-Vol.1) God made man in His own image. However, ever since the fall of Adam and Eve, men have been molding God into their image. (see Fruit Of The Forbidden Tree-Vol.1) God does not change and neither does His Word. "Evolved Christians" can try to ease their own consciences by misrepresenting God's Word, but that doesn't make them any more right than the slave owners.

Last week the Center for Medical Progress released the first of what will be several videos revealing a secret practice of Planned Parenthood. (see Evil Is As Evil Does) It revealed the Senior Director of Medical Services quite casually discussing how she purposely crushes the head and lower parts of babies when aborting them so as to preserve their vital organs to sell. She also discloses how she carefully skirts laws restricting partial birth abortion as well as the selling of body parts from an aborted baby. In their response to the video, officials at Planned Parenthood did not deny they are harvesting organs from the aborted babies. They merely apologized for the "tone" of the executive in the video.

Planned Parenthood then deflected attacks at their barbaric behavior by attacking the group exposing them, claiming it is a pro-life, propaganda attack video that had been highly edited. A compliant media ran headlines adamantly proclaiming Planned Parenthood was *not selling aborted baby parts while others ignored the appalling discovery altogether. Unfortunately for them the second video made public this week shows the organization's top doctor haggling over the price of the "tissue samples." As Soren Kierkegaard once said, "There are two ways to be fooled. One is to believe what isn't true; the other is to refuse to believe what is true." As additional videos are released, it will become extremely difficult for Liberals to continue the mantra that Planned Parenthood has no blood on its hands.*

I can understand the initial reaction of pro-abortion activists defending Planned Parenthood. They have spent their lives promoting the organization, believing that they were supporting an honest and humanitarian group. How can you believe that the group you trusted, defended, and promoted is everything your political opponents said it was, a human butcher shop? My sympathies ran dry when I discovered that some Liberal websites started circulating an article this week encouraging women to donate their aborted baby's body to science. Some are so invested in their sin they are willing to fall further and further down the rabbit hole of evil instead of facing the reality of their beliefs.

To sit back and accept this atrocity to human life is no better than the Germans who knew of the death camps and said nothing.

During the Bush Administration, Nancy Pelosi, along with other predominate Democrats, repeatedly insinuated that Bush and Republicans were Nazis. Liberal supporters outright called Bush "Hitler", complete with posters of him in a Nazi uniform and a Hitler mustache. As I described in my letter about Margaret Sanger (Sanger And Eugenics And Socialism Oh My), Hitler began his reign of terror by eliminating mentally and physically handicapped people. (see Finishing The Master Race-Vol.4) Hitler did not come up with this idea of the perfect race on his own. He followed the Progressive policies put forth right here in America by predominate Democrats such as Woodrow Wilson, Teddy Roosevelt and the sainted founder of Planned Parenthood, Margaret Sanger.

Following in the footsteps of history, a Liberal Princeton professor Peter Singer just divulged in an interview that he believes Obamacare should withhold care from disabled infants, which would basically kill them. He claims it's not so much about the monetary cost as it is about relieving the burden on parents and society,

believing his methods are representative of a compassionate people. Singer also confessed, "So we are already taking steps that quite knowingly and intentionally are ending the lives of severely disabled infants." If we follow the pattern of history then we realize it did not take long for the Nazi Party to evolve from slaughtering the disabled of any race to killing everyone of a specific race. His "compassion" ended in the deaths of 6 million Jews and 5 million other undesirables. Hitler's "compassion" evolved from Margaret Sanger's promotion of terminating any human weeds, including Negros. (see Holocaust: Then And Now) Again, an entire race of people. Different roads, different flags, same destination.

The second piece of the Progressive/Nazi puzzle was just proposed by General Wesley Clark, a former Democrat presidential candidate. He wants to imprison people like we did with the Japanese in World War II. (see Forgotten Atrocities of World War II-Vol.4) Anyone who has been radicalized or is disloyal to America, he argues, should be confined. It is a message that resonates with people when they are afraid. However, it leads down very dark roads. In the case of Democrat Franklin D. Roosevelt, he didn't just imprison radical and disloyal Japanese Americans, he imprisoned ALL Japanese Americans. The important question is, who gets to decide who the radicals and disloyal citizens are?

In my point of view, Clark just described himself, the media, Obama and his administration, Nancy Pelosi, Harry Reed and the vast majority of radical, Liberal Hollywood. Clark spoke of terrorists but never uttered the words "Muslim" or "Islam". Knowing that this administration for the past six years has argued that Tea Partiers are radical terrorists, that Republicans are disloyal traitors, that white people are oppressive supremacists and that Christians hate everybody, how long would it take for authorities to come after people like me if a bill were actually passed to do this? As a military commander, it's quite telling that Wesley Clark would mirror policies of WWII. Roosevelt pointed his crosshairs at Japanese Americans, not German Americans, even though we were at war with both. Hitler used the same tactic to imprison, torture, exterminate, and conduct experiments on Jews. Margaret Sanger targeted Negros with abortion before they were even born.

While Jews were in German Concentration Camps, Nazis used the prisoners to conduct "scientific" research. (see Evil Is As Evil Does) It's no coincidence this is how Planned Parenthood is dismissing their harvesting of fetal organs. Margaret Sanger promoted and supported both policies. It is murder, pure and simple, and profiting from the "leftovers" is evil in its most unadulterated form. Planned Parenthood and the Democratic Party's official policy should be, "So what, the Nazis did it." In fact, they are saying that in their very silence on the topic.

The Democratic Party has supported this practice for decades, arguing that embryonic stem-cell research is a benefit of abortion. Why are they not showing public support for Planned Parenthood now? Could it be that embryonic stem-cell research has been going on for over 40 years with no successful results? Or is it that Democrats know how incredibly disgusted the American people are by these videos, even though their lawmakers still want to fund it? Pro-life advocates, on the other hand, adamantly support adult stem-cell research, which has resulted in countless amazing medical advances and doesn't require the death of an innocent baby.

Liberty, after reading my previous letters, the revelation of Planned Parenthood's actions should sicken you, but it should not surprise you. This is consistent with standard operating procedures for the Progressive movement. Human life through the lie of evolution has been reduced to nothing more than a clump of tissues to be tossed aside at the whim of those who believe they are far superior and more evolved. Planned Parenthood is trying to cover their actions and their conscience by saying they are donating the tissue and only receiving processing and handling fees in return. This claim was decimated in the second video where the Planned Parenthood doctor negotiated the price for the organs. You don't negotiate a cost when you are just covering expenses. You can spin your actions all you want, but in God's eyes evil is evil.

Under Republican President Abraham Lincoln, 360,000 Northern soldiers gave their lives to end slavery in the Confederate States led by Democrat President Jefferson Davis. (see Sibling Rivalry-Vol.7) America went to war and sacrificed 250,000 lives in Europe to stop the horrific and disgraceful practices of Hitler and the Nazi Party. Now the same Progressive moment that supported Sanger and Hitler is embedded in the highest positions of this country and forcing the same disgusting policies on the American people. So far 55 million American babies have given their lives in the mass genocide know as Roe v. Wade.

I will continue to proclaim the value of life, every life, every chance I get. I know that I will never be able to completely eradicate the murderous practice of abortion. I probably won't be able to close even just one clinic. Regardless, I will never hurt an abortion doctor or demean women who have had the procedure. These are lost souls in desperate need of finding peace in the Savior, Jesus Christ.

Where I must draw the line is allowing the government to take the tax dollars of American citizens to fund Nazi death camps in America. Funding Planned Parenthood with tax money means all Americans have blood on their hands, forced to pay for the slaughter of primarily black babies. In New York City today, more black babies are aborted than are allowed to live. (see Suffering In Utopia-Vol.7) Well done, Margaret Sanger. Well done, Democratic Party. All Americans *are forced to participate in this abomination against God. It is here that I take a stand. It is here that everyone who believes All Lives Matter should stand.*

If these videos don't stop the governmental funding for Planned Parenthood, than maybe the truth of Margaret Sanger gaining support for her organization by speaking at KKK rallies will. The KKK, who have been tied directly to the Confederate Flag, are also tied directly to Planned Parenthood as well. (see <u>How The South Was Won</u>) It's time to distance ourselves from our Confederate racist history once and for all. If TVLand can't show <u>The Dukes of Hazard</u> because there is a Confederate flag on the roof of the car, then why in the hell are my tax dollars going to an organization that began because of the support of the KKK?

Defund Planned Parenthood Now! All Lives Matter!

That's my 2 cents.

Love,
Mom

July 31, 2015

Dear Liberty,

On the day the Supreme Court forced same-sex marriage on the country, supporters waved rainbow flags in the streets. (see *What Is Love?*) Facebook enabled a transparent rainbow icon to be placed over your profile picture in celebration. Within hours, the administration changed the lighting scheme on the White House to that of a rainbow. Interestingly enough, it took them 5 days to lower the flag to half-mast when 1 navy and 4 marine recruiters were gunned down by a terrorist just 2 weeks ago. It's an intriguing time for what we take pride in.

Whether these proud advocates realize it or not, their use of the rainbow is a deeper rejection of God than they ever imaged.

To understand this we must examine the significance of the rainbow by going back to the beginning. Most people, religious or not, are familiar with Noah and the Flood story. Over 500 cultures in every nook and cranny of the globe have a worldwide flood account. Many skeptics argue the fable started in one ancient culture and was passed around to other societies. In basically all the tales, there is a hero who saves some people on a boat. Most refer to animals, food storage and a sacrifice made by the hero at the end. At the time the original tale was supposedly spread, there were no books, no phones, no Internet. They didn't move around much and even if they did they were not dragging along stone tablets. Epics were passed down entirely by oral tradition for thousands of years. Civilizations existed all across the globe. The only way for a Middle Eastern story this ancient to flourish, even in the most isolated tribes in Africa and the Americas, was if there was a common genesis between all these cultures. Many skeptics want to dismiss the flood story as just legend with no basis in reality, but logic would dictate that with so many cultures having this particular story, no matter the region of the world, would go to validate the story, not forsake it. The flood account had to be passed down from father to son, grandparents to grandchildren, starting with the group that lived through it.

Thanks to Walt Disney, many of us know and love such wonderful fairy tales as Snow White, Cinderella, Rapunzel, Sleeping Beauty, and many more. Growing up I believed, as most do, that Disney and his company developed these wonderful tales. It is well-known to those aware of the history of Disney, Walt adapted those stories from the Grimm Brothers' fairytales. Most stop there, though, crediting Jacob and Wilhelm Grimm as the original authors. Just because the Grimms were the first to write the stories down doesn't mean they were the inventors of the fairytales either. Those who do their own research discover Jacob and Wilhelm spent years gathering these long-held regional fables from the community. They simply put these pre-existing stories into print.

It is relevant to note even well-known local fairytales didn't become widely told until the Grimm Brothers and the printing press gave them the ability to spread across the globe. (see <u>All In Due Time</u>) This again gives more support that the flood story was not just a fable but an actual event experienced by common ancestors of all cultures. I use this example to illustrate that sometimes you have to dig a little deeper and a little harder to understand the whole truth.

This can be said about the Noah account. Many attribute its origin to the Sumerian epic of Gilgamesh, commenting on the specific Babylonian version from the Sumerian region. What is interesting is that Babylon was in modern day Iraq, about 30 miles from Bagdad. It was settled by Cush (which means "Let us rebel"). Cush was Noah's grandson. His father was Ham, who along with Noah was one of the few survivors of the flood when he boarded the ark. Even so, he rejected both Noah and God's authority, passing down his rebellion to his son Cush who extended it to Nimrod. At the time of Nimrod, the people of Babylon said, "Come, let us build ourselves a city and a tower with its top in the heavens, and let us make a name for ourselves, lest we be dispersed over the face of the whole earth." (Genesis 11:4) After God saw what they were doing, He said, "Behold, they are one people, and they have all one language, and this is only the beginning of what they will do. And nothing that they propose to do will now be impossible for them." At this point he split their language so they could not communicate and spread them over the world. And with them, the people took their histories.

So, it is no surprise to me that the Babylonians and surrounding Sumerian area would have an amazing amount of consistency with the Noah story. Just as it is no surprise that they have just as many errors when compared to the Biblical narrative. The important part is that we can connect Babylon directly to Noah and his descendants, albeit rebellious ones, where many place the beginning of the tale.

Just like with the Grimm stories, there are similarities throughout the different versions flood account, but they do get distorted the further they get away from the source. It is like a game of telephone where one whispers a phrase or sentence into another's ear, who passes it on until you get back to the source. It never comes back the same. Though many of the flood narratives have a hero who built an ark and saved a few remnants of mankind from a catastrophic flood, the reasoning for the disaster has two major differences between God-fearing religions (Judaism, Christianity, and Islam) and other cultures. One, God spoke directly to Moses who then recorded the world's history from Creation. All other accounts were passed down by oral history from generation to generation which, as already discussed, led to inaccuracies and errors. Even if Moses' personal knowledge of the story was incorrect, God rectified any mistakes giving Moses a complete and precise depiction of history.

Second, God revealed how He became disgusted and infuriated enough with man's immorality that He decided to destroy the ungodly people. Finding faithfulness in Noah, God spared him and his family from the annihilation of creation hoping to start over with a righteous leader. All other cultures in some form or another excuse mankind for their role in the cause of the flood. Blame is often placed on the selfishness of the gods of the culture while crediting the hero as being either a partial god or gaining immortality. Even Hollywood butchered the story in a recent "Noah" movie turning it into an agenda driven, global warming propaganda piece. They depicted Noah as a hatefully man, disgusted with God and mankind, who almost murders his own grandchild, who did not even exist at the time of the flood. Not wanting to admit that we are a sinful, unrighteous, immoral people, we ignore and deny the truth in efforts to sooth our own ego.

After God destroyed all life outside of those preserved on the Ark and the rain stopped, He promised Noah that He would never again pass such judgment on His creation regardless of how immoral and unrepentantly sinful they became. He attached that promise to the rainbow so whenever we look at it we should remember not only God's promise that He would never destroy the world with a flood again, but the reason for the flood in the first place. God's promise in the flood story is another similarity consistent across cultural lines.

Which leads us to the rewriting of history and meaning of the rainbow. About 150 years ago, homosexuals began using bright colors to communicate their preferences to others. They would often wear such items as a green carnation, yellow socks, or a pink triangle, a symbol adopted from the Holocaust mark homosexuals were forced to wear.

Judy Garland, a huge supporter of the LGBT community, fostered a rainbow connection to the group. Gay men flocked to her performances where "Somewhere Over the Rainbow" became a cult classic for the movement. After World War II, many started referring to themselves as "friends of Dorothy," a reference to Judy's role in "The Wizard of Oz." Judy was reported as saying, "When I die I have visions *of fags singing 'Over the Rainbow' and the (American) flag at Fire Island being flown at half mast." It would be another 9 years after her death before the now popular rainbow flag was designed for the colorful community.*

In the late 1970's artist Gilbert Baker of San Francisco combined several bright colors used by the LGBT community as an 8 strip flag. Each color had it's own significance: pink = sex, red = life, orange = healing, yellow = sunlight, green = nature, blue = art, indigo = harmony, and violet = the human spirit. Hot pink was often hard for flag makers to find so Baker dropped it. He also dropped indigo, or unity, to make the number of stripes even. It seems appropriate as the LGBT has been demonstrating anything but unity with others as their protests, demands, and lawsuits against those who choose to hold differing religious views. And thus, the rainbow flag was born.

By using the rainbow as their trademark, the LGBT community is taking a symbol of forgiveness and hope for eternal life despite our sins, and is shoving it right back into God's face. And like the original story of Noah, the more this story is told the more it changes the original meaning. God is very clear when he states, "You shall not lie with a male as with a woman; it is an abomination." (Leviticus 18:22) "If a man lies with a male as with a woman, both of them have committed an abomination; they shall surely be put to death; their blood is upon them." (Leviticus 20:13) It's like they are taunting God with their sin, rather than asking forgiveness. It is the adulteress proud of her cheating.

Liberty, man has been rejecting God's rainbow promise since Ham stepped off the Ark. As much as it pains my heart to see this willful repudiation, it is actually an opportunity for us to share the message of God with those celebrating their sin. They are now out in the open with it. Let us be, too. We as Christians must utilized the door that God has opened for us. It starts with the phrase, "Let me tell you what the rainbow means to a dying world."

With the help of the Holy Spirit, you may very well make a rainbow connection with a lost soul searching for a lifesaving promise.

That's my 2 cents.

Love,
Mom

August 6, 2015

Dear Liberty,

    As chaotic as America seems today, it is not the first time citizens have experienced such strife and discord with their own countrymen. The land was literally divided.

    In the beginning of the Civil War, events did not go well for the anti-slavery North. Lincoln and the Union Army suffered defeat after defeat. The power of the armies of the Southern states steered Northward, threatening to overtake Washington DC and reshape the Nation. If circumstances didn't change, the Stars and Bars would surely fly over the White House and secure slavery as the way of life for all in the young country. (see How The South Was Won*)*

    Both sides were confident that God was behind their struggle. Lincoln, however, was faced with a sobering reality. "I have been driven many times upon my knees by the overwhelming conviction that I had no where else to go. My own wisdom and that of all about me seemed insufficient for that day." This realization led him to refocus his efforts. "My concern is not whether God is on our side; my greatest concern is to be on God's side, for God is always right." Lincoln put this understanding to action and asked the people to join him in one simple act - A Day of National Humiliation, Fasting, and Prayer. He issued the following proclamation:

A Day Of National Humiliation, Fasting, and Prayer in The United States Of America on April 30, 1863

WHEREAS, the senate of the United States, devoutly recognizing the Supreme Authority and Just Government of Almighty God, in all the affairs of men and of nations, has by a resolution, required the President to designate and set apart a day for National prayer and humiliation:

And whereas, it is the duty of nations as well as of men, to owe their dependence upon the overruling power of God, to confess their sins and transgressions, in humble sorrow, yet with assured hope that genuine repentance will lead to mercy and pardon; and to recognize the sublime truth, announced in the Holy Scriptures and proven by all history, that those nations only are blessed whose God is the Lord:

And, in so much as we know that, by His divine law, nations, like individuals, are subjected to punishments and chastisements in this world, may we not justly fear that the awful calamity of civil war, which now desolates the land, may be but a punishment inflicted upon us for our presumptuous sins, to the needful end of our national reformation as a whole People? We have been the recipients of the choicest bounties of Heaven. We have been preserved, these many years, in peace and prosperity. We have grown in numbers, wealth, and power as no other nation has ever grown. But we have forgotten God. We have forgotten the gracious hand which preserved us in peace, and multiplied and enriched and strengthened us; and we have vainly imagined, in the deceitfulness of our hearts, that all these blessings were produced by some superior wisdom and virtue of our own. Intoxicated with unbroken success, we have become too self-sufficient to feel the necessity of redeeming and preserving grace, too proud to pray to the God that made us! It behooves us, then to humble ourselves before the offended Power, to confess our national sins, and to pray for clemency and forgiveness.

Now, therefore, in compliance with the request, and fully concurring in the views of the Senate, I do, by this proclamation, designate and set apart Thursday, the 30th day of April, 1863, as a day of national humiliation, fasting, and prayer. And I do hereby request all the People to abstain on that day from their ordinary secular pursuits, and to unite, at their several places of public worship and their respective homes, in keeping the day holy to the Lord, and devoted to the humble discharge of the religious duties proper to that solemn occasion.

All this being done, in sincerity and truth, let us then rest humbly in the hope authorized by the Divine teachings, that the united cry of the Nation will be heard on high, and answered with blessings, no less than the pardon of our national sins, and the restoration of our now divided and suffering country, to its former happy condition of unity and peace.

In witness whereof, I have here unto set my hand, and caused the seal of the United States to be affixed.

Done at the city of Washington this thirtieth day of March, in the year of our Lord one thousand eight hundred and sixty-three, and of the Independence of the United States the eighty-seventy.

By the President:
ABRAHAM LINCOLN

Following this simple show of humility by a President, and a nation of people willing to do likewise, the tide of the war shifted. Prior to the National Day of Prayer, the Union won only two battles. After the National Day of Prayer, the Union suffered only two defeats.

Perhaps we are at a time that such a humble act of national prayer could again turn the tide that is leading to the slaughtering of Christians, Jews, and homosexuals in the Middle East. (see <u>Holocaust: Then And Now</u>) It may reawaken our hearts to call on God and turn from the slaughter of children through abortion. Over the past 40 years this national disgrace, hidden under the mask of women's rights, has killed more babies than the entire population of Canada.

As activists across the nation are ripping God from our schools, public areas and government, the country is falling faster and farther into a hell on earth. The solution is simple. It is time once again to be driven to our knees and search out God's will, not ours. (see <u>God's Divine Providence</u>-Vol.3) We need to submit ourselves to His wisdom and His righteousness.

"If my people who are called by my name humble themselves, and pray and seek my face and turn from their wicked ways, then I will hear from heaven and will forgive their sin and heal their land." 2 Chronicles 7:14

That's my 2 cents.

Love,
Mom

August 13, 2015

Dear Liberty,

In a recent interview, CNN anchor Chris Cuomo attempted to play the "gotcha game" with Presidential candidate Senator Marco Rubio. Cuomo insinuated Rubio's "no exception" view on abortion in the previous night's debate was contradictory to a bill he presented that allowed abortions in cases of rape and incest. He arrogantly stated, "So, it seems that you had your own record wrong," before inviting Rubio to correct himself. As Rubio pointed out, Cuomo was completely wrong on his assessment. Rubio patiently explained how he compromised on a bill that included exceptions, something Democrats demand Republicans do no matter what the issue, because the bill stopped some abortions even if it did not go as far as Rubio wanted.

At this point the conversation turned to the question of the beginning of human life and science. Cuomo argued, "you're deciding when it is human life," apparently not realizing that he is doing the same thing. While Cuomo maintained scientists don't know when human life begins, Rubio again gracefully explained the truth. Ignoring the facts, Cuomo turned to a tiresome liberal talking point and insisted Rubio abandon his faith and support science, as he said he does as a Catholic. Except, the science is pretty definite on this one. There is no doubt when the human egg and human sperm meet, there is one thing and one thing only it can be - a human life. It's been that way for over 6000 years. Until empirical evidence demonstrates it can became anything else, then science has proven it is a human life.

Cuomo continued to demand that Rubio forget faith and follow science, apparently believing the two are mutually exclusive. What he fails to realize is anyone exploring real science is actually open to every possibility. Cuomo, by his own admission, refuses to even consider the possibility of life beginning at conception, labeling it as strictly a religious understanding. That is the true definition of a science denier.

But before we completely dismiss Cuomo, let's go ahead and look at the science.

An egg by itself does nothing. After it's release from the ovary, if it is not fertilized, it breaks apart and is expelled from the woman. Likewise, if sperm are not ejected by the male, they naturally *break down and are absorbed back into the body. Apart, neither the egg nor the sperm evolve or develop into anything else.*

When an egg and a sperm meet though, and the sperm successfully fertilizes the egg, an immediate biological reaction happens. It's important to note that the voyage alone the sperm needs to travel to get to the egg is an enormous feat in and of itself. Also, because of a thick layer surrounding the egg, those tired little guys still have to get through the tough coating to penetrate the egg. So it takes a very healthy and determined sperm to make the trip and break through this wall. This process is not an easy, effortless, insignificant task that should be thoughtlessly discarded like an unwanted toy. Pregnancy is a miracle, plain and simple.

Once fertilized, the egg begins dividing and multiplying and a new life, called a zygote, has started. Within days, the baby's DNA is mapped out. After 6 weeks, the heart is beating, arms and legs are formed, and the brain, spinal cord, eyes and lungs are well on their way. By 11 weeks the baby is almost completely formed. Vital organs are functioning, bones are hardening, and it's genitalia are beginning to develop.

Through scientific study of DNA, we know how a person's hair color, eye color, height, and other physical features are determined by the merging the information obtained from the mother and the father. I remember learning that in 8th grade science class. These traits begin formulating as soon as the egg and sperm unite. Just because we don't know a baby's sex until the 20th week does not mean that's when it is determined. The sex of a baby is defined by whether an X- or Y-chromosome sperm fertilizes the egg. It's that simple. It's science.

A few months ago when Bruce Jenner received the Arthur Ashe Courage Award for coming out as a transgender named Caitlyn, Cuomo praised him for his braveness in denying his identity that was determined by science. Bruce was designed as a man. Cuomo was so proud society seems eager to accept those who defy the science regarding their gender. For Cuomo to approve of Bruce's identity change because he "feels" like his is a woman is completely unscientific. Science is not about feelings, it's about evidence. To insist Bruce be referred to as a "she" even though he still has his male genitalia is a complete denial of science. If Cuomo wants to play "gotcha" with someone's inconsistencies, he needs to look in the mirror.

Pro-abortionists like Chris Cuomo insist that human life does not begin until late in the pregnancy if at all. Many consider a baby just tissue until the moment it is born. One feminist blogger even dedicated an article to contending a fetus is actually a parasite. If at 11 weeks a baby is almost completely formed with functioning organs, with what scientific reasoning can you say it is still just tissue? If science doesn't know when life begins then how can they be so confident as to when it can end?

It's not that people like Cuomo are purposely denying science while at the same time trying to claim it as a basis for their argument. They do it because they have chosen to deny God, even some of those who proclaim to be Christian. Many say they are believers, but then insist most Biblical teachings are mythical and folklore. Which causes me to ask, what is their faith truly based on? If they were to honestly open their minds to the facts about the creation, then they would have to accept that there is a creator. That would then undoubtedly prove God existed, which would completely destroy their whole world view and their ability to act like a god themselves.

Cuomo continued to insist that Rubio was using faith and not science to influence his political decisions. Rubio unashamedly confessed his faith "teaches me to care for the needy, my faith teaches me to respect and love even my enemies. People should hope that my faith influences my political position." He went on to profess that faith, "teaches me that God knew us when He formed us in the womb." Rubio concluded "the science is clear that when there is conception, that is a human life in the early stages of its total development and it's worthy of the protection of our laws. I'm not in favor of destroying human life because people somehow are going to obscure human life."

Amen, Senator Rubio!

That's my 2 cents.

Love,
Mom

August 21, 2015

Dear Liberty,

Liberating Letters
The**Facts**Paper.com

In Planned Parenthood (PP) video #6 by the Center of Medical Progress, Melissa Farrell, Director of Research for Planned Parenthood Gulf Coast, admits, "It would be exciting too if you needed it (fetus) dissected, because LaShonda and I are the most Curious George of the group. I know it's sickening on some level, but it's fun... it's just that those of us who are into medicine and nursing, things that other people find gross, we enjoy. Obviously."*

When people are able to dismiss the beginning of life, the development of life, or life itself, they can then justify such actions as abortion. (see When Does Life Begin?) When this ideology goes unchecked, the mind is able to rationalize even more grotesque actions against humans, especially when done under the guise of science. This is evident in the continued Democrat support for PP but also in Nazi Germany with Josef Mengele. (see The Axis Of Evil?)

Dr. Josef Mengele, known as "Uncle Mengele" to his unsuspecting victims and "the Angel of Death" to everyone else, was a member of the Nazi party. After being wounded in 1942 at age 31 and declared unfit for duty, he volunteered to serve in a concentration camp. Upon arriving in Auschwitz, he seized an opportunity to turn humans into lab rats. Mengele charmed the children by giving them candy and clothes with a smile before transporting them to his medical laboratories where he perform horrific experiments.

Without anesthesia and while the victim was still alive, Mengele operated on hearts, removed organs and limbs, and performed other surgeries on the helpless specimens. This is similar to PP's now exposed pre- and post-abortion practices. As this week's video reveals, former StemExpress technician Holly O'Donnell describes how she cut open a baby's face to extract its brain while its heart was still beating. Dr. Ben Van Handel, the Executive Director of Novogenix Laboratories, LLC, the company that harvests tissue from PP abortions, admits that sometimes the baby's heart is still beating even after their procedure is done.

Mengele's victims were injected with lethal germs or exposed to various stimuli to monitor their reaction. Some were isolated to determine toleration. Both physical and psychological endurances were tested, examined, and analyzed. Mengele reveled in torturing twins by transfusing their blood with each other and even tried combining a pair to make them Siamese. As stated in _Josef Mengele, Angel of Death_, "Once Mengele's assistant rounded up 14 pairs of Gypsy twins during the night. Mengele placed them on his polished marble dissection table and put them to sleep. He then proceeded to inject chloroform into their hearts, killing them instantaneously. Mengele then began dissecting and meticulously noting each and every piece of the twins' bodies." (http://auschwitz.dk/Mengele.htm) How is this event any different then the excitement and enjoyment Melissa Farrell expressed in what she does with fetuses, yet she is being praised where Mengele was condemned?

Mengele performed sex change operations, a practice once considered mutilation and now deemed a right by today's Progressives. He forced incestuous pregnancies, which today's activists consider a staple cause for free abortions. Mengele also performed numerous sterilization experiments, which he learned from eugenicists here in America. (see _Finishing The Master Race_-Vol.4)

Viewing the Jewish population as a sub-human existence, Mengele convinced himself that his "scientific" experiments were just that, science. In 1960 he still proclaimed, "I personally have not killed, injured or caused bodily harm to anyone," insisting he had committed no crime but instead that he himself was a victim of a great injustice. This sentiment is eerily reflected in the defenses given by today's abortionists who don't even consider fetuses human, let alone sub-human.

As repugnant as Mengele's torturous experiments were, he and the Nazis were only continuing the policies of George Bernard Shaw and the praised champion of women's rights and Planned Parenthood founder, Margaret Sanger. Liberals love to call their political opponents Nazis yet it is their heroine that inspired the inhuman practices of the Germans as well as those happening in PP today. (see _Sanger And Eugenics And Socialism, Oh, My_)

We will never know the depths and extremities of Mengele's torture and death as his notes were destroyed after the war. It is estimated that as many as 1.5 million children were murdered during the Holocaust but no one knows for sure. (see _The Forgotten Rescue_-Vol.6 and _Code Name Jolanta_-Vol.6) These were not only Jewish children, which makes up about 1.2 million. Gypsy children were also killed along with thousands of handicapped children. (see _Finishing The Master Race_-Vol.4)

As noted in _The Axis of Evil_ letter, the mentally and physically handicapped were the first targeted by the Nazi regime, a view some

133

Liberals are now beginning to promote again. But as appalling as this figure is, PP has performed over 55 million abortions in the past 4 decades. And now with the realization of the tissue and organ harvesting they are conducting, it makes this reality even more horrendous. PP is continuing the work Margaret Sanger started and Josef Mengele expanded, and it is all done in the name of science. They have set up for themselves an unending supply of samples at taxpayer expense, no less. They unlawfully allow a longer gestation period and ignore a mother's reservations so their precious specimens can be retrieved and sold for a hefty profit. What they have ultimately sold is their soul.

Liberals continue to grasp to the argument that PP be funded by the government because they give necessary services to women such as mammograms. In reality, PP does not do mammograms. They refer women to other doctors for the test. But revealing the truth would dismiss advocates like Sen. Kirsten Gillibrand (D-NY) who told reporters she will continue to support PP and has no intention of watching the videos. Sorry, Ms. Gillibrand, you will still be held accountable even if you try to stay ignorant of the facts. Spewing the usual Liberal talking points, she claims women receive affordable health care at PP that they can't receive elsewhere. This is another Progressive lie. Free and low-cost healthcare clinics exist all over the country that have no ties to abortion and provide vital services to women. And as Ben Carson reminded America, Obamacare was passed to allow affordable healthcare for everyone, so the Left's arguments are running very thin on both truthfulness and morality.

Carson also stated when asked about the recent PP revelations, "Well, maybe I'm not objective when it comes to Planned Parenthood. But you know, I know who Margaret Sanger is, and I know that she believed in eugenics, and that she was not particularly enamored with black people. And one of the reasons that you find most of their clinics in black neighborhoods is so that you can find way to control that population. And I think people should go back and read about Margaret Sanger, who founded this place — a woman who Hillary Clinton by the way says she admires. Look and see what many people in Nazi Germany thought about her."

To excuse Planned Parenthood of their wickedness because they provide some positive services is like overlooking Hitler's atrocities towards the Jews because he designed the Auto Bahn.

Evil is Evil. Period.

That's my 2 cents.

Love, Mom

August 27, 2015

Dear Liberty,

    In a secretly recorded video, Hillary Clinton revealed to several Black Lives Matter activists that she doesn't believe in changing hearts. She believes in changing laws. Here in lies the crux of the difference between Liberals and Conservatives, Progressives and Constitutionalists, slavery and freedom.

    Professor Peter Viereck illustrated it in his book Unadjusted Man *as "The liberal sees outer, removable institutions as the ultimate source of evil; sees man's social task as creating a world in which evil will disappear ... The conservative sees the inner unremovable nature of man as the ultimate source of evil; sees man's social task as coming to terms with a world in which evil is perpetual and in which justice and compassion will both be perpetually necessary. His tools for this task are the maintenance of ethical restraints inside the individual and the maintenance of unbroken, continuous social patterns inside the given culture as a whole."*

    Progressives like Hillary believe man's behavior can be regulated through law. They believe morality, their morality not God's, can be controlled through government enforcement. There is no interest in trying to convince people their way is right, partly because they think the masses are too stupid to accept it. They instead bully and force the population into conforming to their beliefs.   The recent same-sex marriage ruling is a perfect example. Progressives know the American people overwhelmingly reject the practice, so liberal State, Federal and Supreme Court justices spat on the law and the Constitution and forced their agenda through the courts. (see What Is Love? *and Founding Documents-Vol.7) Many claim America was moving towards same-sex marriage anyway as state after state started allowing it, but that is a false representation. Voters overwhelming rejected the idea when given the chance to cast their ballot. It was judges who overruled the election results and allow it anyway.*

    It is the same with the Affordable Care Act, or Obamacare. Even today over 53% of Americans still think it is horrible for the country, but the administration, Congress, and the Supreme Court worked in concert to force through and uphold an unconstitutional law even at the objection of the majority of the people.

Supporters in both of these cases, like Hillary, often abandon trying to win over objector's minds and smugly contend we have to mindlessly accept it because "it's the law." Abortion is legal at this time too, but just because it's the law doesn't make it right.

On the flip side of Hillary's statement, Progressives don't respect the rule of law either. It is a tool to be used for their own benefit and to control the populace. The law didn't prevent Hillary from illegally setting up her own private email server as Secretary of State or when she wiped that server clean before surrendering it under subpoena. Obama praises lawbreakers like Trayvon Martin, Michael Brown (see *Just The Facts, Ma'am-Vol.1*), and Freddie Grey (see *Useful Idiots*), holding them out as heroes and martyrs even though they have been proven criminals. When the law is really needed, this administration rewards those promising to destroy and kill us, like China, Cuba and Iran, by removing all legitimate sanctions designed to keep their behavior in check.

Progressives convinced themselves they have man's moral authority which can be imposed on the masses. It is how they can advocate that killing a baby in the womb is principled and refusing to bake a wedding cake for a gay couple is unconscionable. (see *We Reserve The Right To Refuse Service-Vol.1*) Deep down Hillary Clinton and those continuing to support Planned Parenthood as increasingly disturbing videos are released actually do understand the power in changing hearts. (see *The Axis Of Evil* and *Evil Is As Evil Does*) This is why Liberals and Progressives have to shove their ideology down the throats of all people through legislation and then publicly destroy anyone who refuses to comply. They know that the vast majority will outright reject this practice of evil, as they rightly should. Progressives can't let the truth be known about the inhuman practices taking place with the aborted and as we now know some living babies. To them, abortion is the law and that's the end of it. Even the simplest question is irrelevant to them - If these fetuses are just tissue and are not connected to human life, then what is the purpose and benefit of harvesting and doing experiments on them? (see *When Does Life Begin?*)

Liberty, America was founded on the basis of the rule of law instead of totalitarianism, but it was driven by the principles of self-governing to follow that law. It was a concept never before tried and only possible when people are guided by a strong internal moral compass, not an external dictator. Our founding fathers were very clear that it was imperative God be the arrow of our compass if we wished to remain a free, self-governing nation. Progressives have removed that arrow and replaced it with their own god, the government, as we were also warned about.

"Only a virtuous people are capable of freedom. As nations become

corrupt and vicious, they have more need of masters." Benjamin Franklin, Signer of the Declaration of Independence and the Constitution. (see Spirit Of Conciliation-Vol.7)

"Men, in a word, must necessarily be controlled either by a power within them or by a power without them; either by the Word of God or by the strong arm of man; either by the Bible or by the bayonet." Robert Winthrop, Speaker of the U. S. House

"Religion and morality are the essential pillars of civil society." George Washington. (see God's Divine Providence-Vol.3)

"The Christian religion, in its purity, is the basis, or rather the source of all genuine freedom in government. . . . and I am persuaded that no civil government of a republican form can exist and be durable in which the principles of that religion have not a controlling influence." Noah Webster, author of the first American Speller and the first Dictionary.

"The moral principles and precepts contained in the scriptures ought to form the basis of all our civil constitutions and laws. . . All the miseries and evils which men suffer from vice, crime, ambition, injustice, oppression, slavery, and war, proceed from their despising or neglecting the precepts contained in the Bible." Noah Webster

"The Bible is the best of all books, for it is the word of God and teaches us the way to be happy in this world and in the next. Continue therefore to read it and to regulate your life by its precepts." John Jay, Original Chief-Justice of the U. S. Supreme Court

"Whereas true religion and good morals are the only solid foundations of public liberty and happiness . . . it is hereby earnestly recommended to the several States to take the most effectual measures for the encouragement thereof." Continental Congress, 1778

"The only foundation for a useful education in a republic is to be aid in religion. Without this there can be no virtue, and without virtue there can be no liberty, and liberty is the object and life of all republican governments. Without religion, I believe that learning does real mischief to the morals and principles of mankind." Benjamin Rush, Signer of the Declaration of Independence. (see A Dream Within A Dream-Vol.4)

"Why should not the Bible regain the place it once held as a school book? Its morals are pure, its examples captivating and noble. The reverence for the Sacred Book that is thus early impressed lasts long; and probably if not impressed in infancy, never takes firm hold of the mind." Fisher Ames, author of the final wording for the First Amendment (see Founding Documents-Vol.7)

"Human law must rest its authority ultimately upon the authority of that law which is divine. . . . Far from being rivals or enemies, religion and law are twin sisters, friends, and mutual assistants. Indeed, these two sciences run into each other." James Wilson, Signer of the Constitution and U. S. Supreme Court Justice

We must continue to turn our focus back to the Lord and reject the misguided illusion of human superiority. Elitists in both parties have used their bully pulpits to push an ideology that concludes that some humans are more important than others. It's why Black Lives Matter activists are infuriated if you say, "All Lives Matter". It's why the media crucifies Christian business owners for living their faith and not participating in a gay wedding yet forgives Muslim terrorists who kill in the name of Allah. It's why so many accept Planned Parenthood murdering babies for the mother's convenience. They ignore and fight the realities revealed in the Center for Medical Progress videos because they know the damning evidence being exposed can and will change the hearts of the American people, including some who consider themselves pro-choice. (see *The Axis Of Evil*)

We are living out the concerns our founding fathers cautioned us about 200 years ago. Removing God from our government, as well as our lives, removes morality and responsibility from society. When that happens people demand justice from the government instead, an institution more than willing to dictate, and enforce what the masses can and will do. The power to govern is eradicated from the citizens and thrust upon a small minority of elites who have no regard for the will of the people. We see this over and over in politicians who promise specific action if they are put in power and then ignore their promises once there. Instead they pass laws that take freedoms and liberty away from the people and give themselves more and more control.

When hearts are changed, governmental power is lost. When hearts are changed, lives are spared. When hearts are changed, souls are saved. And that is our goal, Liberty. We are not to force our beliefs down other's throats, but show them the love, understanding and forgiveness through the blood of Christ. We are to be an example so the Holy Spirit can change their hearts and minds to focus on the one true God. When we put our trust and faith in the Lord, our hearts will influence our behavior. You will not need laws and regulations to tell you what is right. Your conscience, guided by the Word of God, will direct your actions.

One of our most powerful ways of witnessing is by the way we live our lives. By it, you can change the world, one heart at a time.

That's my 2 cents. Love, Mom

September 4, 2015

Dear Liberty,

You are growing up in a culture that has perverted, distorted and degraded the precious gift of marriage and sex. Societies have gone through this time and time again. God destroyed Sodom and Gomorrah for their love and embrace of homosexual sex and rape, which was a total rejection of God. Queen Jezebel convinced her subjects abundant sex, including orgies, would make them closer to the gods. In Greece, before the fall of the Roman Empire, both single and married males were expected to take a young boy as a lover. In fact it was considered abnormal if they didn't. In the 60's America was introduced to 'free love', where even couples were encouraged to have open marriages allowing multiple sexual partners at their spouse's blessing. So what constitutes a proper marriage and use of sex?

Islam commands that the wife is property of the husband. In fact, any male family member has dominance over the women, including sons over mothers. Women cannot get a passport on their own, drive a car or show their face. Husbands can beat their wives if they do not submit to their sexual advances. Fathers can commit a mercy killing if their daughters kiss a boy. Females are punished if they leave the home unescorted by a male. Mothers are forbidden to correct their son's behavior and punished for doing so. Males are allowed to rape and molest children while wives are stoned to death for committing adultery. In fact, under Sharia Law, a female rape victim should be murdered for having sex out of wedlock. ISIS members pray on their knees before and after brutally raping girls as young as 9. During the assault they whisper in the girls ears that Allah not only gives the man the right to do this, but it will make the man closer to Allah.

The secular world is trying to remove marriage from society and pushing the concept of 'free love' harder than ever. We are inundated with images in magazines, music, TV, and movies where sex has become a casual past-time instead of a beautiful, loving act between a husband and wife.

In the 50's, Lucy and Ricky in 'I Love Lucy' had single beds that you rarely ever saw them in. Fifty years later, sitcoms make jokes that characters switch partners so quickly they didn't even have time to change the sheets. Brad Pitt and Angelina Jolie are held up as a model

Hollywood couple despite the fact their relationship began while he was still married to Jennifer Aniston. Furthermore, Brad and Angelina were praised for refusing to get married, even though they had several children together, until homosexuals were given the same opportunity.

Today's youth are being fed a steady diet of sexual immorality. It is promoted that it is natural to sleep around as long as you make sure to 'protect' yourself. Feminists, under the guise of sexual freedom, promote birth control as a right that others must pay for, including abortion. Murdering unborn babies is not birth control or taking responsibility. It is an abomination of God's purpose for us.

Feminists supported and applauded Sandra Fluke in 2012 when she demanded the government provide free birth control so women can be sexually promiscuous without taking personal responsibility. As accepted fashion designs get skimpier and more revealing, sexual freedom is deemed victorious. Society then demeans and degrades the male population as they increasingly view women simply as sex objects. Women demand they be allowed to have sexual freedom and then are furious when a man sees them that way. They are horrified when boys who are excited by girls flaunting themselves around, actually respond to the girl's advances. Rape is never acceptable but society ignores the danger girls are putting themselves in. You can only dangle meat in front of a lion and deny him access for so long before he attacks.

In the secular world, responsibility, commitment, and humanity have been irradiated from people's view of one another. We are brainwashed to believe that our only service is to ourselves. Others are there solely to please us. It's no excuse but it's no wonder more and more males are seeing females as nothing more than a conquest, just like in the animal kingdom. They are not living, breathing human beings who should be loved and honored. (see <u>Marriage Is What Brings Us Together Today</u>)

In Christ's kingdom, we are shown the truth. Throughout the Bible, the relationship between Christ and the church is compared to a groom and his bride. Prophets like Isaiah continually warned the people of Israel about "prostituting" themselves with other gods. God considered their worship of these false gods as infidelity.

Jesus said, "and the two will become one flesh. So they are no longer two, but one flesh." (Mark 10:8) Paul wrote in 1 Corinthians 6 why this relationship is so important. A human's body is a temple of the Holy Spirit, bought at a price through the blood of Christ. "All other sins a person commits are outside the body, but whoever sins sexually, sins against their own body." When two people come together, they make "one flesh, But whoever is united with the Lord is one with him in spirit". The two people make an everlasting bond. Those choosing to sleep with multiple partners are damaging their souls, whether they are heterosexuals or homosexuals. When a couple splits, that bond is fragmented. When this is done multiple times, the body and soul become severely damaged and splintered. No wonder so many people feel so broken, hollow and alone these days.

Ephesians 5 explains God's intent for a husband and a wife. First, Paul instructs both parties to "Submit to one another out of reverence for Christ." Our first requirement is that neither party be superior, but each partner should be submissive to the other. He then specifically coaches each spouse, starting with the wife. "Wives, submit yourselves to your own husbands as you do to the Lord. For the husband is the head of the wife as Christ is the head of the church, his body, of which he is the Savior. Now as the church submits to Christ, so also wives should submit to their husbands in everything." Many feminists use this passage to accuse the church of oppressing women and allowing the man to be dominate, yet claiming this completely ignores the first "submit to each other" command.

If critics were to continue reading, they would realize that God has an even stricter directive for the groom. "Husbands, love your wives, just as Christ loved the church and gave himself up for her to make her holy, cleansing her by the washing with water through the word, and to present her to himself as a radiant church, without stain or wrinkle or any other blemish, but holy and blameless. In this same way, husbands ought to love their wives as their own bodies. He who loves his wife loves himself. After all, no one ever hated their own body, but they feed and care for their body, just as Christ does the church—for we are members of his body. 'For this reason a man will leave his father and mother and be united to his wife, and the two will become one flesh.' This is a profound mystery—but I am talking about Christ and the church. However, each one of you also must love his wife as he loves himself, and the wife must respect her husband." (Ephesians 5:25-32)

If anyone has a "war on women" (see War On Women), it would be those who have willingly divorced themselves from God's intention for marriage. They fail to realize that God is not making the man a dictator as Islam does, but gives the couple a recipe for a relationship that requires both parties to work responsibly together in their respective roles, be forgiving, and be representatives of their faith. How can a man love a woman he just met in a bar? How can a woman respect a man who left her bed before the sun came up?

If critics would take the time to honestly study the love and devotion God commands us to give to our spouse, they would realize their impression of God is not at all what they thought. If a woman respects her husband, she will trust his guidance. If a man loves his wife, he will consider her thoughts and feelings in his leadership. Like

Christ, he is to be ready and willing to lay down his life for her. You don't sacrifice yourself for someone you consider property. You sacrifice yourself for what you hold dear, for what you cherish and put on a pedestal, just as Christ did for us. If people would only follow the commands of God, domestic violence would be non-existent.

We, as the Christian Church, are the bride. Christ is our groom. But there is a third participant in marriage - God. Christ tells his disciples that there are many rooms in His father's house "and if I go and prepare a place for you, I will come back and take you to be with me that you also may be where I am." (John 14:3) The bride and groom will live in God's house. He is an active member in the marriage bond. Jesus commanded, "Therefore what God has joined together, let no one separate." (Mark 10:9) The state doesn't unite the couple, God does. This makes Him, not the government, party to it. (see *Marriage Is What Brings Us Together Today*)

At the time of Christ, when an engagement was announced, the groom would leave and prepare a home for him and his new bride. Even though they were just engaged, the promised commitment was still as binding as a marriage. When the house was ready, the groom would return for a wedding ceremony and feast. The newlywed couple would then depart to their new home. When Christ used this analogy, it was a vivid description on how He views His relationship to the church. First, He and His bride are committed to each other even in His absence. Second, He was going to leave for a time to prepare our home in Heaven. Third, He would return to gather His bride and take her to His father's house.

Liberty, your father and I will do what we can to shield you and protect you from what God has told us is a very harmful and dangerous behavior, but the decision to reject this conduct will be yours. I was fortunate enough that I had parents that let it be known to me that these types of activities are not God-pleasing. I decided early on that I would follow God's plan for me and not society's. I prayed many times for a good, God-fearing man that would love Him as much as I did. God answered my prayers and your father and I have been together for 27 years. While many of our friends were experimenting with sex and some getting pregnant, your father and I had decided long before we even started dating that we would hold to God's loving intent for us.

Satan is working hard, though, while our groom is away to entice us in any way he can. He wants us to forget about Jesus. He wants us to forget our vow and seek the pleasures of other gods, whether that be money, fame, vengeance, or flesh.

You will be tested and because you are a child of God, Satan will target you even harder. Our prayer for you is you will stay strong.

Find strength in God's word and seek guidance from us and other family members, your pastors, and other believers in troubling times. Study, ask questions and seek answers. Know what you believe and hold firm.

I am so thankful I made my decision early to follow God's plan for marriage. I have never regretted it. It would have been very easy to fall to temptation if I had not. Both your father and I had wonderful examples of loving, Christian parents and grandparents. I pray your father and I are as good of examples as our parents were, and will be for you.

That's my 2 cents.

Love,
Mom

September 10, 2015

Dear Liberty,

Many regard the Pilgrims as the first missionaries of faith in the New World. They are also credited with bringing the concept of self-governance to the shores. The fact is the mission of the very

first English settlers in the land was to spread the Gospel and do it freely from under the chains of England.

Over 100 years after the discovery of the Americas, King James I formed the Virginia Company on April 10, 1606, with the purpose of funding immigrants to the New World. The company was divided into two sections, the London Company and the Plymouth Company. A charter was drawn up stating the mission and goal of the company. As one section states: "We greatly commending, and graciously accepting of, their desires for the furtherance of so noble a work, which may, by the Providence of Almighty God, hereafter tend to the Glory of his Divine Majesty, in propagating of Christian Religion to such People, as yet live in Darkness and miserable Ignorance of the true knowledge and Worship of God..." (see God's Divine Providence-Vol.3) In other words, part of their focus was to spread the Gospel of Jesus Christ to the natives.

On April 26, 1607, one hundred and four men and boys, including the famous Captain John Smith, reached the New World on the ships Susan Constant, Godspeed, and Discovery. They landed on what is now Cape Henry and spent a month searching for the proper location for their colony. Their new settlement, called Jamestown, becoming the first permanent English colony in North America. Though Plymouth Company established the Popham Colony in Maine a few days later, it failed and disappeared just after a year. No other colonies were established in the New England area until the Pilgrims landed in 1620. (see Thanks Be To God-Vol.1)

While the animated Disney movie Pocahontas depicts John Ratcliffe driving a British flag in the ground upon making landfall, the first colonists actually planted a wooden cross on Virginia Beach at Cape Henry. While kneeling on the cross, Pastor Robert Hunt offered the prayer: "We do hereby Dedicate this Land, and ourselves, to reach the People within these shores with the Gospel of Jesus Christ, and so raise up Godly generations after us, and with these generations take the Kingdom of God to all the earth. May this Covenant of Dedication remain to all generations, as long as this earth remains, and may this Land, along with England, be Evangelist to the World."

Upon arrival, there were tensions between the Jamestown colonists and the 14,000 Algonquian Indians under the leadership of Chief Powhatan. Powhatan ruled over several tribes in the Chesapeake area and desired Jamestown to become part of his domain. The colonists built James Fort but struggled with disease, food and Indian attacks. The English's resistance did not sit well with the Chief but did not make relations with the Indians impossible either. John Smith worked with the natives and secured food for the men, saving the colony from starvation.

In December of 1607, Smith and two companions were captured while exploring and mapping the Chickahominy River region. The Powhatan warriors delivered the prisoners to their Chief. After killing the other two colonists, Smith recounts in his book <u>Generall Historie</u> (1624) that "two great stones were brought before Powhatan: then as many as could layd hands on him [Smith], dragged him to them, and thereon laid his head, and being ready with their clubs, to beate out his braines, Pocahontas the Kings dearest daughter, when no intreaty could prevaile, got his head in her armes, and laid her owne upon his to save him from death: whereat the Emperour [Powhatan] was contented he should live... ." Pocahontas was not only successful in saving Smith's life, she convinced her father to safely return him to Jamestown. She was just 13-years-old at the time.

By January of 1608, less than half of the original settlers were still alive. That month, 70 more English settlers arrived but they failed to bring sufficient provisions. The colony continued to struggle over the next several months while more people arrived without supplies. Representing her father, Pocahontas often visited Jamestown and usually with gifts of food.

On September 10, 1608, things changed for the settlement. Already a strong leader in the community, John Smith was officially elected council president of Jamestown, Virginia. He believed greatly in the Biblical instruction that, "The one who is unwilling to work shall not eat." (2 Thessalonians 3:10). Under his strong leadership, work ethic and self-governing standpoint, Jamestown began to produce, grow and become self-sufficient. Smith was not loved by everyone, though. After a mysterious gunpowder accident, Smith was forced to return to

England in October of 1609, never to see Virginia again.

While Smith was around, relations between Powhatan and the settlers were somewhat stable but not perfect. Shortly before he left, conflicts arose that began the First Anglo-Powhatan War. Because of the hostilities, Pocahontas was told that Smith had died. She disappeared soon after, reportedly marrying Kocoum and moving to a secret village for safety reasons. Samuel Argall discovered her location, abducting her on April 13, 1613, and took her to Henricus. His purpose was to hold her for ransom. His demands included the release of English prisoners Powhatan held captive, along with returning stolen weapons and tools. The Chief released the Englishmen, but failed to return all the stolen items resulting in Pocahontas' continued captivity.

As we say, though, the Lord works in mysterious ways. Rev. Alexander Whitaker traveled to Virginia in 1611 with the sole purpose of sharing the Gospel with the natives. (see The Apostle Of Virginia-Vol.4) He wrote, "One God created us: They have reasonable souls and intellectual faculties as well as we. We all have Adam for our common parent." During her time in Henricus, Pocahontas was put in Whitaker's care who ministered to her and taught her English through reading the Bible. She soon embraced Christianity and was baptized with the name "Rebecca", thus becoming the first native convert in the Americas.

After her abduction, her marriage to Kocoum was terminated due to either his murder, or Powhatan tradition that ends a marriage after a kidnapping. Either way, Pocahontas was no longer a married woman. During her time in Henricus, she met and fell in love with John Rolfe, a widower who lost his wife and child several years earlier in Bermuda on his voyage to the New World. He reached America and became a tobacco farmer. He spent years developing new varieties of tobacco, which became the Colony's first export cash crop. This resulted in Rolfe becoming a prominent and wealthy member of society.

In March 1614, Pocahontas was given an opportunity to speak to several of her senior Native American leaders not including the Chief. She criticized her father for putting tools and objects over her life and then revealed that she preferred to stay with the settlers. A month later she married John Rolfe at a Jamestown church. And thus, the American dream begins with the first native Christian convert and a self-made entrepreneur.

Though some use her kidnapping as a reason to denounce the founding of the country, her marriage to John allowed improved Native American and colonists' relationships. It resulted in the six-year "Peace of Pocahontas" period where natives and English lived in peace.

Rolfe and Pocahontas took their young son, Thomas, to England in 1616 to promote and raise money for the Virginia Company. Her conversion to Christianity gave hope to those in England for spreading the Gospel of Jesus Christ across the globe. The first Native American to travel to England, Pocahontas was very well received and even met King James and Queen Ann. She became famous in her own right in the Old World with statues and paintings commemorating their respect for her.

Their union was also a testament to inter-racial marriage. John Rolfe quoted 2 Corinthians 6:14 in his quest to marry Pocahontas, "Do not be yoked together with unbelievers. For what do righteousness and wickedness have in common? Or what fellowship can light have with darkness?" It was her faith in Christ Jesus that made them equal as partners, not their ethnic background. (see Marriage Is what Brings Us Together Today)

After 7 months overseas, Rolfe was ready to get back to his tobacco farm. The family set sail but had to return to shore when Pocahontas became gravely ill. She died in March 1617, in her husband's arms and was buried at Saint George's Church in Gravesend, England.

Back in Jamestown, Smith's model of self-governance was taking root and growing. Many believe the idea of breaking from the crown originated with the Patriots and our Founding Fathers in the mid-1700's. The truth is the basis for self-governance was embedded in the Charter of 1606 by stating individuals in this colony: "shall HAVE and enjoy all Liberties, Franchises, and Immunities, within any of our other Dominions, to all Intents and Purposes, as if they had been abiding and born, (that's God-given, inalienable rights) within this our Realm of England, or any other of our said Dominions." It is this language, along with the Mayflower Compact of the Pilgrim's in 1620, that inspired and supported the Founder's purpose for the Declaration of Independence. (see Thanks Be To God-Vol.1, America's First Founding Document-Vol.3, Happy Independence Day-Vol.1 and Founding Documents-Vol.7) From the beginning, the desire for freedom and liberty was written in the hearts and minds of the American settlers. (see Independence: It's In Our DNA) The harder kings put their foot on America's neck, the more determined she became to have her freedom.

On July 30, 1619, the first representative legislative assembly convened in Jamestown. So from the start, America was based on a "government of law and not of men." By March 1622, after an Algonquian attack that killed 300 settlers, and severe debt of the Virginia Company, King James rescinded the Virginia Company Charter and consequently any God-given rights that went with it. He made Virginia a Crown Colony, appointing his own governor in 1624.

King James may have taken liberty and freedom away in Jamestown, but it was alive and well in Massachusetts with the Pilgrims and there was no way to prevent its spread.

Historians generally agree the Geneva Bible came to the New World in 1607 with Captain John Smith, as evident with his push for self-reliance and self-governance. (see <u>All In Due Time</u>) Rev. Whitaker's surviving sermons show he referenced the Geneva Bible in his preparations. (see <u>The Apostle Of Virginia</u>-Vol.1) Away from the prying eye of the crown, people were free to study the notes of the Reformers included in the best selling Bible. (see <u>The Knock Heard 'Round The World</u>-Vol.1) The result was an increased skepticism to the crown and monarchy's role in governing the people. Despite King James attempt to hide God's warnings against monarchs with his Kings James Version, Americans embraced the true words of individualism in the Bible with all reliance on God.

The language of the Charter of 1606 gave the New World freedom as an independent, Christian county and nothing was going to stop it. Christian common law and spiritual liberty are woven into its DNA. It is only in the past 100 years that Progressives have erased these important and freedom-giving facts from our schoolbooks in attempts to write the history they want. They have lied, denying the influence of God and the Bible in our formation. They know that as with the rejection of the crown, the truth shall set us free.

Liberty, if you don't know the truth it's easy to believe anything. Evil is eager to put the shackles of social and economic slavery around your ankles and control your every move, including who you worship. America was blessed once because the people landing on its shores understood the importance of putting God first. Satan has been fighting from that time to take that blessing from us. We, as with the Jamestown settlers and the Pilgrims, have a country before us again that is ignorant and unaware of the saving grace of our Lord and Savior Jesus Christ. We don't need to travel to a far away nation to be missionaries anymore. There our millions of Pocahontas' in our own country right now.

Let's get to work.

That's my 2 cents.

Love,
Mom

September 17, 2015

Dear Liberty,

   While July 4th is a pivotal day for our country, it was on this day in 1787 that the backbone of our nation's governing system was cemented with the U.S. Constitution.

   The nation had built up a substantial debt fighting the Revolutionary War. The First Continental Congress allowed the government to print money of which it actively did. By the end of the war, the bills had depreciated so much simply because there were so many of them, they were turned into a joke with the common phrase "not worth a continental".

   As George Washington and the Continental Army fought King George III, the 13 colonies gathered for the Second Continental Congress to agree on the Articles of Confederation, the first American Constitution. (see Founding Documents-Vol.7) It was a simple document but it had its issues. The only means of revenue for the new government was taxation but since the Articles did not grant enforcement powers, most states did not pay. Those who did contribute barely covered the interest owed for their state. Adding in states producing their own currency, the economy of the new nation was failing fast. The country was on the verge of bankruptcy and she was barely 10 years old. (see *Reading The Riot Act-Vol.5*)

   For America to survive on the world stage, there had to be some common unity between the states. The Articles did establish a structure for the states to vote on proposals affecting the country, but it allowed any one state the ability to veto a bill. It also lacked instruction on managing affairs, specifically internationally, of the nation and failed to provide the guidance and support needed from a strong, central but still limited, government. Seeking a resolution, another Constitutional Convention was called. State legislatures chose 74 delegates to attend but only 55 showed up on May 25, 1787, in Philadelphia, Pennsylvania. (see *Spirit Of Conciliation-Vol.7*) The original purpose was to amend the Articles of Confederation. The delegates soon realized the best action was to start over with a new Constitution.

   As demonstrated in *Jamestown: A City Upon A Hill-Vol.1* and *Thanks Be To God-Vol.1*, the concept of self-governing was instilled in the hearts of Americans from the very first settlers. (see *Independence:*

It's In Our DNA-Vol.1) The new Constitution highlighted this concept, beginning with the words "We the People". It was this phrase that set the stage for the historical document that grants rights and power to the citizens, not a person or entity. (see Founding Documents-Vol.7)

Establishing the people's control over the government and not the other way around, the delegates designed a central government consisting of 3 "separate but equal" branches: Legislative, Executive, and Judicial. Care was taken to make sure each branch had their own specific duties and authorities, as well as precise restrictions and boundaries. "Checks and balances" were developed instructing each branch to keep the other branches within their limitations. (see The New Trinity-Vol.3) Included were measures, specifically impeachment, to remove anyone who abused or overstepped their boundaries, whether it be a Congressmen, Justice, or President.

The delegates worked through the hot days of summer in Philadelphia fighting, arguing, compromising and developing an amazing document. (see Spirit Of Conciliation-Vol.7) As Jefferson is the "Father of the Declaration of Independence", James Madison was given the honor of authoring the majority of this instrument, which earned him the title "Father of the Constitution". (see Founding Documents-Vol.7) Forty-one delegates were present on September 17th when the Constitution was presented for signatures. Three refused to sign at the time with thirty-nine putting their name on the document. Upon exiting the proceedings, Benjamin Franklin was asked, "Well, Doctor, what have we got—a Republic or a Monarchy?". Franklin replied without hesitation, "A Republic, if you can keep it."

Many states were skeptical regarding the new Constitution and wanted more clarity on the rights of personal freedoms. More importantly, they desired additional limits on the federal government in its authority and further restrictions to reduce their ability to abuse its power. Also sought was the retention of some powers to the states and to the citizens. After the Constitution was ratified in 1788, Congress moved to address these issues. James Madison proposed 39 Amendments of which Congress approved twelve on September 25, 1789, with eventually 10 being ratified by the states. These ten clauses became known as the Bill of Rights, the first of which gave ultimate freedom of speech and religion to the citizens. (see Ratifying Liberty-Vol.4 and Founding Documents-Vol.7)

"Congress shall make no law respecting an establishment of religion, or prohibiting the free exercise thereof; or abridging the freedom of speech, or of the press; or the right of the people peaceably to assemble, and to petition the Government for a redress of grievances."

To be able to sustain the First Amendment, Americans were given the Second Amendment. (see Founding Documents-Vol.7)

"A well regulated Militia, being necessary to the security of a free State, the right of the people to keep and bear Arms, shall not be infringed."

After fighting a war against a King who not only controlled religion but executed those who spoke against him, the Founding Fathers of the Country made sure that the people of America would be free to speak and worship as they choose. But the only way to secure that freedom was to guarantee a tyrannical government couldn't overpower them. This was achieved by giving citizens the right to defend themselves, not against intruders and other citizens, but from a government seeking to become a totalitarian governing body. (see Gun Control: The First Steps Of Tyranny-Vol.3)

The delegates borrowed elements and ideas from other documents, including the Declaration of Independence and the Articles of Confederation. (see Founding Documents-Vol.7) As a whole, though, the Constitution of the United States of America was an unprecedented governing contract that had never been seen before. It was an agreement that limited the powers of the national government, giving the control to the states and personal rights to the citizens of the country. The Constitution and Bill of Rights were very specific in not informing the federal government what it could do, but what it couldn't. (see Founding Documents-Vol.7) They are explicitly meant to tie the hands of those writing, enforcing, and judging our laws to prevent them from hindering our liberties and freedoms.

President George W. Bush ushered into law a bill honoring the 39 brave men who signed the document. It designated September 17th Constitution Day, which America first celebrated in 2005. How fantastic we are re-familiarizing ourselves with such an important document. It's easy for a government to take away freedoms that citizens aren't even aware they have. But God help those who try to remove liberties while citizens are wide awake.

That's my 2 cents.

Love,
Mom

September 24, 2015

Dear Liberty,

Freedom. She could taste it. Araminta and her brothers had quietly slipped off the plantation in Dorchester County, Maryland, unnoticed. The 90-mile trip to Philadelphia was physically taxing and fraught with the constant fear of capture. Her brothers began to have second thoughts as a $300 bounty was put on their heads and posted in the <u>Cambridge Democrat</u> newspaper. It was enough to turn anyone around. Anyone except Araminta, that is.

Araminta, or "Minty", was placed in a very difficult position. She was as close as she had ever been to freedom, yet she couldn't let her brothers venture back on their own. Risking her own capture, Minty traveled back with her brothers to ensured their safe return before setting out again, this time alone, on that fateful September day in 1849.

Running through the woods Minty recalled how close her family had been to freedom already. Her father, Benjamin Ross, had been freed at age 45 upon the death of his owner. With a wife and children still enslaved, he had little choice if he wanted to keep the family together. Working for his former owners as a timber estimator and foreman seemed to be his only option. Minty herself had technically been born free as her mother, Harriet Green, had also been released by a previous owner before her birth. Maybe it would have been better if she hadn't hired that lawyer to look into her mother's status. At least they wouldn't have discovered the will Harriet's new owners ignored. Even Minty's husband of 5 years was a free man yet would not come with her on her liberating journey.

Branches and twigs scrapped and tugged at her skin, as if holding her back to the life of captivity she had always known. As she raced through the forest towards her deliverance she was taken back to a morning as a young child when she was lashed 5 times before breakfast. The scars of that day, both mental and physical, still remained with her these 20 years later. Just a little further and that life would be nothing but an unpleasant memory.

She coughed and wiped her forehead with her sleeve, praying her recent illness did not return, stealing what energy she still had. Sickly slaves were not desired property, let alone good escapees. As she smoothed her hair back, her hand brushed the head injury she received as a teenager. It seemed like yesterday she defended the slave who left the plantation without permission. She just could not bring herself to hold him down so the overseer could whip him. The iron weight he hurled at her, striking her unconscious, would forever imprint her life with severe headaches, seizures, and narcoleptic episodes. But all would be all right soon. She said a prayer to God for strength and faith, took one last drink of water and then set her sights on the Northern Star.

There wasn't any difference in the landscape when she stepped from Maryland into Pennsylvania. The birds sang the same songs and the trees swayed in the same wind. There was no fanfare or celebration. But from the moment Minty's foot touched the ground in the free state of Pennsylvania, her life completely changed. She had reached the Promise Land.

When she became a wife, she took her husband's name. It seemed appropriate to make a similar revision now. Admiring her mother's boldness, Minty decided to use her mother's name as well. Goodbye to the slave life of Arminta Ross. Welcome to the free life of Harriet Tubman.

As Harriet gained her own freedom, the Underground Railroad was doing its best to provide safe passage for escaped slaves in search of freedom. It was hindered in September of 1850, when the Fugitive Slave Act was passed, requiring the capture of escaped slaves in Northern states. (see Abolishing Mistakes-Vol.6) Law enforcement officials were forced to cooperate in the search and arrest of runaway slaves regardless of how they felt personally about the issue. Sizable rewards enticed many to grab any Negro they saw which sometimes included legally free blacks. Those who provided food and shelter could now be punished with steep fines and possible jail time. Fugitive slaves and free blacks fled to Canada, with the tracks of the Underground Railroad soon following behind.

Her first mission was to return to Maryland to retrieve her niece, Kessiah, and her family. Over the next 8 years she earned the title of 'Conductor' of the Underground Railroad, guiding at least 19 trips back into slave states. During the course of conducting the railroad she brought her parents, several siblings and family members, along with hundreds of other souls to a life of liberty in the North.

When she returned, it was to the home lent to her by Senator William H Seward. Seward, a member of the newly formed abolitionist Republican Party, was as determined to end slavery as she was. (see Birth Of A Movement-Vol.1) She could never repay him for offering his house to her on the outskirts of Auburn, New York, so she could retrieve her parents from Canada to come live with her in a free state. She could only offer thanks to God for such a man and a political party established on the primary objective to abolish slavery.

Her years of conducting the railroad had led to the freedom for many, but also a $40,000 bounty on her head. This reward made each crusade into the South even riskier than the one before.

She knew she was preparing for her last voyage into the South to rescue slaves yearning for the freedom she so treasured. Straightening up her room, she found herself humming, "Go Down, Moses". Pausing for a moment, she realizing how powerful and strengthening this spiritual had been to the refugees during their travels. Young and old affectionately referred to her as the "Moses of her people," as she led the exodus of Negros out of bondage and to the land of liberty.

Before leaving her home, she reached for her most important item, her trusty pistol. Checking the barrel, she held the gun with a steady hand, sure of her ability to defend herself when required. She never would have used it on her brothers, but she could never risk any of her other travelers changing their minds. She mouthed her mantra, "Dead Negros tell no tales." More than one escapee had had that pistol in their face and told "you'll be free or die a slave". The risk to herself and the entire Underground Railroad if a slave returned or was caught was too great and would not be tolerated. She never lost a traveler or allowed one to turn back. She took one last look at her room, took a deep breath, and shut the door.

Harriet looked out across her little tract of land she just purchased from Senator Seward. He was so generous to let her stay there for two years but Seward had taken a great risk selling her the home, as it was illegal to do. For the first time Harriet had hope for the future as members of his new party were honest in their efforts to help the Negro and view them as equals. Prayers were needed for the upcoming election next year. Her conducting days were over but she was in no way done with her service.

The summer heat was beginning the rise on the June 1863 day as Harriet scouted the Combahee River shoreline from her gunboat for rebel placed torpedoes. Harriet left her home, which had become a place of refuge and shelter for poor and needy Negros, to offer her services to President Lincoln and the Union Army at the beginning of the war. Cooking for and nursing soldiers was noble, but guiding an expedition into South Carolina to free slaves and disrupt rebel supply lines was the lifeblood of America's Moses. She glanced over to her friend Col. James Montgomery, whom she personally requested to command the 150 Negro Union soldiers of the 2nd South Carolina regiment in this mission. It didn't faze Harriet this was the first armed expedition led by a woman. No, her heart was beating to the rhythm of "My people must go free."

As the Union gunboat made its way up the river, slaves fled from the fields afraid that they would be spotted by a ship commanded by the horned and tailed Northern soldiers. But as the slaves saw Harriet standing at the bow of the lead ship, they broke from the tree line, waving to the ships. Word quickly spread among the slaves that these were "Lincoln's gunboats come to set them free". Upon that revelation the Negros grabbed what clothes, food, and other supplies they could and sprinted towards the boats. Harriet laughed with joy as women ran with pigs, chickens and children hanging from their necks and dresses. Over 700 slaves rushed the gunboats scrambling for a coveted spot to freedom. True to her character, America's Moses made sure not a soul was left.

Harriet continued her work of service and kindness, along with suffrage and activism, until being admitted to the 'Harriet Tubman Home for the Aged' built on land she gave to the African Methodist Episcopal Zion Church in 1903. (see Hoosier Daddy-Vol.5) Surrounded by family and friends, she declared, "I go to prepare a place for you," just before she took her last breath on March 10, 1913. She was now truly free.

The 1869 publication of the Sarah Bradford book entitled, Scenes in the Life of Harriet Tubman, brought Harriet revenue sales, donations, recognition, and much needed financial relief, but her heart always seemed to be greater than her pocketbook. She died virtually penniless. A genuine hero, she rightly received a burial with military honors at Fort Hill Cemetery in Auburn. Her tombstone reads: Servant of God, Well Done.

In 1990, Congress passed a bill signed by President George H. W. Bush declaring March 10th Harriet Tubman Day. New York State established it as a holiday in 2003.

Liberty, life is not perfect. Everyone has hardships and setbacks, but what determines our character is our reaction and our perseverance in those struggles. Harriet Tubman was a slave. She received debilitating injuries and unthinkable treatment, yet throughout her life she happily and eagerly served God. God was her master, not a slave owner. It is this devotion, this love, this servitude that we are also commanded to willing take upon our shoulders as followers of Christ. And when you get weak or discouraged, look to the Cross and remember the sacrifice of the perfect servant. He will give you strength.

That's my 2 cents.

Love,
Mom

October 1, 2015

Dear Liberty,

Evolutionists and science fiction aficionados alike are rejoicing this week following NASA's announcement confirming flowing water on Mars. NASA has suspected for a long time that ice caps existed on Mars. They just recently discovered in certain times of the year, which coincide with warm periods, that there are dark streaks on the surface. NASA concluded these streaks are flowing water as they emit light waves consistent with water. Without taking any actual samples, this can only be an educated guess. It is also unknown where the water actually comes from, so these are just plausible speculations.

The NASA scientists have no concrete empirical evidence for their theories, but those theories are considered gospel by all who have enough faith to believe them. This revelation provides enough evidence for them that life did or could exist on Mars. Their childhood dreams of "My Favorite Martin", "Mork & Mindy", "Close Encounters of the Third Kind", and "The Martian", interestingly enough released Friday, could actually be true. While all these productions are categorized as "Science Fiction", too many opt to focus on the "science" part of that description instead of the more accurate "fiction" part.

For decades man has gravitated to the idea that intelligent life exists somewhere out in the universe. Evolutionist and atheist Richard Dawkins, knowing spontaneous generation was debunked by Louis Pasteur, contends aliens brought life to Earth. (see <u>The Science Is Settled</u>) What he can't answer though, is how did the alien life-form begin? Many, like Dawkins, choose to believe aliens built such structures as the pyramids and Stonehenge because they can't explain them otherwise. Accepting man was smart enough to design and construct such amazing architectural feats in a time when humans was supposed to be evolutionarily primitive would destroy the narrative of their entire belief system. Man could not have been smarter thousands of years ago than he is now because he was not as evolved. Otherwise, man would have had to have a period of devolving, which in the evolutionary world is not scientifically feasible.

Evidence of the possibility that the tiniest microbe may have the slightest chance to cling to life on some distant planet has elated the evolutionary world to new heights. On the other hand, a 20-week-old fetus with a brain, a beating heart, lungs, kidneys, arms, legs, eyes, ears, fingers, and toes is just a parasite with only the potential to become a human being. (see *When Does Life Begin?*) Evolutionists have more faith in a minute chance of an organism spontaneously generating to life on Mars than DNA evidence validating life beginning at conception. (see *The Science Is Settled*) Science supposedly still has yet to demonstrate that unborn children are humans, however scientists are desperate to use the body parts of murdered babies for scientific research to further knowledge of mankind.

Bill Nye, The Science Guy, just released a video arguing that a fertilized egg must first attach to the uterine wall before it can become human. PBS, his former home, says singled-celled organisms "are some of the most important life forms on Earth." A single cell defines life in evolution, but apparently not in human biology. If not at conception, when exactly when does a human become a human? We have thousands of years of data proving that no human woman has ever given birth to anything other than a human baby, but scientists and media dismiss empirical evidence as inconclusive. On the other hand, Climate Change hypotheses and theories based on computer models generated by manipulated and falsified data are unequivocally supported because it fits their personal worldviews. Taking a moment to think logically, Liberty, who are the science deniers?

The recent media reports quote NASA scientists consistently using words like "hypothesized", "suspect", and "theorize" throughout their statements. Nevertheless they still confirm flowing water on Mars. Furthermore, the director of planetary science at NASA, Jim Green, claims that millions of years ago Mars had "an ocean two-thirds the size of the northern hemisphere and a mile deep." He also surmised, "Mars suffered a major climate change and lost its surface water," due to some mysterious catastrophe. The mainstream media lapped it up without an ounce of journalistic curiosity as to how he scientifically concluded any of his findings. Where is his evidence? Where is the science? It doesn't matter because he brought in Climate Change. Yet, they can look at a fully intact aborted baby in a petri dish and say it is not human life.

A theoretical unidentified catastrophe on Mars goes unchallenged, but honest scientific evidence pointing to a global flood happening on this planet is tossed aside like an aborted fetus. (see *Leap Of Faith*-Vol.3 and *Evolution Explodes*-Vol.4) Ignored are the nautical fossils found well above sea level. Dismissed are the perfectly preserved fossils resulting from rapidly buried plants and animals indicating a massive flood. Disregarded are impeccably maintained trees discovered spanning through several sedimentary layers that supposedly took eons to develop. This fact alone blows the whole "millions of years" theory out of the water. Trees could not have lived and grown that long to have numerous layers build up around them. Yet the scientists *presenting these facts are ostracized while those suppressing the evidence are given Pulitzer Prizes. Again I ask, who is actually denying the science here?*

Liberty, what this all comes down to is very simple. It began when Satan convinced Eve to take the fruit from the Tree of Knowledge of Good and Evil. (see <u>Fruit Of The Forbidden Tree</u>-Vol.1) Sin immediately infested the human DNA with the impulse to reject God. We cling to things that don't make any logical or scientific sense while eagerly denying indisputable proof of God's existence. We cheer at the slightest possibility that life has the tiniest likelihood of existing on another planet, yet we vigorously challenge the life that actually exists right here inside our mothers, our sisters, our wives, and our daughters.

Abortionists are attacking the Center for Medical Progress (CMP) claiming their videos were edited, saying they are against women's health and just want to stop Planned Parenthood (PP) out of spite. (see <u>The Axis Of Evil</u> and <u>Evil Is As Evil Does</u>) Democrat Representative Nancy Pelosi, who receives large political donations from PP, refuses to watch the videos yet maintains they are doctored and wants the CMP investigated. Abortion supporters are distancing themselves from the actual issue as much as possible, trying to distract the American public with insults, accusations and denials. The leftist media, Democratic Party and Hollywood are doing all they can to help PP hide from the toxic truth of what they are doing God turned on the lights and the cockroaches are scattering, still trying to conceal themselves in the shadows.

Intellectual curiosity has been abandoned for ideology and political correctness. Through DNA, science proves a fetus is and can only be a human, yet those who profess this are called the science deniers. Jim Green can declare water existed millions of years ago on a planet no one's ever been to and he is heralded as brilliant. Anyone daring to reject Green's claim or just simply ask for any sort of evidence are also accused of denying science. But how can you deny what hasn't even been presented? People will do whatever they have to do to disregard and reject God, even if it means accepting and defending the indefensible.

Convinced it gives verification that God does not exist, many are desperately clutching to the remote possibility that life did or could exist outside of our planet. Yet God is making it pretty clear that He is more in control than ever. Throughout history God has been subtle when first calling His people back to Him. Eventually, God puts the evidence plainly in our face. It is no different today. God is being so incredibly obvious. It is not a coincidence that in the same week NASA speculates life's faint chance on Mars, Planned Parenthood's president is being questioned by Congress on their practice of selling baby parts. Simply put, this is Creation vs. Evolution. It is time to decide. Are we going to believe facts or science fiction?

Liberty, it is easy to get caught up in the agenda driven propaganda being forced on people all over the world. A narrative has been created for evolution, climate change and abortion, which has nothing to do with science. Anyone diverting from this agenda is attacked and destroyed. The primary strategy of name calling, such as "science denier", "religious fanatic", or simply "hater", is just a way of shutting down opposition. If that doesn't work then the personal attacks and accusations begin. Once these tactics are resorted to you know you have won the argument. Notice the tactics have nothing to do with science? That doesn't mean the opposition has any intention of backing down though. You must always search for the truth, seek out the facts and never be afraid to stand for, present, and defend them over and over and over again. Because yes, there is intelligent life out there. And we were made in His image.

That's my 2 cents.

Love,
Mom

October 9, 2015

Dear Liberty,

A horrific tragedy occurred in Oregon on October 1st. A very seriously demented 26-year-old entered Umpqua Community College and forced students to lie on the ground. One by one he told his victims to stand and answer the question, "What religion are you?" Those responding with Christianity were rewarded with a bullet in the head.

Obama's immediate response was to politicize the tragedy. He demanded real gun control in America, suggesting we follow Australia's lead. Unfortunately, Australia's gun control was actually gun confiscation. Obama claimed it eliminated gun violence. Hours after this statement, a gunman opened fire on a police department in Australia killing two. Obama maintained areas with rigorous gun laws are the safest in the country.

Oregon is already a gun control utopia and yet this mass killing happened despite such laws. In fact, several of the cities with the strictest gun laws are the most violent, such as St. Louis, Baltimore and Washington D.C. His 12-minute propaganda was full of inaccuracies and outright lies designed to manipulate the American people regarding gun facts, never acknowledging the real root of the problem. If this issue was truly about gun control then every day there should be massive protests in cities like Chicago where upwards of 50 people are shot in a weekend.

As I wrote in my letter <u>A Change of Heart</u>, Progressives believe they can force a person's morality through legislation. Any change seen in an individual by such laws is false, insincere, and therefore not binding to the person. Gun control is just such a deceptive issue. (see <u>Gun Control: The First Steps Of Tyranny</u>-Vol.3) It has no real effect unless citizens address the genuine internal cause.

Since the founding of this country there has always be a respect and acknowledgement of God. (<u>The United Church And States Of America</u>-Vol.6) Over the past several years there has been an obvious shift to reject God. If you reject God, you reject his laws, which are foundational to our nation. There is no reason to respect yourself or others. Life has been devalued with many playing gods themselves in deciding who gets to keep theirs.

As an example of how far off course our country has veered, hundreds just gathered in Detroit in July to praise the unveiling of a new Satanic monument. This week, Oklahoma secretly removed a Ten Commandments monument in the dead of night. We have been erasing God from our culture for 50 years at an exponentially increasing rate. Is it any wonder that as the Liberal Progressives push harder and harder to villainize Christianity, while embracing everything that is ungodly, that these acts of violence are increasing?

They want to blame the NRA and guns, yet guns have been around since the beginning of the country. Kids use to take their guns to school and were involved in gun clubs yet we did not have incidents like this. Gun murders are actually down except in gun free zones and gun controlled cities. What has changed? (see It's Not What's In Your Hand, It's What's In Your Heart)

We are removing God and becoming a secular humanist society that embraces openly worshiping Satan, excuses radical Islamists, but eagerly condemning Christians and Jews. Progressives started going after Christians because they didn't participate in a same-sex wedding. (see We Reserve The Right-Vol.1) In the Charleston shooting, the gunman attacked the oldest African-American church in the country. (see Their Deaths Were Not In Vain) The Oregon shooter confessed he hated organized religion, wanted to serve Satan, and murdered the Christians while only wounding others. In the Middle East, ISIS is massacring Christians by the hundreds and thousands. (see Holocaust: Then And Now) Our Administration is responding with one, big yawn.

Evil loves death. It's not the gun that kills people. It is a black heart that seeks to end life no matter what the means. Abortion doctors do it with a vacuum. Rapists do it with knives and ropes. Spouses do it with poison, knives, pillows, and any other device at their disposal. Many even do it to themselves with a rope, car, or drugs. ISIS carries out their evil deeds by slitting the throats of their victims, bombs, burning them, or drowning them. Death is not picky about evil's choice of weapon.

Those demanding gun control have decided that an inanimate object is responsible for deaths while ignoring and actually contributing to the true problem, the removal of God from our lives. Liberty, Christ told us "If the world hates you, keep in mind that it hated me first," John 15:18. This moment in time epitomizes Christ's meaning, especially in America.

There is a solution though - A sure fire, concrete solution. It was given to us directly from God in 2 Chronicles 7:14. "If my people who are called by my name humble themselves, and pray and seek my face and turn from their wicked ways, then I will hear from heaven and will *forgive their sin and heal their land."*

I pray with all my heart America and the world wake up and heed this promise before God completely turns his back on us and lets us live in the "utopian" world we have carved out for ourselves.

Regardless of what the rest of the country or the rest of the world does, I will stand with those students in Oregon and proudly declare, "I am a Christian!"

That's my 2 cents.

Love,
Mom

October 23, 2015

Dear Liberty,

When President Warren Harding and Vice-President Calvin Coolidge took office in 1921, the economic health of America was in critical condition. Still trying to recover from The Great War, the unemployment rate was a staggering 11.7%. During Progressive Democrat President Woodrow Wilson's term, the national debt skyrocketed from $1.5 billion to $24 billion, partly due to the expenses of World War I, while the Gross National Product plummeted from $91.5 billion to $69.6 billion in just one year. These conditions were profoundly worse than the years leading to the Great Depression and overwhelmingly more disastrous than the economic climate Obama inherited in 2009, despite the political mantra against the Bush presidency.

Upon taking office, Harding and Coolidge did not spend their time or effort blaming Wilson for the country's woes. Instead, they rolled up their sleeves and got to work. They stood on principles, not propaganda, and implemented a very simple, very liberating agenda: cut federal spending dramatically and reduce the burden on both individuals and businesses by lowering taxes and reducing regulations.

Unfortunately, Harding's administration was riddled with corruption and scandal, which began to greatly hinder his objectives. That changed after his sudden death in 1923 as Coolidge quickly brought integrity and morality back into the Executive Branch.

The only president to be born on the 4th of July, it was fitting Coolidge held so strong to the Founding Father's vision for our country knowing "American ideals do not require to be changed so much as they require to be understood and applied." He believed that "Three very definite propositions were set out in its (Declaration) preamble regarding the nature of mankind and therefore of government. These were the doctrine that all men are created equal, that they are endowed with certain inalienable rights, and that therefore the source of the just powers of government must be derived from the consent of the governed." (see Happy Independence Day-Vol.1, Inalienable Rights-Vol.5 and Founding Documents-Vol.7)

Unlike his Progressive predecessors Teddy Roosevelt and Woodrow Wilson, Coolidge was a strong believer in small, limited federal government. Because of those previous administrations, many believed the president's job was to constantly make demands, advance policy and push agendas. Coolidge rightful understand that America should be guided by the citizens, not an overactive president or elite group of Congressmen. "Our country was conceived in the theory of local self-government. It is the foundation principle of our system of liberty." (see Independence: It's In Our DNA-Vol.1) He was so reserved in his demeanor it was once quipped that "Silent Cal," as he became known, could be "silent in 5 languages."

The Progressive mindset believes it is the government's job to "spread the wealth around" but Coolidge understood and warned of the dangers and oppressive nature of this perspective. "The individual, instead of working out his own salvation and securing his own freedom by establishing his own economic and moral independence by his own industry and his own self-mastery, tends to throw himself on some vague influence which he denominates society and to hold that in some way responsible for the sufficiency of his support.... This is not local self-government. It is not American. It is not the method which has made this country what it is. We cannot maintain the western standard of civilization on that theory. If it is supported at all, it will have to be supported on the principle of individual responsibility." Coolidge's policies prove that the most effective way to raise people out of poverty is to give them the liberty, freedom and responsibility to live their own lives.

In his 150th Anniversary speech of the Declaration of Independence, Coolidge quite eloquently dismembered the Progressive argument of progress. "It is often asserted that the world has made a great deal of progress since 1776, that we have had new thoughts and new experiences which have given us a great advance over the people of that day, and that we may therefore very well discard their conclusions for something more modern. But that reasoning can not be applied to this great charter. If all men are created equal, that is final. If they are endowed with inalienable rights, that is final. If governments derive their just powers from the consent of the governed, that is final. No advance, no progress can be made beyond these propositions. If anyone wishes to deny their truth or their soundness, the only direction in which he can proceed historically is not forward, but backward toward the time when there was no equality, no rights of the individual, no rule of the people. Those who wish to proceed in that direction can not lay claim to progress. They are reactionary. Their ideas are not more modern, but more ancient, than those of the Revolutionary fathers."

The Progressive view of abortion promotes we are not all equal. A mother's right to be free of the burden of a child is greater than the baby's right to live. Furthermore, the theory people can be made equal through governmental redistribution is not progress but a return to the parochial and supremacy ideology of generations before us who used political status and power to enslave the population.

Coolidge held firm that "Governments do not make ideals, but ideals make governments. This is both historically and logically true. Of course the government can help to sustain ideals and can create institutions through which they can be the better observed, but their source by their very nature is in the people. The people have to bear their own responsibilities. There is no method by which that burden can be shifted to the government. It is not the enactment, but the observance of laws, that creates the character of a nation." He believed this so strongly he vetoed 50 bills, including a farming subsidy that would have helped farmers in his own home state, insisting, "It is much more important to kill bad bills than to pass good ones." (see Views And Vetoes-Vol.5)

As a result of Coolidge's policies, the Revenue Acts of 1921, 1924, and 1926 reduced the highest income tax rate from 73% to 24%. To make sure the federal budget was balanced, Coolidge reduced federal spending by almost 50%. These two policies allowed Coolidge to pay off much of America's debt and run federal surpluses during his entire administration. He believed, "A government which lays taxes on the people not required by urgent public necessity and sound public policy is not a protector of liberty, but an instrument of tyranny. It condemns the citizen to servitude."

Life as we know it began because of the Coolidge presidency. Under his guidance, America experienced a nationwide economic boom known as the "Roaring 20's". Lower taxes allowed business owners and entrepreneurs to use their money to hire more workers, increase production and services, expand their business and grow the economy, as "after all, the chief business of the American people is business". The public sector shrunk while the private sector exploded. Wages naturally increased, rising 37%, resulting in the emergence of the middle-class. (see Fording The Way-Vol.5)

Coolidge's small government strategy allowed millions of families to rise out of poverty and enjoy a profitable living for the first time. Americans purchased their first cars, electricity became a staple in urban homes, and families reveled in a never before seen disposable income to buy luxuries such as radios, phones and refrigerators. Often characterized as a Scrooge by his critics, Coolidge's conservative approach actually oversaw one of the most productive and abundant times in American history.

In 1924, Coolidge's son developed a blister while playing tennis on the White House lawn. Considered a minor annoyance today, this simple ailment led to an infection and the death of Calvin Coolidge Jr.

While it did not affect Coolidge's governing ability or focus, it personally tore him apart. He lamented in his autobiography, "if I had not been President he would not have raised a blister on his toe.... I do not know why such a price was exacted for occupying the White House." He had completely lost the desire to continue the job. Even though he was considered the overwhelming favorite to win a landslide victory, Coolidge announced in 1927 he would not seek another term. In typical Coolidge humility, his declined by saying, "We draw our presidents from the people. It is a wholesome thing for them to return to the people. I came from them. I wish to be one of them again."

Republicans chose Herbert Hoover, who had served under Harding and Coolidge as Secretary of Commerce, to replace Coolidge. Despite having never held an elected office, Hoover easily won his party nomination and the national election. Eight months into his administration, the Wall Street Crash of 1929 sent the nation into a panic. Instead of holding firm to his predecessor's conservative economic policies of keeping expenses and taxes low, especially at lean times, Hoover began growing the government. He expanded public works programs by over a billion dollars, including funds to the building of the Hoover Dam.

To pay for such spending growth and keep a balanced budge, Hoover increased corporate and income taxes, raising the top bracket from 25% to 63%. As a result, unemployment naturally rose. Adding insult to injury, Congressional Republicans passed the Smoot-Hawley Tariff Act, which raised tariffs on imports. Despite sever opposition from economists, business executives and Hoover himself, he signed the bill into law. In retaliation, other countries imposed their own tariffs on American goods, which severely hindered America's economy further. What should have been a natural and temporary economic adjustment turned into the basis for a sweeping victory for Progressive Democrat Franklin D. Roosevelt and his promise of a New Deal.

Where Coolidge cut taxes and spending, giving the money back to the people, FDR pushed through a series of domestic programs expanding government, spending, and taxing which he said gave a "more equitable opportunity to share in the distribution of national wealth". FDR's actions prolonged the Depression for many years longer than it should have. Obama followed the same path with his 2009 Stimulus bill with much of the same results, a bloated government, skyrocketing debt, and plummeting economic conditions. Other countries experienced the same economic hiccup America had in 1929, but the United States is the only country where it lasted so long and was so deep that it is known as the "Great" Depression.

To pull America out of the Progressive spin it is in today, we don't need a Hoover (Romney, Bush) or Roosevelt (Clinton, Sanders).

America needs someone with the same principles, spirit, focus, and desire of our Founding Fathers. As Coolidge summarized, "The American Revolution represented the informed and mature convictions of a great mass of independent, liberty-loving, God-fearing people who knew their rights, and possessed the courage to dare to maintain them." We need a president who supports entrepreneurship and believes successful business owners improve our economy. Not one who demeans businesses and depicts profits as evil. We need someone who understands and respects the rights and liberties granted to the people through the Constitution and is willing to fight for them. (see Founding Documents-Vol.7) We need a Calvin Coolidge. Several excellent candidates are running that fit this description perfectly. The question is will America wake up in time and choose one as our next president.

Coolidge described our country's greatness and the path to its preservation in the conclusion of his Declaration speech. "We live in an age of science and of abounding accumulation of material things. These did not create our Declaration. Our Declaration created them. (see Founding Documents-Vol.7) The things of the spirit come first. Unless we cling to that, all our material prosperity, overwhelming though it may appear, will turn to a barren scepter in our grasp. If we are to maintain the great heritage, which has been bequeathed to us, we must be like-minded as the fathers who created it. We must not sink into a pagan materialism. We must cultivate the reverence, which they had for the things that are holy. We must follow the spiritual and moral leadership that they showed. We must keep replenished, that they may glow with a more compelling flame, the altar fires before which they worshiped."

That's my 2 cents.

Love,
Mom

October 31, 2015

Dear Liberty,

LiberatingLetters **2¢**

TheFactsPaper.com

The Reformation began on October 31, 1517, when Martin Luther nailed 95 theses to the Wittenburg Church door. (see *The Knock Heard 'Round The World-Vol.1*) The first settlers and pilgrims brought the religious freedom obtained because of the Reformation to America's shores and used it in the formation of American governance from the very beginning. (see *Jamestown: A City Upon A Hill* and *Thanks Be To God-Vol.1*) These events could not have been as impactful or even possible if it had not been first for the invention of the printing press.

During the 13th Century, Chinese "block-printing" reached Western civilization and was eagerly embraced. It was effective and allowed for multiple copies of documents to be made at the same time. But since each new print needed to be carved out of wood, which usually split after some use, the practice was very time consuming and extremely expensive.

In the early 15th century, former stonecutter and goldsmith Johannes Gutenberg decided there had to be a more productive, cost effective way to print material. Adapting the concept of block-printing, Gutenberg first developed a sturdy material that would cast well and be durable in a press. Instead of molding full pages or even words, Gutenburg reduced the blocks to one letter each that could be easily rearranged as needed. Words and sentences could be quickly edited without having to re-block the entire page. This allowed the letters to have a much longer printing life than the limited use wooden blocks advanced by the Chinese. In addition to discovering a more efficient way to set type, Gutenberg had to also develop printing ink, the setting of type, the press itself, binding for the books and putting all these steps together.

Since he was using borrowed money and knew his first project needed to be his most important, as it may be his only one, Gutenberg chose the Bible. The first Gutenberg Bible consisted of two volumes of which around 200 copies were made. He first sold them at the Frankfurt Book Fair in 1455 for the cost of three times the average clerks salary.

Over the next 50 years, acquisition of the printing press spread across Europe. By the turn of the century, about 2500 cities had one of the coveted machines. The advancement, disbursement, and ease of obtaining information because of the printing press has only been equaled by the invention of the internet.

Yet, for his efforts, Gutenberg died in poverty. His financial backer and business partner, Johann Fust, lost patience with Gutenberg, complaining he was just spending money and not producing the promised Bibles. Fust sued Gutenberg for the return of his investment. The court sided with Fust and ordered the printing press, equipment and half of the completed Bibles be turned over to Fust. Gutenberg eventually began a second printing shop but all financial gains from his most prized project were gone.

By the time Luther came along the effectiveness of the printing press was immeasurable. When Luther posted his 95 theses, it received little more than a quick glance from those who read the local "bulletin board," possibly because the document was written in Latin. Several of Luther's friends recognized the importance of his statement and translated it into German. It was because of the printing press, though, that the translated pamphlet was able to spread across Germany in two weeks and throughout all of Europe in two months. The printing press allowed for Luther's arguments to go from a local, confined discussion to a European wide movement.

As I stated in The Knock Heard 'Round The World(Vol.1), Bibles at the time were primarily written in Latin. Before the printing press, Bibles were hand written which took years to produce just one. Even though Gutenberg's Bible was a little more accessible, it was still in Latin. Luther realized this fact helped give the church the power they had over the people in their spiritual knowledge. Just as he was able to examine the Bible and understand God's word through personal study, Luther wanted to give that same opportunity to the German people. While in exile, Luther translated the Bible into German using the original Greek and Hebrew as his sources.

There were earlier translations in German, but even with the printing press there were other obstacles in their way of widespread distribution. One main hindrance was Archbishop Berthold of Mainz. He claimed it was not possible to accurately convey the proper meaning of God's word from Greek or Latin into German. He also proclaimed laymen and women were not able to understand the Bible anyway. Because of this on January 4, 1486, he prohibited the unauthorized printing of any sacred or scholarly books, specifically the German Bible, in his diocese.

There were prints made of the other Bibles, but with the Reformation and Luther's ability to pull together High German and

Low German language, his translation spread across Germany as quickly as his 95 theses. (see *Here I Stand*-Vol.4 and *England's Luther*-Vol.6) Hans Lufft, a German printer and publisher in Wittenberg, began printing Luther's first complete edition of the Bible in 1534. It is estimated about 100,000 copies were printed over the next 40 years, which was an extraordinary amount for that time. This does not include the immeasurable number of copies from reprints. The Gospel was delivered to millions of people through God's written word at a rate never before experienced in history.

Johannes Cochlaeus, a German humanist, champion of Romanism, and leading opponent of Luther, offhandedly complimented Luther's translation when he lamented that "Luther's New Testament was so much multiplied and spread by printers that even tailors and shoemakers, yea, even women and ignorant persons who had accepted this new Lutheran gospel, and could read a little German, studied it with the greatest avidity as the fountain of all truth. Some committed it to memory, and carried it about in their bosom. In a few months such people deemed themselves so learned that they were not ashamed to dispute about faith and the gospel not only with Catholic laymen, but even with priests and monks and doctors of divinity."

This statement highlights how the Bible and Gospel was "spread by printers", a notion not reasonably obtainable before the printing press.

While Luther ministered to the Germans, other reformers such as John Calvin, were leading the English Protestant Reformation. Just as Luther had to go into hiding in Germany, English reformers were forced to flee to Geneva, Switzerland, for protection from the church and crown. Several English scholars gathered and like Luther, returned to the original texts for their translation. (see *England's Luther*-Vol.6) The result was the Geneva Bible that was first printed in 1560. This Bible was extremely significant because for the first time it included chapters and verses. This allowed the reader to cross-reference one verse with other related verses. The Geneva Bible also included scriptural study guides, book introductions, maps, tables, illustrations and comments from reformers. To include all these features was just not practical before the printing press. Because of all these attributes, the Geneva Bible became known as the very first Study Bible.

England began printing the Geneva Bible in 1575 and it was the first Bible ever to be printed in Scotland beginning in 1579. That same year Scotland passed a law requiring every household that was able to buy a copy. By that time the printing press had made the cost so low that even the lowest-paid laborers could obtain one for less than a week's wages.

All this had to take place as it did so when Captain John Smith came to the New World in 1607, he would be able to bring his copy of the Geneva Bible with him. Ministers, such as Rev. Alexander Whitaker, who came to witness to the Native Americans, were able to easily bring their Bibles as well. (see *The Apostle Of Virginia*-Vol.4 and *Jamestown: A City Upon A Hill*)

Years later the pilgrims, under the leadership of William Bradford and his 1592 Geneva Bible, built their civilization around God's instructions. This is very evident in the Mayflower Compact as illustrated in *Thanks Be To God*. (see *America's First Founding Document*-Vol.3 and *Founding Documents*-Vol.7)

Liberty, when studying history it is evident that God's will is always being done. God's timing is perfect. The printing press had to be invented and established before Luther posted his 95 theses. His actions would have been completely insignificant if his friends had not started distributing his words with the help of the printing press. Once that Pandora's Box was open, Europe began to spread the Gospel in various languages. By the time the first settlers, including the pilgrims, ventured to the New World, often the only possession they brought was their copy of the Bible.

We cannot always expect visible results of our efforts in our lifetime. The process from the invention of the printing press until the Geneva Bible hit the shores of America took over 150 years. Furthermore, Gutenberg and many of the reformers died poor men. Our mission is not about money, though, it is about souls. And just like Gutenberg, Luther, Calvin, Smith, Whitaker and Bradford, we all have our parts to play. You were born at this time for a purpose. Just remember to keep your focus on His glory and not yours.

That's my 2 cents.

Love,
Mom

November 5, 2015

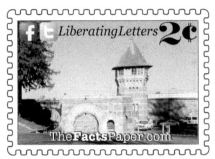

Dear Liberty,

At the turn of the 15th century, Spanish Jews were under persecution from King Henry III of the Castile-Leon region in Spain. They were given the ultimatum of baptism or death. Choosing Catholicism over execution, these Jews became known as Conversos. As with any forced conversion, the change for many was only surface deep. (see <u>A Change Of Heart</u>) Privately, they continued to practice their Jewish faith earning them the derogatory label of Marranos. Spain's anti-Semitism grew as speculation intensified that all Conversos were false converts.

With the marriage of Ferdinand II and Isabelle I in 1469, the kingdoms of Aragon and Castile-Leon were united as one region. The Iberian Peninsula, which consisted of Spain and Portugal, was completing the Reconquista reclaiming the area for Christianity. The Moors (Muslims), who had attacked and conquered them some 770 years before, were almost completely removed from the area. (see <u>A Crusade For The Truth</u>) The Spanish Roman Catholic Church and the Spanish monarchies had become indivisible. It was believed if you vowed allegiance to one, you were vowing allegiance to the other. Desiring political unity within their empires, King Ferdinand and Queen Isabelle pressured Pope Sixtus IV into issuing an Inquisition. More importantly, they insisted the church relinquish control of it to the government.

On November 1, 1478, the Pope relented and signed a Papal Bull creating The Tribunal of the Holy Office of the Inquisition. He granted individual monarchs sole authority in appointing inquisitors in their kingdoms. Historically, the Catholic Church conducted Inquisitions on baptized members only to cleanse the church of false Catholics. The interrogations were conducted by church officials and convicted parishioners were usually sentenced to simple acts of penance. The Spanish Inquisition was different because it was controlled by the powerful hand of the secular government, even though church officials were appointed to leadership roles.

The state quickly began to abuse its power, targeting citizens outside of the Catholic faith. Unlike Inquisitions under church authority, the government controlled Spanish Inquisition terrorized anyone not conforming to the Catholic monarchy, including Jews, Muslims, and *even Christian Protestants. Events such as this is exactly why the Founding Fathers made it paramount that the authoritative powers of the church and state were kept mutually exclusive. (see Separation Of Church And State) It is also why Sharia Law is so incredibly dangerous.*

A major turning point of the Spanish Inquisition occurred on October 17, 1483. Under duress from the crown, the Pope appointed Tomas de Torquemada the first grand inquisitor of Spain. Torquemada was a long-time close spiritual consultant of the monarchy and had been instrumental in advocating for the Inquisition from behind the scenes. Even though the Pope resisted many of the state's tactics, leaders in the church, such as Torquemada, used the state to enforce their personal beliefs and agendas. Once in control, Torquemada turned the Inquisition into the infamous, oppressive tribunal known in history.

Torquemada aggressively targeted Marranos and added Moriscos (Islamic converts), Jews, and Moors in his crosshairs. Believing all these groups presented a religious and social threat to Spain, he was determined to achieve religious purification. In addition to prosecuting crimes of heresy and religious abandonment, Torquemada provided inquisitors twenty-eight new articles that extended violations to blasphemy, homosexuality, polygamy, witchcraft, and more. He also authorized the use of torture to acquire evidence.

Exploiting his connection with the monarchy, Torquemada convinced the King and Queen to issue a decree on March 31, 1492, forcing Spanish Jews to once again choose between baptism or exile, even though the Catholic faith strictly prohibited forced baptisms. Over 160,000 Jews were banished from Spain.

As the Inquisition dragged on, new Protestant Christians rising out of the Reformation were quickly exterminated. (see The Knock Heard 'Round The World-Vol.1) While the rest of Europe experienced the spread of religious freedom, Spain continued to purge itself of any opposing view. With no one else left to attack, the inquisitors eventually turned on their own Catholic members.

In the same way Ferdinand and Isabelle used Catholicism, the Left uses climate change. It is their religion. Earth is their god, evolution is their creation story, abortion is their sacrament and Global Warming is their great commission. Opposing the official religious beliefs of the Spanish state was considered a threat to the state itself. The Global Warming Progressive Left agrees and are reacting the same way.

The more the evidence mounts against their theories, the harder activists try to silence their opponents. Their actions, accusations and demands for retribution are no different than the reprehensible methods of the Spanish Inquisition. Using intimidation, threats and punishment to force conversion or suffer the consequences, their tactics mirror those of Torquemada. They are even going as far as soliciting the government to help propagate their cause. Unfortunately, this administration embraces the activists advocating punishment and oppression on those who do not conform to their religion and bow to the altar of climate change.

As their science continues to fall apart, Global Warming activists proceed to turn up the heat. (see Actions Speak Louder Than Words-Vol.1) Environmentalist Robert F. Kennedy, Jr., complained a year ago, "I wish there were a law you could punish (skeptics) with. I don't think there is a law that you can punish those politicians under." The Obama Administration is actually working on that. In a speech earlier this year, Al Gore declared the proposed federal cap-and-trade system would punish companies exceeding their carbon-emission limits. "We need to put a price on carbon to accelerate these market trends...And in order to do that, we need to put a price on denial in politics."

In September, twenty Global Warming scientists stepped up their propaganda. Instead of just implying skeptics should be punished, they are demanding it. These scientists insist Obama prosecute those who dare have an opposing opinion and throw them in jail. Employing their same old tired accusations, they implied skeptics' findings are influenced by research funded and supported by the fossil fuel industry. Yet Global Warming scientists' backing is never analyzed. It is widely known federal grants flood laboratories corroborating man-made climate change while anyone publishing a report to the contrary is stripped of their funds and sent to the back of the science lab.

A few weeks ago John Kerry resurrected the Left's mantra that anyone who denies climate change should be disqualified from holding political office. Apparently someone who continues to exam the empirical evidence of climate change is too inept to be politician. Yet one who blindly accepts the theory as fact, slamming the door on all scientific evidence that disproves that theory, is eagerly welcomed in the ruling class.

It has been said before if you want to control an issue, control the language. The Associated Press fell in line two months ago and are doing their part. In their official "usable terms" list, the AP changed the labels used for those refusing to swallow the Progressive agenda. (see Everything Free But Speech-Vol.1) According to Paul Colford, the AP VP and Director of Media Relations, "We are adding a brief description of those who don't accept climate science or dispute the world is warming from man-made forces...Our guidance is to use climate change doubters or those who reject mainstream climate science and to avoid the use of skeptics or deniers." Colford defended the change admitting their scientists complained that man-made Global Warming skeptics "aren't skeptics because 'proper skepticism promotes scientific inquiry, critical investigation and the use of reason in examining controversial and extraordinary claims.'"

As I explained in great detail in The Science Is Settled and The Science Is Settled, Part II, to close your mind to opposing science is the true definition of a science denier. Skepticism is the natural, healthy process of science but since the Left still has to destroy dissenters, they just change the terms.

If the science was there to support man-made climate change than the facts would stand on their own. The truth is, they're not. The theory is falling apart as more and more evidence surfaces confirming the data and models are manipulated, falsified and out-right made up. The only other option they have is to destroy those who are shining a light on the truth. But, isn't that how Satan always works?

Liberty, mankind loves to believe it is evolving and progressing into a more advanced and intelligent being. But as history proves, mankind continues to repeat the same cruel, primitive, oppressive deeds as thousands of generations before us. And after all this time, I have yet to find one instance where the oppressors were on the right side of the argument.

"For the sake of Christ, then, I am content with weaknesses, insults, hardships, persecutions, and calamities. For when I am weak, then I am strong." 2 Corinthians 12:10

That's my 2 cents.

Love,
Mom

November 11, 2015

Dear Liberty,

    The allied forces were crushed under the German onslaught that threatened all of Europe. The allies were in desperate need for American reinforcements as they battled from trench to trench and faced certain death the moment they entered no man's land. (see Big Red Won-Vol.5 *and* Leading From The Trenches-Vol.5) *The tide of World War 1 began to turn as American General "Black Jack" Pershing and his troops arrived in St. Mihiel in September 1918. Pershing then led the AEF in the Meuse-Argonne Offensive in October and early November. (see* A Reluctant Hero-Vol.4) *The effectiveness of this attack so dismembered the German defensive positions that they were forced to negotiate an armistice.*

    John "Black Jack" Pershing remains the highest ranked military General, sharing the Title 'General of the Armies' with only General George Washington himself. (see A Tale Of Two Soldiers-Vol.3) *Pershing's leadership skills were evident from his beginning at West Point. Even as an average student, he quickly rose to the rank of First Captain, the highest possible cadet rank, and his classmates elected him class president of 1886. He graduated 30th out of 77 but was commended by General Wesley Merritt for his "superb ability". Upon graduation the 26-year-old was sent to Fort Bayard in the New Mexico Territory as a Second Lieutenant.*

    From Fort Bayard, Pershing spent the next five years participating in several successful campaigns against Indian tribes. Because of his skills as a commander, he was assigned to the University of Nebraska-Lincoln, as a Professor of Military Science and Tactics. While there he obtained a law degree and was promoted to first lieutenant.

    In 1895 he was assigned the command of the 10th Cavalry Regiment, one of the original Black "Buffalo Soldier" units. A few years later, while instructing at West Point with the tactical staff, his strict and rigid style led the indignant cadets to nickname him "Nigger Jack", due to his connection with the 10th Cavalry. Though the name later changed to "Black Jack", his famous moniker was not a term of endearment, but derision.

    When war broke out with Spain in April of 1898, Pershing was reunited with the Black soldiers of the 10th Cavalry in active duty. At the time, Assistant Secretary of the Navy, Theodore Roosevelt, resigned his position in order to organize a regiment of cowboys and college men, dubbed the "Rough Riders", to fight in the war. Due to a mix-up when leaving Tampa, half of his cavalry regiment and all their horses were left in Florida. Teddy Roosevelt and his "Rough Riders" charged up San Juan Hill on foot, accompanied by Pershing and his Buffalo Soldiers. Pershing's gallantry at San Juan Hill was immediately noticed by Roosevelt and eventually by the entire military. (see A Tale Of Two Soldiers-Vol.3) "Black Jack" received the Silver Citation Star in 1919 for his actions, which was later upgraded to the Silver Star decoration in 1932.

Over the next several years, Pershing served commands in Cuba, Puerto Rico, Philippines and Japan of which he was cited for bravery on multiple occasions. Roosevelt, who became President in 1901 upon the assassination of William McKinley, knew well of Pershing's skills and valor. When Pershing returned to the states in 1903, Roosevelt appealed the Army General Staff to promote him from captain to colonel. Though it was agreed Pershing should serve as a colonel, the tradition of promotion in the military at the time was seniority-based, not merit-based. The Army General Staff rejected Roosevelt's petition.

As President, Roosevelt only had the authority to promote Generals. To circumvent the military structure Roosevelt turned to the United States Congress to authorize a diplomatic posting. Pershing was assigned to Tokyo as military attaché in 1905. Before leaving, he married Helen Frances Warren, the daughter of Republican Senator Francis E. Warren, who also happened to be chairman of the Military Appropriations Committee.

When Pershing returned to the U.S. in the fall of 1905, Roosevelt nominated Pershing to Brigadier General, which Congress approved. In doing so Pershing skipped over three ranks and 835 higher seniority officers. Even though the move was not unprecedented, it did not stop the accusations of political ties over military abilities. Roosevelt addressed the criticisms, noting "To promote a man because he married a senator's daughter would be an infamy; to refuse him promotion for the same reason would be an equal infamy."

Over the next several years, Pershing and his family were bounced around the world with only one of his four children being born in the United States. In December of 1913, Pershing was commissioned to San Francisco to command the 8th Brigade at the Presidio. He was there only a few months before the tensions on the American-Mexican border resulted in the brigade being deployed to Fort Bliss, Texas.

After over a year apart, Pershing sent for his family in August of 1915. While the final arrangements were being made, a fire in the

Presidio claimed the life of his wife and their 3 daughters. The only surviving family member was his 6-year-old son Warren. Devastated, Pershing buried his family in Wyoming before returning to Fort Bliss with his son and his sister, Mary, to resume his command.

During his time at Fort Bliss, Pershing formed a political friendship with Pancho Villa, who sent his condolences after the death of his wife and daughters. But in March of 1916, Villa attacked the town of Columbus, New Mexico, after the United States chose to support Venustiano Carranza over him. Despite obstacles from both the American and Mexican governments, as well as insufficient supplies, Pershing led 10,000 troops, including your great-grandfather, in the Mexican Punitive Expedition to track down Villa. The troops infiltrated 350 miles into Mexico in a quest to capture Villa. Though they tracked Villa, they were unable to ever capture him. Despite the failure to apprehend Villa, Pershing was promoted to Major General in September of 1916.

When the United States entered World War I in April of 1917, President Woodrow Wilson selected Pershing as the Commander of the American Expeditionary Force (AEF) with a promotion to full General. (see The Day America's Neutrality Sank-Vol.4 and Duty First-Vol.4) Even though Democrat President Wilson and Secretary of War Newton D. Baker gave him full delegation of authority, their political and racist "separate but equal" policies tied Pershing's hands in regard to utilizing black regiments along with other American troops. "Black Jack's" past experience leading black units alongside white units let him know the quality and bravery of such troops. (see The Birth Of A Nation-Vol.2 and Separate But Equal?-Vol.6) However, unlike Republican administrations, Pershing was forbidden to allow black units to participate with the American forces. Even though the Buffalo Soldiers were the first Americans to fight in France in 1918, Pershing was forced to assign them under French command, separate from the other American Forces, where they remained for the duration of the war.

Pershing began building an American Army using many of the soldiers that helped him on the Mexican border. Assigned to the 2nd Machine Gun Battalion, your great-grandfather sailed to France in June of 1917 as part of the 1st Infantry Division. (see A Hero's Story-Vol.1) Among the very first troops to enter the war, these soldiers became known as "The Fighting First" as well as "The Big Red One" (see Duty First-Vol.4), due to their shoulder patch displaying a red number one on army green. On July 4th, days after arriving in France, Pershing marched through Paris with members of the 2nd Battalion and 16th Infantry to raise the spirits of the French. Stopping at Lafayette's tomb, Pershing's aide, Colonel Charles E. Stanton, declared, "Lafayette, we are here!" (see A Hero Of Two Worlds I & II-Vol.5)

Pershing quickly discovered the English and French were not interested in waiting for a strong American Army to be assembled. The Europeans simply wanted men. The French initially trained the first American divisions, but Pershing refused to allow this to remain a permanent arrangement. American's fought in concert with Allied leadership until Pershing was able to organize a full American Army. Still insisting the AEF fight under American command, Pershing did loan out some divisions to Allied forces during critical times in the spring of 1918. It wasn't until August of 1918 that the American Army was completely under Pershing's direct command.

It only took Pershing's Army four months to put the final blows on the German forces. (see A Reluctant Hero-Vol.5 and Cracking The Code-Vol.6) All other members of the Central Powers had declared a ceasefire. Much to Pershing's dismay, the Allied Supreme War Council accepted Germany's truce in November. He wanted the Allies to continue fighting until an unconditional surrender was obtained, even sending the Council a letter demanding as such. President Wilson was eager to end the war, though, before the mid-term elections.

"The Great War" was officially over on the 11th hour of the 11th day on the 11th month of 1918. (see Veterans Day-Vol.1) Barely evading a serious reprimand by Wilson's administration, Pershing soon after apologized for his boldness to the Council. Years later, many agreed Pershing was right in his strategy, including President Franklin D. Roosevelt.

Pershing returned to America a celebrated war hero. Recognizing his outstanding leadership in creating a powerful national Army from the ground up, Congress approved the formation of a new rank, General of the Armies of the United States, which Pershing was promoted to in 1919. In the history of the country, he is the only living general to hold this rank. Pershing chose to wear four gold stars as his insignia but still outranks the rank of five-star General of the Army, created in 1944. In 1976, during our country's 200th Anniversary, President Gerald Ford posthumously promoted General George Washington to the same rank of General of the Armies. Pershing and Washington are the only two men in history to hold such a rank. (see The Man Who Refused To Be King-Vol.1)

Realizing good military leaders make good Commander in Chiefs, a movement began across the nation to nominate Pershing for President in 1920. He refused to campaign, but said he "wouldn't decline to serve" if the people choose him. However, due to his military service under Wilson, many Republicans considered him too closely connected to Wilson's Democrat policies. The party nominated Ohio Senator Warren G. Harding instead. (see The Forgotten President)

Pershing was appointed Chief of Staff of the United States Army in 1921. During his three years of service, he created a national network of military and civilian highways, known as the Pershing Map. His actual proposal was never adopted. However, the Interstate Highway System enacted by Dwight D. Eisenhower in 1956 overwhelming favored his design.

Forced to retire on his 64th birthday on September 13, 1924, Pershing published his memoirs, _My experiences in the World War_. This not only brought him additional fame but the 1932 Pulitzer Prize for history. Pershing moved to Washington D.C. in 1944, where he died at Walter Reed Hospital on July 15, 1948. He was laid to rest in Arlington National Cemetery among the soldiers he commanded in Europe. *(see _The Birth Of A Cemetery_-Vol.7)*

Liberty, William Shakespeare once wrote, "Be not afraid of greatness; some are born great, some achieve greatness, and others have greatness thrust upon them." Pershing was not the best student, but he sought out the best education he could. He was given assignments with the odds stacked against him and he prevailed. His troops and cadets often bulked at his strict military discipline, but he stuck to his principles because he knew it meant their lives. He never sought to be great, he just sought to do what was right.

On this Veterans' (Armistice) Day we should bow our heads to all those who have given their lives for our freedom. *(see _Veterans Day_-Vol.1)* May we not make their sacrifice in vain.

That's my 2 cents.

Love,
Mom

November 20, 2015

Dear Liberty,

LiberatingLetters **2¢**

TheFactsPaper.com

    In the 1960s, college students and activists were convinced they were the most enlightened generation ever. Many proudly chanted, "Make Love not War," protesting the Vietnam War. They shouted "baby killer" at returning Veterans while also insisting abortion is a women's reproductive right. They burned their bras, celebrated "free love," and promoted peace, love, and kindness.

    At the same time, Weather Underground terrorist, Bill Ayers, preached change through discourse, anger, and intimidation. Along with the Black Panthers, he rejoiced in terrorizing to force oppression. Bombing the U.S. Capital, the Pentagon and police departments, Ayres escaped prison on a technicality. Undercover cop, Larry Grathwohl, exposed Ayers' utopian Weather Underground plans in a 1982 documentary. At the time, Ayers believed they would overtake the government. After which patriotic Americans would have to go to re-education camps where any capitalist refusing to change would be eliminated. Ayers had told the group 25 million Americans would be a good start.

    After their violent, terroristic ways failed, Ayres and his radical comrades reorganized their strategy. Realizing their reeducation camps already existed they started to infest, overtake, control, and implement their propaganda machine peacefully. Universities opened their arms to Ayres and his wife, Bernadine Dohrn, despite their domestic terrorism past, which is where Ayers eventually met Barack Obama.

    Colleges and Universities transformed from institutions of higher education to institutions of reeducation. (see "Higher" Education-Vol.3) Values and principles parents taught and instilled in their children are quickly replaced with extreme left-wing ideology. Students are no longer taught how to think, but what to think. Having been brainwashed to believe that certain ideas must be accepted, anyone not conforming is actually seen as a threat. Their response to those threats is to bully their opponent into submission using "political correctness". Under this radical indoctrination, they are convinced systematically eradicating free speech actually achieves more freedom.

    A few months ago, University of Missouri (Mizzou) student Payton Head claimed a truckload of whites drove past him somewhere off campus and shouted the "N" word. Stories of a swastika drawn in feces on a dorm wall began circulating around campus. Jonathan Butler, a Missouri grad student, began a hunger strike until the University's President, Tim Wolfe, resigned for not providing a "safe learning environment."

The movement remained somewhat stagnant until thirty football players were convinced not to play until demands were met, even though no proof or validity of the instances were given. Knowing it would cost the college a million dollars for each forfeited game, University leadership surrendered within hours, forcing the president to resign. Their victory ignited similar protests at colleges all across the country.

The next day Head terrified students, warning them to stay away from open spaces and windows, claiming the KKK was on campus. Students insisted classes be cancelled on Wednesday as they feared for their safety. Within a day Head admitted he lied about the warning but the damage was already done.

It would be one thing if Payton Head was just an ordinary student making such claims, but Head is the student body President, black, openly gay, upper middle class, and recently voted Homecoming King. If this horrible racism really existed at Mizzou, why did Head have to fabricate examples of it? Head is also active in the Black Lives Matter (BLM) movement and met with President Obama at the White House with other activists. (see The Birth Of A Nation 2016-Vol.3)

As a former intern for Rahm Emmanuel in his hometown of Chicago, Head's tactics are taken straight from Saul Alinsky's Rules for Radicals disciples, Emmanuel, Obama and Ayres. He knows his racism accusations are completely bogus but to forward his narrative he was forced to lie. But he wasn't the only one. The real reason Jonathan Butler, whose top railroad executive father earned $8.4 million last year, protested was because he is about to lose his free school health care due to Obamacare. Butler helped remove the school president because he is going to suffer from the policies pushed through by the same radicals this whole movement aligns themselves with.

Continuing the "political correctness" agenda, student body Vice-President admitted she is just "tired of hearing that first amendment rights protect students when they are creating a hostile and unsafe learning environment." (see Founding Documents-Vol.7) Her president outright lied about the KKK targeting students. It is now suspected he lied about being called the "N" word. Motivations behind the swastika have become suspect, including whether it actually happened. Students are being manipulated and threatened with lies intended to force them into demanding action. Who here is "creating a hostile and unsafe learning environment?" Even with the resignation of Tim Wolfe, protesters continue to march demanding justice for Michael Brown (see *Just The Facts, Ma'am*-Vol.1) and Trayvon Martin. (see *A Change Of Heart*-Vol.2) What do those incidents have to do with the students in Missouri?

On the heels of the KKK lie, protesters swarmed the Dartmouth College library chanting "Black Lives Matter". Innocent students studying and working in the library were commanded to stand. Anyone not complying were ripped out of their chair. Some were thrown against the wall, and white supporters and non-supporters alike were yelled at in their face and called racial slurs.

At a meeting days later, the protesters argued they didn't feel safe because of the negative media coverage. The vice-provost Ingle-Lise Ameer apologized to the protesters because "There's a whole conservative world out there that's not being very nice." Does she realize the conservative media she was criticizing was their own independent *Dartmouth Review* who broke the story? She demonized other Dartmouth students while kowtowing to BLM bullies.

For other activists, the "free love" movement has evolved into the "free everything" campaign with demands for free college tuition, current student loans forgiven, and $15 an hour campus jobs. Million Student March Organizer Keely Mullen, when asked how their free college requirement would be paid for, responded, "The 1%," insisting taxing them 90% was right and fair. Following being told taxing them 100% still wouldn't be enough to pay for her demands, she stated, "If we're to the point where the rich is paying 100% on their taxes then we're on the road to socialism." When retold it's not enough, she just said, "Yeah, I don't believe that." The facts mean nothing to her.

Mullen claimed to be from an "incredibly working class family" that is "already on numerous forms of government assistance and is basically scraping by in order to get (her) through college." Except her father sent her to an expensive high school and has a $1 million home. Keely also failed to mention she organized the march through the "Socialist Alternative," a Marxist group. Keely, like Head, is a complete liar. Their agenda is their lifeblood and they are ruthless on how they achieve it.

Riding high on what they considered to be a productive week, the terroristic BLM movement showed their true colors when a handful of cowardly, demented ISIS terrorists attacked several venues in Paris on November 13th. (see *Wolves In Sheep's Clothing*) Over 120 people were killed with hundreds more wounded. As attention and headlines dropped the manufactured crisis in Missouri, the activists' hatred was exposed tenfold. Their concocted claims of victimization were smashed by real victims and they were furious. Phrases such as "F___ Paris" were tweeted repeatedly before overwhelming pressure from responders forced many of these tweets to be removed. Some equated the KKK threat as equal or greater to the Paris attack even though it had already been proven a hoax. They believe their highly questionable, if not outright made-up, accusations of racism and victimization are more important, more fearful and more deadly than the terrorists that slaughtered and wounded hundreds of innocent lives, regardless of race, creed, color, or religion.

What many have yet to realize is the BLM movement is just as willing to use violence to force the changes they desire as ISIS is. Last month BLM leader Blake Simons warned if the Constitution was not destroyed and replaced with one that serves all people, America "will get the bullet." Conform or be eliminated, just like Ayres said. This is no different from ISIS entering Christian homes and giving the ultimatum of converting or die. ISIS is beheading Christians; BLM is targeting and executing police, much like Ayres, and white people.

I'm not denying that racism exists, but these spoiled, often middle-class or rich activists, have no concept what true, honest racism really is. To them, someone who says "No, I don't believe that' is equivalent to Democrat Gov. George Wallace blocking black students from entering the University of Alabama vowing "Segregation forever." (see Separate But Equal?-Vol.6)

These millennials equate a derogatory name with not being able to sit at a lunch counter. Their movement relies on people seeing themselves as victims who cower in the corner because someone called them a name. They have been conditioned to embrace minority groups such as homosexuals, transgenders, illegals, and even terrorists, as they can all claim victimhood. Yet it is their duty to demonize Christians and conservatives, as they have been labeled the enemy.

While hippies discarded bras, today's male activists are strapping them on and demanding access to women's bathrooms. The Civil Rights Movement would have died if these activists were leading it. They don't want the proven change brought about as Martin Luther King Jr. did, with love and peace. They want the violent, forced tactics Malcolm X tried and failed. (see Free At Last?)

These students claim they want college to be a "safe" place to learn from each other, but what they see as safe is to not feel offended, nervous, uncomfortable, or threatened by opposing beliefs. (see Safe Spaces-Vol.6) They resolve the only solution is to not allow those opinions they can't accept. Why? Because that's what they are TOLD to think.

They want everything to be free, except speech.

Liberty, no one can offend you unless you let them. What do you really learn from someone who totally agrees with you? How are your principles ever challenged and strengthened if someone doesn't make you defend them? How do you truly know what you believe deep down if you aren't ever allowed the opportunity to honestly fight for it? How strong are you really if you feel that uncomfortable by someone else's opinion? Challenge yourself and learn HOW to think. Question everything and verify for yourself. Don't ever give someone power over you by controlling your mind. It's your life. Own it!

That's my 2 cents.

Love,
Mom

November 25, 2015

Dear Liberty,

After the horrific ISIS terrorist attack on Paris on November 13th, evidence surfaced that several of the terrorists entered Europe under the guise of refugees. (see <u>Everything Free But Speech</u>) Following this staggering revelation, instead of pausing to consider a similar threat in the United States, Obama announced America will be placing even more Syrian refugees on the fast track to importation.

The country erupted in arguments whether Obama is compassionate or traitorous. The media immediately circled the wagons along with many Liberal Democrats arguing that it would be un-American to turn away these poor exiles. Charges were launched against Republican Presidential candidates who suggested we should suspend the refugee program, as there is no way to properly vet the Syrians.

Senator Ted Cruz stated that America should focus on rescuing Syrian Christian who are being targeted, crucified, and massacred by ISIS. Whoopi Goldberg and Joy Behar of "The View" quickly pounced, restating Liberal misinformation, citing that both Hitler and Timothy McVey were Christians that did equally despicable atrocities. This tired Liberal talking point is designed to distort truth, playing well to a uniformed audience. It is well documented that both of these men eagerly admitted they were not Christian. Behar also asserted that Cruz's statement is "not very Christian." Can she honestly not see Cruz believes in rescuing Christians from their persecutors while stopping the import of those very same persecutors here? The Muslim refugees have several sympathetic Islamic countries they can flee to close to their own homes, culture, and language. On the other hand, "safe spaces" for Christians in the Middle East are evaporating quickly.

The morning of the Paris attack, Barack Obama commented, "I don't think they're (ISIS) gaining strength. What is true, from the start our goal has been first to contain and we have contained them. They have not gained ground in Iraq and in Syria they'll come in, they'll leave. But you don't see this systemic march by ISIL across the terrain." (see <u>The Ottoman Empire Strikes Back</u>-Vol.4) His clear lack of understanding, or unwillingness to admit the truth, is supported by his statement after the attack, "The terrible events in Paris were obviously a *terrible and sickening setback. Even as we grieve with our French friends, however, we can't lose sight that there has been progress being made."*

Both of these statements go to prove how completely incompetent Obama is on foreign affairs. He is either refusing to recognize or is actively supporting the threat that radical Islam places on the world. This was proven in a speech where he had harsher words for Republicans than ISIS. "We are not well served when, in response to a terrorist attack, we descend into fear and panic. We don't make good decisions if it's based on hysteria or an exaggeration of risks." An interesting statement coming from an administration that boldly claimed, "you never let a serious crisis go to waste."

Knee jerk reactions are the bread and butter of a community organizer. Rather than carefully examining the facts involving the arrest of a friend, he took the opportunity to make a racial claim as if he was taking to the streets in 1955 Montgomery, Alabama. (see <u>Walking To Freedom</u>) "Not having been there and not seeing all the facts...it's fair to say that the Cambridge police acted stupidly." As he readily admitted, facts aren't important, the agenda is. He later sparked the flames of discontent like any good Fabian Socialist when he said, "If I had a son, he'd look like Trayvon Martin." Martin "could have been me 35 years ago." Seeing another opportunity to cause racial strife without waiting for the facts, he stated "I urge everyone in Ferguson, Missouri, and across the country, to remember this young man (Michael Brown) through reflection and understanding." Michael Brown had died after robbing a convenience store and fighting a police officer. (see <u>Just The Facts, Ma'am</u>-Vol.1) Who he was didn't matter. What color he was did. Obama's statements directly fed the "Black Lives Matter" formation. (see <u>Birth Of A Nation 2016</u>-Vol.3)

To challenge Republican candidates proposing that the United States stop accepting Muslim refugees from Syria, he said, "When individuals say we should have a religious test and that only Christians, proven Christians should be admitted, that's offensive." It's interesting what Obama claims is offensive. What's offensive is Muslims beheading or crucifying Christians. What's offensive is Islamic extremists promising death and destruction to the infidels. What's offensive is Islamists murder of homosexuals and raping and enslaving of women. What's offensive is radical Islamist strapping on bombs and walking into theaters to blow up Muslims that aren't Islamic enough. What's offensive is the president will not even admit that any of this is happening. Why should there be a religious exception to refugees from the Middle East? There are no Christian members of ISIS, period.

In desperation, Democrats are comparing the Muslim refugees to Jews seeking refuge from Hitler and the Nazis just prior to World War

II. Democrat President Franklin D. Roosevelt rejected the refugees sending them home to suffer the fate of the concentration camps and gas chambers. (see Voyage Of The Damned-Vol.3 and Remembering The Holocaust-Vol.3) Democrats argue this is equal to rejecting the Syrian Muslims. It's not. It's the Christian Syrians that are the "Jews" in this scenario and again, a Democrat president is flat out denying them access. The dangerous truth is Obama is demanding the acceptance of today's Nazis.

During WWII, Roosevelt set up internment camps for Japanese-Americans. (see Forgotten Atrocities Of World War II-Vol.4) After the Pearl Harbor attack, we had no idea who might be here sympathizing with their homeland. (see A Date Which Will Live In Infamy-Vol.3) It was a very unfortunate time in American history, but totally understandable. It is the president's supreme responsibility to defend citizens against possible attacks, both foreign and domestic. Though many can argue Roosevelt went too far with the camps, Roosevelt's actions were based on the security of the country. Obama is doing the complete opposite, providing transportation, medical care, and housing to those who would do us harm.

Obama mocked Republicans, stating, "Apparently they are scared of widows and orphans coming into the United States of America." If Obama would care to read even just a few of his briefings, he would know that about 80% of the refugees are healthy males of military age. Any president truly concerned about the safety of his people instead of his "fundamental transformation of America" agenda would be trying to find out why these men want to come here instead of staying and fighting for their country. Does he even wonder why they aren't bringing their families with them? Trey Gowdy summed it up perfectly. "The President says we're scared of widows and orphans, with all due respect to him, what I'm afraid of is a foreign policy that creates more widows and orphans." Rand Paul reminded us, "The Boston bombers came here as refugees. We coddled them, we gave them free stuff, we gave them free housing, and yet, they decided to attack us, so there's a great risk." Exactly, gentlemen.

Terrified of killing even one civilian, pilots recently confirmed that Obama has blocked 75% of airstrikes against ISIS. This inept policy has allowed ISIS to get a firm hold in the Middle East, recruit, grow, and kill. Since the Paris attack, pressure has intensified so much he finally started going after ISIS's funding by bombing oil tankers. Forty-five minutes before hand, though, flyers were dropped warning of the incoming strike. In a similar fashion, Democrat President Bill Clinton refused to go after Osama Bin Ladin after the 1993 World Trade Center attack and it eventually led to 3,000 deaths on September 11, 2001. (see Never Forget-Vol.1) Obama's refusal to act has enabled ISIS to strengthen and intensify, granting the terrorist group the freedom and time to plan and prepare the caliphate their faith so passionately preaches.

It's honorable Obama doesn't want to inflict even one civilian casualty. However, he shows absolutely no regard for the number of American civilians he is willing to place in harm's way by risking bringing even one terrorist onto our soil. Islamic terrorists purposely hide among civilians. They attack from homes, schools and Mosques, knowing that we will not return fire on such buildings. Why would they view hiding among refugees any differently? They clearly don't, as Paris has proven. In Syria, 70 percent of the Muslims support the actions and agenda of ISIS. Here it's just the White House and the Liberal media, and even some of them are waking up.

We have been told since 2008 that Obama is the smartest president ever. If that is so, how can he be so incompetent in his efforts against ISIS? It forces one to wonder what Obama's true motives really are. We now know the Benghazi attack was because of guns this administration was running to Syria to support rebels to oust Assad. Those guns went directly into the hands of rebels now known as ISIS. Obama supports "Black Lives Matter," who I demonstrated in last week's letter (Everything Free But Speech) are using the same tactics as ISIS. One can only conclude that the common denominator between the birth of BLM and ISIS is Barack Obama. It's not that he doesn't understand the threat. Any honest analysis of Obama's actions and statements proves he's nurturing it.

On this week of Thanksgiving, we need to be thankful for the freedoms we have. Let us remember that the Pilgrims came to this country as refugees seeking freedom from the tyranny and persecution of the crown of England. (see Thanks Be To God-Vol.1) We do want to help and support others seeking protection, but not of the risk of loosing the very freedom those Pilgrims brought to the shores of this country. Over 60% of Americans understand this danger and do not want Syrian Muslims scattered throughout our country as we do not have an accurate vetting system to ensure the safety of our citizens. If only 1 percent of those Muslims that come into the country want to harm us we are looking at 850 invaders brought here by our own

President. 850 waiting for the moment they are told to go. That is a risk the President seems quite comfortable taking. Even some staunch Liberal Democrats are breaking with Barack here. Senator Diane Feinstein, ranking Democrat on the Senate Intelligence Committee, disputed Obama when she stated, "I have never been more concerned. ISIL is not contained. ISIL is expanding. They just put out a video saying it is their intent to attack this country. I think we have to be prepared."

I pray this country opens its eyes and falls on its knees before the Good Lord and asks forgiveness before He lets us reap what we have sown.

That's my 2 cents.

Love,
Mom

December 3, 2015

Dear Liberty,

Stepping off the bus after paying her toll, Rosa headed towards the rear entrance to get back on. She waited her turn to board the door for colored riders before finding a seat at the front of the "colored section". Her back and fingers ached from sewing for hours. It had been a long day and Rosa was ready to get home. Little did she know her day had just begun.*

Rosa eyed the bus driver in his mirror as he drove the route she knew by heart. Even closing her eyes, she knew every stop and every turn. Rosa wondered if he recognized her as the woman he physically threw off the bus 12 years ago for refusing to get off after paying just to re-enter from the back. She opened her eyes to notice the "white section" had filled. Her muscles tensed knowing what would happen if another white entered the bus.

It did not take long until Rosa's fear became reality. The bus driver promptly told the blacks in their first row to give up their seats. Rosa had been fighting for months the rule that the "white section" can move at whim while blacks are forced to stand on the bus even if no whites are riding. At first, none of Rosa's seatmates moved. That was until the bus driver started heading back. The other three riders then quietly slid out of their seats but Rosa stayed firm. "I'm tired and I've had enough," thought Rosa, but she was not referring to her physical state. She sat there, staring straight ahead. "Move," demanded the bus driver. "Not today," thought Rosa.

She recalled the other two women who refused to get up over the past several months. She knew the result of such defiance, but she was also insulted by the continued enslavement of complying. As secretary of the Montgomery Chapter of the NAACP (National Association for the Advancement of Colored People), Rosa had been working hard to rid the South of the racist, separate and unequal Jim Crow laws as well as other segregation practices flamed during the Progressive Democrat Woodrow Wilson Administration. (see A Tale Of Two Leaders-Vol.5, Separate But Equal?-Vol.6, The Birth Of A Nation, and How The South Was Won)

When Rosa got up that brisk December 1st morning, she had not planned on changing the country. She, like other Southern blacks, just wanted to be treated with a little dignity. Now Rosa had to make a decision. Was she going to continue to allow these unconstitutional laws to stand, or was she going to take a stand? Even while the cops were putting her in handcuffs she didn't think this would be any different than those arrested before her. But just like with Rosa, perhaps the time had come for many to make their voices heard.

The next few hours were a blur for Rosa. E. D. Nixon, the NAACP chapter president, quickly posted bail, putting his house up on bond, and began mobilizing those in his organization. Activists, along with pastors, met and coordinated a boycott of the Montgomery bussing system on Rosa's court date, Monday, December 5th. Pamphlets were distributed that night announcing the boycott for Monday. Ministers rallied their congregations during church services.

Seventy-five percent of bus patrons were black. Nixon hoped the boycott would send a message with 90% of the black community participating. The lost revenue made a statement, but not a change. Black leaders regrouped that evening and formed the Montgomery Improvement Association (MIA), electing an unknown 26-year-old minister as their president, Martin Luther King, Jr. (see Free At Last-Vol.2)

A simple list of demands was made: First-come, first-served seating with whites filling from the front and blacks from the back, more frequent and convenient stops in black communities, black drivers in predominantly black routes, and basic human courtesy to the black community.

After requests were again dismissed, King proposed the continuation of the boycott until demands were met. Nixon's strategy was to challenge the segregation law in court. He passed on utilizing the other two young women's arrests, feeling they were not a good face for their cause. A pregnant teenage girl couldn't be used as a moral crusader. Rosa was another story. A well-respected and liked member of the community, she was a woman both blacks and whites could unite behind. The NAACP filed a lawsuit with Parks as the plaintiff arguing the law was unconstitutional.

Under the peaceful and respectful leadership of Martin Luther King, the black community held together for the boycott while the case went to court. Taxi services participated in the beginning, charging black patrons the 10-cent bus fare until the city sued them and won. The MIA organized a large carpool system while many chose to simply walk to their destinations.

Blacks in Montgomery understood the evils of racism and looked it square in the face, not with hate or contempt, but with determination and peace. They could have stormed the bus stations or became abusive on the busses. They would have made the news but they would not have gained support. Instead, under King's influence, protestors choose to take the extra time to walk from place to place not for themselves, not for their own satisfaction or glory, but to obtain dignity for their children and grandchildren. Where Rosa's generation was forced to walk while whites rode busses to school, blacks now willingly volunteered to walk for freedom and liberty.

During the time of the boycott many of the activist leaders were targeted. Both Nixon's and King's homes were bombed, yet neither one returned with violence. King's peaceful approach to change was making all the difference in the building of the foundation of the Civil Rights Movement.

On June 5, 1956, the Montgomery federal court sided with the NAACP, ruling the segregation laws violate the 14th Amendment passed in 1868. (see Founding Documents-Vol.7) Appealing the verdict, the city of Montgomery continued to reject the MIA's demands as the case advanced to the Supreme Court. Victory was secured on December 20, 1956, with the Supreme Court upholding the lower court's ruling. The yearlong boycott was over. King called for an end to the Montgomery Bus Boycott the next day.

Last Friday, Black Lives Matter (BLM) protesters marched in the streets of Chicago demanding justice for Laquan McDonald by disrupting Black Friday shopping. McDonald was high on PCP, brandishing a knife and suspected of breaking into cars the September 2014 night Officer Jason Van Dyke shot him. Such facts mean nothing to the BLM movement. Van Dyke's indictment last week coincidently set off protests in Chicago at Thanksgiving time just as Ferguson had done one year earlier. (see Just The Facts, Ma'am–Vol.1)

Friday also brought the indictment of Corey Morgan, who lured 9-year-old Tyshawn Lee into an alleyway and executed him. There were no calls for justice for Lee in the weekend protests. Morgan, along with two other gangbangers, targeted Lee, the son of a rival gang member, in a retaliatory slaughtering. Morgan and his friends riddled Lee's body with bullets even though he raised his hands in a vain attempt to defend against the onslaught of handgun rounds. Why is Lee's death irrelevant while BLM protested the death of a thief armed with a knife? They were also eerily silent as eight Chicagoans were killed and twenty wounded during their protest weekend. Over 2700 shootings and more than 440 deaths have occurred in Chicago this year alone yet McDonald's is the only one protested. Don't Black Lives Matter? Apparently, only if cops are involved.

Nixon would be mortified that BLM not only chose Michael

Brown as the face of their movement, but that they continue to cling to slogans like "Hands Up, Don't Shoot" when the facts prove that did not happen. (see *Just The Facts, Ma'am*–Vol.1) They still refer to him as the "gentle giant" even after the video of him robbing a store and assaulting the owner minutes before his death was released. This just makes those defending Brown look ignorant and untrustworthy. The majority will not support a cause based on a criminal. Nixon purposely waited for a Rosa Parks, not jumping on the first opportunity. He chose the best opportunity. Nixon would be ashamed that Payton Head lied about the KKK being on the University of Missouri campus, sending black students into a panic. It diminishes true examples of racism and real acts of heroism such as Rosa Parks. King would be embarrassed by the BLM activists who swarmed Dartmouth library and verbally and physically assaulted innocent students regardless of their support of the movement. (see *Everything Free But Speech*)

The actions of Nixon, Parks, and especially King prove they would not have supported the BLM movement. King famously said, "I have a dream that my four little children will one day live in a nation where they will not be judged by the color of their skin, but by the content of their character." Does that sound consistent with BLM activists declaring that the "All Lives Matter" slogan is racist? Unlike Black Lives Matter, these amazing people, along with countless others, fought for the desegregation of busses, lunch counters, schools, water fountains, restrooms, concert seating, everything. Today's activists at Mizzou are regressing back to the times of "separate but equal". (see *Separate But Equal?*-Vol.6) They are willingly segregating themselves because they are too afraid of being offended, demanding a "safe space" where no one can hurt their feelings. Well what if Rosa Parks had felt that way? or Nixon? or King?

Liberty, every generation has its time to stand for truth, liberty, and equality. The problem is there are those out there who want to manipulate eager activists into standing for lies, oppression, and disunity. This is the difference in choosing a community organizer as your movement's leader instead of a minister. If you are not sure which group to follow, then look to Christ for your answer. Would Christ have supported Rosa Parks' stand for truth, or Payton Head's deception? Remember Satan is the father of all lies. Did Christ demonstrate peace and patience or upheaval and suppression? King knew all this and patterned his actions after the victor of this fight, Christ. King won with his leadership of peace and non-violence. He won because he fought for equality, not to get even. (see *Free At Last?*)

That's my 2 cents.

Love,
Mom

December 10, 2015

Dear Liberty,

When your grandparents were growing up, it was not uncommon for school children to take their guns to school. Gun racks hung in the back truck window with a shotgun at the ready. Homes, especially in rural areas, had a gun hanging over the mantle, set for easy access, a tradition from frontier days. Many students belonged to gun clubs, spending their after school hours practicing and perfecting their shots as well as learning gun safety.

Today, schools are not only "gun-free" zones, children are suspended for simply making the shape of a gun out of their fingers. They are expelled for playing cops and robbers in the playground. Yet with all these precautions, school and other "gun-free" zone shootings appear to be on the rise. So what's different between now and the days when guns were as common as a backpack or lunchbox for a student?

The answer is simple, Liberty. As the Liberal, politically correct Left demanded guns be removed from schools, they were simply following God out the door as well. Liberals demand students be punished for even the thought of a gun, yet file lawsuits against any teacher who might utter the words, "Thou Shall Not Kill." Children are indoctrinated into accepting the gun as evil without any acknowledgement to what is in their heart.

On December 2, two suspects entered a building in San Bernardino, California, and opened fired on a room full of people enjoying a Christmas party. To the media and Liberal dismay, the killers turned out to be a husband and wife ISIS supporting Muslim couple.

Instead of addressing the reality of this massacre, Liberal Progressives, as they always do, used the opportunity to further their agenda regardless of facts. Hillary Clinton, Mark O'Malley and others began calling for stricter gun laws before the bodies were even cold. Accusations against the NRA were leveled while the police were still searching for the suspects. Obama weighed in lecturing America about our need for even more restrictions on citizens' access to guns while insisting this had nothing to do with Islam. (see <u>Gun Control: The</u>

First Steps Of Tyranny-Vol.3) Once again the radical ideology of hate from the extremist Muslims was completely ignored and Americans were the ones demonized.

In the die-hard Liberal mind, it is the gun that kills. If guns were gone, there would be no more killing. Overriding truth with propaganda, they have no comprehension that pipe bombs at the murder site and the suspects' home completely expose the inaccuracy of their ideology.

Gun control activists seem to be ignorant that evil people can kill with knives, spears, arrows, cannons, ropes, and fire. Eight terrorists, consisting of both men and women, carried out a massacre in Kunming, China, in 2014 with just knives, killing 33 and injuring 140. There are several other instances of mass murder in China, Japan, South Korea and Europe involving knives where the strictest gun control laws exist. The honest truth is that knives are much more easily accessible than guns, especially in an impulsive situation. Fertilizer and fuel created a simple explosive in Oklahoma City in 1995, resulting in 168 deaths. The Boston Marathon bombing in 2013 involved two improvised pressure cooker explosives. Nineteen Islamic terrorists carried out the worst foreign attack on American soil on September 11, 2001, with nothing more than box cutters and planes. (see *Never Forget-Vol.1*) Killers don't squabble over their weapon of choice. Their goal is death.

The New York Daily News' cover the day after the San Bernardino massacre was "God isn't fixing this." They ridiculed Ted Cruz, Rand Paul, Paul Ryan and Lindsey Graham for offering their prayers, accusing these politicians of pandering to a right-wing extreme gun policy. While Christian prayers are jeered, Democrats are cheered when they hit their knees in mosques. "Democratic lawmakers are planning to attend prayer services at a Washington-area mosque (12/4/15) that has been accused of acting as a front for Hamas and that served as the home of terrorist spiritual leader Anwar al-Awlaki, who reportedly mentored two of the 9/11 hijackers." (*The Washington Free Beacon*) *The New*

York Times praised their compassion and understanding.

Others jumped into the fray, mocking Christians and God while arguing the dangers in the world are getting worse. Can't any of them see the correlation between the world's arrogant denial of God, removing Him from every aspect of our lives, and the increase in occurrences such as this latest tragedy? Obama admits he defines Christians by the Christian Crusaders. As I argued in *A Crusade For The Truth*, these campaigns began as a response to the over 400 years of Muslim invasions, slaughters and overthrows of Christian cities and territories that started with Mohammad's direction and blessing. Obama sees Christianity as a religion of hate while claiming that he is one. Then again, how could he feel any other way after spending 20 years in a church led by Rev. Jeremiah Wright?

While over 80% of the nation's citizens consider themselves Christian, even though a good portion of them do not attend church or belong to a particular denomination, it is the atheists and the Muslims that this administration supports. Christian bakers, florists, and wedding chapels are targeted and run out of business for not wanting to participate in same-sex marriages. (see *We Reserve The Right To Refuse Service*-Vol.1) Any mention of God in a school could lead to grounds for expulsion, suspension, or termination. The Attorney General just threatened to prosecute anyone who spoke out against Islam because of this recent attack. A *New York Daily News* columnist followed up the insulting "God isn't fixing this" story by tweeting, "That Jew got what he deserved," referring to a Christian/Messianic Jew killed by the Islamic extremists, simply because he supported the NRA. The Left and this administration will criticize Christians wanting to live their faith, calling them bigots and Islamophobes, while defending Muslims, atheists, and their own intolerance every single time.

During his 2008 campaign, Obama mocked middle-America Christians, stating, "They get bitter, they cling to guns or religion." He later apologized for his wording, but not for his opinion. We have had presidents before who may not have been the most faithful Christians, but we have never had one so hostile to the predominate faith in this country while pandering to those who have proven to be at war with us time and time again.

During this administration, hostility towards God and Christianity has exploded like never before. Fifty years ago boys carried guns to school and there was never a concern for mass murders. Guns hung freely and unlocked in many homes, yet the owners were not compelled to use them because of a disagreement with a neighbor. Why? Because of the Bible they had open on the table. The Word of God curbed our morality, instilling in us the respect for life. Sermons on Christ's love, forgiveness, and personal responsibility were heard every week in church and often from the mouths of our leaders.

Even if students were not getting it at home, they were at least getting the Ten Commandments at school. Too many have stood by while a small minority took that away. Teachers used to have parental and school support to reprimand those behaving badly. Now kids are coddled and pandered to, allowing them to continue their aggressive behavior well into adulthood, developing into a generation with no abilities to confront the real world.

Earlier this year, Dylann Roof attended a Bible study at the Emanuel African Methodist Episcopal Church in Charleston. (see _Their Deaths Were Not In Vain_) After sitting with them for an hour, he excused himself to retrieve his firearms. He reentered the church and began shooting, killing nine parishioners. After he was in police custody, he confessed he "almost didn't go through with it because everyone was so nice to him." After only one hour, the love of those Christians was strong enough to make Roof seriously reconsider what he was about to do. If Roof would have had a daily influence of God's love, image how different his life would have turned out. Image how many other lost souls could be found if Christians and God were not so vilified by Democrats, media, and Hollywood.

The gun is a tool. If it had control of itself then guns would be put on trial for murder instead of people. America has gone to sleep and turned from God. The Old Testament is full of accounts of the Jews turning from the LORD, holding fast to other gods and idols, until the time comes that God allows them to experience life without Him. When Israel's kings turned from God, the nation suffered. America and the world have followed the false idols of Israel and have failed to acknowledge the God that made all men equal.

We kicked God out of schools, out of courthouses, out of public buildings and now out of the White House. The further we get from Him the more evil we will reap. We are seeing that play out right now before our very eyes. Until we as a people wake up and accept the truth, the darker our world is going to get.

Liberty, unlike what you are being told by today's Progressives, it's not what's in your hand that kills, it's what's in your heart.

That's my 2 cents.

Love,
Mom

December 16, 2015

Dear Liberty,

   "Blessed are the poor in spirit, for they shall see the kingdom of heaven." George's voice boomed through the village streets causing the coal miners and citizens to stop and search for the source. A small, natural hill was his stage and the blistering cold and wet February English weather was his backdrop. Using his theatrical talents, he departed from traditional monotone sermons and brought the Bible to life. Projecting his voice, his words traveled throughout the city grabbing the people's attention. George recited the story of Jesus, from His birth to His resurrection, with passion and tenderness. From Hell to the cross, George continued to preach the Good News of Jesus Christ as upwards of 200 villagers congregated around. They gathered out of curiosity. They stayed for the message.

   By the time George was finished, the hard, tired, blackened faces of the coal miners were softened and cleansed by the tears that were running down their cheeks. One man approached George after the sermon. Holding his granddaughter's hand, he thanked George for reminding him of the Christmas story. He explained his mother had told it to him when he was a child but he had forgotten it long ago. He never told his children and they never told his grandchildren. The man was so joyful that the gift of the Gospel had been given back to him to share with his family.

   The Church of England had dismissed the villagers of Kingswood as poor, unsophisticated simpletons who reveled in their sin. They were not worth the church's time, like the people in so many other little villages in England, so the church did not bless the area with a parish of their own. As with the reformers of the 16th century, George recognized how the church had grown cold and uncaring, desiring power over saving souls. (see <u>The Knock Heard 'Round The World</u>-Vol.1)

   When George Whitefield had entered the ministry at age 17, it was more of a job than a calling. He had worked for years in the family inn helping his widowed mother, but he desired a profession with more prestige. While attending Oxford, Charles Wesley loaned him Henry Scougal's <u>The Life of God in the Soul of Man</u>, which opened Whitefield's eyes and heart to the love of God. He became on fire for the Lord and believed one's faith should be felt in the soul. He began to understand that one should have a deep relationship with God, not just a fleeting friendship on Sundays.

By the time he was ordained a minister in the Church of England at age 22, his passion for the Word had already begun changing others. Along with the Wesley brothers, John and Charles, the three men inspired the teachings now known as the Methodist denomination. A strong "Calvinist", Whitefield and the Wesley's eventually had several disagreements about theology. Regardless, Whitefield never considered himself anything other than a Christian. His sermons inspired members of many denominations, including Baptists, Presbyterians, Congregationalists, and others.

At the beginning of Whitefield's ministry, churches were eager to have him preach. Whitefield's charismatic style drew in thousands to the pews. He not only revealed the love and sacrifice of Jesus Christ, he also spoke of freedom and personal responsibility for your own faith. The church leaders quickly feared his message was undermining the authority of the church, challenging their power and hold over their parishioners. This attitude expanded across the Atlantic Ocean to the American Churches of England as well.

When Whitefield returned to England from his first trip to The New World in 1739, he was not welcomed in the church's pulpits anymore. Following in the footsteps of Christ's own ministry, Whitefield knew the souls that truly needed the Good News were not those in the pews, but the ones rejected by those in authority. They were the ones being outright ignored by the church. Since he was no longer allowed a venue for the people to come hear him, Whitefield decided to take his message to the people, especially those who did not already know the Gospel. His mission started humbly in the small coal-mining village of Kingswood.

God blessed his endeavor. The day after Whitefield's life changing sermon in Kingswood, he returned to speak again. This time the crowd was 2000 strong. By Sunday, men, women and children had traveled from neighboring villages for an audience of over 10,000. Such huge crowds soon became the norm, rather than the exception. Whitefield became known for his ability to project his voice so loud and so far that groups of tens of thousands could easily hear him as he preached. Although he cultivated a church in nearby Bristol, he realized his true calling was evangelizing.

Turning the church over to John Wesley, Whitefield returned to America by the end of the year. He recognized there was a ripe field in England to preach, but America was the land of milk and honey. He had already begun a ministry with the slaves during his first trip and desired to continue those efforts. Traveling throughout the colonies, Whitefield preached practically every day for months. His sermons, along with efforts of other ministers such as Jonathan Edwards, helped spark the movement known as "The Great Awakening", bringing *thousands to the church. (see <u>Give 'Em Watts, Boys!</u>-Vol.6 and <u>"Higher"</u> <u>Education</u>-Vol.3)*

When in Philadelphia, Whitefield forged a strong friendship with Benjamin Franklin, who saw the importance of Whitefield's sermons even though he was a self-proclaimed Deist.   Franklin published Whitefield's work, allowing his tracts and sermons to reach over half of the colonists.   (see <u>A Tale Of Two Printers</u>-Vol.5)   After one of Whitefield's sermons, Franklin commented, "wonderful... change soon made in the manners of our inhabitants. From being thoughtless or indifferent about religion, it seem'd as if all the world were growing religious, so that one could not walk thro' the town in an evening without hearing psalms sung in different families of every street." Whitefield's ministry and witness to Franklin eventually resulted in Franklin becoming an avid reader of the Bible and member of a Presbyterian church. (see <u>Spirit Of Conciliation</u>-Vol.7) For decades the name George Whitefield was as widely known and respected as Benjamin Franklin himself.

During Whitefield's 1764 trip to America, he warned the colonists there was a "deep laid plot against your civil and religious liberties," coming from England.   Still loyal to the crown, Whitefield also sympathized with the rejected colonists. As with the forgotten coal miners who were nothing more than necessary workers to the elite, Whitefield saw the same abuse happening to the colonists.

As Whitefield and Franklin's friendship grew, so did their understanding and desire for man to be free from the tyranny of government.   England and the Church of England felt the affects of Whitefield and other revivalist ministers and responded with the Stamp Act. (see <u>Tree Of Liberty</u>-Vol.4) When Franklin traveled to England to protest the Act in front of Parliament, he took Whitefield with him to proclaim colonists' rights.   It was directly due to the sermons of a significant number of ministers preaching on freedom and liberty that Americans so widely resisted the Stamp Act. The collection of these bold ministers became known as the "Black Robed Regiment" and was just as great a threat to the crown as any military. (see <u>The Shot Heard 'Round The World</u>-Vol.3, <u>Who Among You Is With Me?</u>-Vol.4 and <u>Give 'Em Watts, Boys!</u>-Vol.6)

As no one is perfect except Christ, Whitefield had his faults. He was an advocate of slavery though he insisted that they should be treated humanely. Teaching his own slaves about Christ, he treated them with respect and dignity. He was extremely critical of those who abused and neglected their slaves. Whitefield gave many sermons to the Negros and was credited for bringing the Gospel and Christianity to the slave population. Many rejected his efforts as they were afraid if the slaves were taught about spiritual freedom and liberty given through

Christ, they would also desire it civilly as well.

Many believe there would not have even been an American Revolution if not for George Whitefield, even though he passed away years before in 1770. Benedict Arnold, before he became a traitor, honored Whitefield on his way to Quebec in September of 1775. (see A Tale Of Two Patriots-Vol.5) Arnold and his troops stopped by the Old South Presbyterian Church in Newberry Port, Massachusetts, where Whitefield is buried. Being a Sunday, the troops worshipped God before Arnold took the officers downstairs to Whitefield's crypt. They opened the casket and each took a piece of Whitefield's clerical collar or wristband to wear in battle. Phillis Wheatley, a slave and poet, honored Whitefield with a poem that sparked his notoriety in both the Old and New World. (see Unshackled Speech-Vol.5)

When the Founders assembled to declare Independence in 1776, Whitefield's work was of major significance. His ministry was so influential that when the Declaration was written, it was not a foreign concept to the American population but simply a statement of principles they learned over years of sermons from their "Black Robed Regiment" ministers. (see Founding Documents-Vol.7) Colonists had been taught the idea of Independence, free from the oppression of the crown and the state church, since Whitefield starting touring the colonies in 1740.

George Whitefield was born December 16, 1714, in Gloucester, England. In his short 55 years he preached over 18,000 sermons, which was an average of 10 a week, speaking to an estimated 12 million people. Traveling to Scotland 15 times, America seven times and Ireland twice, he ignited a passion for God's Word not seen since the days of the apostles. Even though it was taking a toll on his health, Whitefield continued a vigorous ministry till the end. His last sermon was preached in a field, standing on a barrel. Speaking on the insufficiency of works to merit salvation, he was suddenly inspired by the Spirit and cried out in a thunderous voice, "Works! Works! A man gets to heaven by works! I would as soon think of climbing to the moon on a rope of sand." His trip to heaven began the following morning, guided solely on the grace of Christ.

As with the grandfather in Kingswood, America has long forgotten the Gospel. We have fallen from the faith and failed to pass on the salvation of Jesus Christ to our children and grandchildren. This Christmas season let us take a cue from Whitefield and go to the streets, telling of the birth and life of our Lord and Savior Jesus Christ. Let us seek out the lost, as Christ did, and show them the light, preaching of the grace and forgiveness given to us because of a tiny baby born 2000 years ago.

That's my 2 cents. Love, Mom

December 25, 2015

Dear Liberty,

"Help!"

The scream sliced through the house like a cold knife. Henry woke with a start from a peaceful afternoon nap to find his wife in flames. Her dress was on fire and threatening the life of the mother of six. Henry grabbed a rug and desperately tried to smoother the growing flames engulfing his precious love, Fannie. Realizing time was of the essence, Henry covered Fannie's body with his own, suffering burns on his face that would mentally and physically haunt him for the rest of his life.

Despite his best and most heroic efforts, Henry was unable to save her. Fannie succumbed to her injuries the next morning on July 10, 1861. Suffering from his own serious wounds, Henry was unable to even attend his beloved's funeral. He wasn't sure he could maintain his composure anyway.

Henry pulled himself together only because he had to find a way to raise their children. He grew a beard to try to hide his physical scars but he wasn't sure if it was for the sake of others or himself. Two years after Fannie's death, their eldest son Charles, snuck off to Washington D.C. to enlist in President Lincoln's Union army. Initially dismayed, Henry was proud of his son and eventually wrote several of his friends, including Senator Charles Sumner (see <u>The Birth Of A Movement</u>-Vol.1), in support of commissioning Charles as an officer. His efforts were unnecessary as Charles was quickly made Second Lieutenant in the 1st Massachusetts Cavalry.

Charles soon suffered from typhoid fever and returned home to recover. This caused Charles to miss the Battle of Gettysburg. (see <u>The Unforgettable Speech</u>-Vol.5) He rejoined his unit in August, only to receive a life threatening gunshot wound in late November. Henry received word by telegram of his son's condition. He and his son Earnest quickly traveled to Washington through the dreary December weather to retrieve Charles and bring him home for another time of recovery.

On Christmas morning 1863, Henry quietly sat and listened to the bells ringing through the town. Choruses of "Peace on Earth" saturating the air rattled Henry's heart. The turmoil between the North and the South was only matched by the turmoil within Henry's soul still suffering from the loss of his beloved wife and battle scars of his dear son. These words came to mind.

> And in despair I bowed my head;
> "There is no peace on earth," I said;
> "For hate is strong,
> And mocks the song
> Of peace on earth, good-will to men!"

Yet among all the violence, death, pain and despair, Henry was able to find hope.

> Then pealed the bells more loud and deep:
> "God is not dead, nor doth He sleep;
> The Wrong shall fail,
> The Right prevail,
> With peace on earth, good-will to men."

Henry Wadsworth Longfellow expressed a simple message of faith in the last stanza of his poem, "Christmas Bells." In 1872, John Baptiste Calkin rearranged the poem and combined it with a memorable tune to produce the loved Christmas Classic, "I Heard The Bells On Christmas Day."

Longfellow used the phrase, "peace on earth, good-will to men," taken from Luke 2:14. The more precise language is "Glory to God in the highest, and on earth peace among those with whom he is pleased!" (ESV) The angels' praise of peace was not that peace would be felt by the whole earth, but that the birth of Jesus Christ will bring peace to believers.

Since the fall of Adam the world has been living with the curse of sin. (see Fruit Of The Forbidden Tree-Vol.1) As Longfellow was experiencing, this world is full of grief and pain, but God sent the peace of a savior to those who believe. It is a gift of hope and reassurance in a world that often times seems filled with pain. So this Christmas, as things in the world seem completely out of control, find joy and happiness in the Reason for the Season, the blessed peace of Our Lord and Savior Jesus Christ who brings, "peace on earth, good-will to men."

That's my 2 cents.

Love,
Mom

Pictures

Disunity Of The Union
http://lobojosden.blogspot.com/2009/11/non-bilateral-abraham-lincoln.html

What's So Good About Good Friday?
man of the day - Jess @ Flickr (Attribution, ShareAlike)

I Win!
LuMaxArt Golden Guy Trophy Winner; Scott Maxwell
LuMaxArt Linkware Image from thegoldguys.blogspot.com/ *or*
www.lumaxart.com/; Attribution & ShareAlike

References

As Time Goes By
http://en.m.wikipedia.org/wiki/Anno_Domini
http://en.m.wikipedia.org/wiki/0_(year)
http://www.webexhibits.org/calendars/year-history.html
http://www.webexhibits.org/calendars/week.html
http://en.m.wikipedia.org/wiki/Dionysius_Exiguus
http://charlesasullivan.com/1842/dionysius-exiguus-and-the-ad-calendar-system/
http://charlesasullivan.com/2637/bede-on-the-problem-of-1-ad/
http://en.m.wikipedia.org/wiki/Julian_calendar
http://en.m.wikipedia.org/wiki/Gregorian_calendar
http://en.m.wikipedia.org/wiki/Ab_urbe_condita
http://en.m.wikipedia.org/wiki/Era_of_Martyrs
http://www.infoplease.com/encyclopedia/society/nicaea-first-council-of.html
http://www.icr.org/article/meaning-day-genesis/

COEXIST
http://www.theblaze.com/stories/2015/01/07/11-dead-in-shooting-at-french-satirical-newspaper/
http://www.theblaze.com/contributions/islam-is-the-most-violent-religion-in-the-world-but-lets-keep-calling-it-peaceful-anyway/
http://www.theblaze.com/stories/2015/01/11/im-a-soldier-of-the-caliphate-video-shows-french-shooter-swearing-loyalty-to-the-islamic-state/
http://www.redstate.com/diary/matthewclark/2014/12/08/isis-reportedly-beheads-four-christian-children-iraq-refusing-convert-islam/
http://www.theblaze.com/stories/2015/01/10/while-islamic-terrorist-held-hostages-in-kosher-market-muslim-employee-took-several-shoppers-to-safety/
http://www.theblaze.com/stories/2015/01/07/ap-censors-deliberately-provocative-charlie-hebdo-images-heres-what-they-had-to-say-about-selling-piss-christ/
http://www.theblaze.com/contributions/eliana-benador-we-knew-the-violence-in-france-wasnt-over-as-terrorists-target-jewish-shops-and-culture/
http://www.theblaze.com/stories/2015/01/09/french-security-source-suspects-in-paris-terror-attack-steal-car-are-on-move-again/
http://www.theblaze.com/stories/2015/01/08/important-detail-revealed-about-the-french-officer-executed-on-video-by-suspected-islamic-extremists/
http://www.theblaze.com/stories/2015/01/10/the-woman-police-thought-helped-with-the-french-shooting-wasnt-there-now-theres-a-new-theory-about-where-shes-gone/
http://eaglerising.com/13626/muslim-psychos-murder-12-french-satirical-magazine/
http://godfatherpolitics.com/19662/paris-murders-come-excuses/
http://www.theblaze.com/contributions/eliana-benador-vengeful-islamists-massacre-artists-in-the-name-of-their-prophet/
http://www.theblaze.com/stories/2015/01/08/the-reason-the-islamic-faith-bans-images-of-the-prophet-muhammad/
http://www.americanthinker.com/articles/2005/08/top_ten_reasons_why_sharia_is.html

Free At Last?
http://www.biography.com/people/martin-luther-king-jr-9365086#early-years
http://en.wikipedia.org/wiki/Martin_Luther_King,_Jr.
http://www.biography.com/people/malcolm-x-9396195
http://en.wikipedia.org/wiki/Civil_Rights_Act_of_1964
http://www.history.com/topics/black-history/selma-montgomery-march
http://www.fhwa.dot.gov/highwayhistory/road/s09.cfm
http://en.wikipedia.org/wiki/Separate_but_equal
http://www.emancipationproclamation.org/
http://www.blackpast.org/aah/bloody-sunday-selma-alabama-march-7-1965
http://en.wikipedia.org/wiki/Bloody_Sunday_%281972%29
http://www.americanrhetoric.com/speeches/mlkihaveadream.htm
http://www.glennbeck.com/content/articles/article/198/39442/
http://www.gopusa.com/commentary/2014/03/13/when-blacks-voted-80-percent-dem-malcolm-x-called-them-chumps/?subscriber=1
http://www.cbn.com/spirituallife/onlinediscipleship/understandingislam/12th Imam_BaptistPress060817.aspx
http://en.wikipedia.org/wiki/Jim_Crow_laws
http://en.wikipedia.org/wiki/War_on_Poverty
http://canadafreepress.com/index.php/article/40889
http://en.wikipedia.org/wiki/Great_Society
http://www.washingtonpost.com/blogs/fact-checker/wp/2014/11/25/giulianis-claim-that-93-percent-of-blacks-are-killed-by-other-blacks/
http://www.lifenews.com/2014/04/14/african-american-pastor-horrified-when-he-learns-how-abortion-targets-blacks/

Robbin' Hood
http://en.wikipedia.org/wiki/Robin_Hood
http://fair.org/blog/2015/01/22/obama-as-robin-hood-sherwood-be-nice/
http://www.history.com/topics/british-history/robin-hood

The Color-Blindness Of Slavery
http://topconservativenews.com/2012/03/americas-first-slave-owner-was-a-black-man/ http://hudsonrepublicancommittee.org/?page_id=573
http://en.m.wikipedia.org/wiki/Anthony_Johnson_(colonist).
http://www.usconstitution.net/consttop_slav.html http://www.colorado.edu/ibs/eb/alston/econ8534/SectionIII/Galenson,_The_Rise_and_Fall_of_Indentured_Servitude_in_the_Americas.pdf
http://en.wikipedia.org/wiki/Headright
https://www.ocf.berkeley.edu/~arihuang/academic/abg/slavery/history.html
http://en.m.wikipedia.org/wiki/Indentured_servant
http://www.scoilgaeilge.org/academics/slaves.htm
http://www.dailykos.com/story/2013/12/27/1265498/-The-slaves-that-time-forgot
http://en.m.wikipedia.org/wiki/Oliver_Cromwell
http://www.project2019.com/blkmayflower.htm
https://floridairishheritagecenter.wordpress.com/2010/06/17/slavery-and-the-irish/
http://en.wikipedia.org/wiki/Slavery_in_the_United_States
http://www.todayifoundout.com/index.php/2013/08/the-first-legal-slave-owner-in-what-would-become-the-united-states-was-a-black-man/
http://www.thefreedomtrail.org/educational-resources/article-rise-and-fall-

of-slave-trade-part1.shtml
http://www.globalresearch.ca/the-irish-slave-trade-the-forgotten-white-slaves/31076

Sanger and Eugenics and Socialism, Oh, My

http://www.issues4life.org/blast/2012086.html
http://en.wikipedia.org/wiki/Margaret_Sanger
http://www.biography.com/people/margaret-sanger-9471186
http://www.blackgenocide.org/sanger.html
http://www.lifenews.com/2013/03/11/10-eye-opening-quotes-from-planned-parenthood-founder-margaret-sanger/
http://www.u-s-history.com/pages/h1676.html
http://www.dianedew.com/sanger.htm
http://margaretsanger.blogspot.com/
http://margaretsanger.blogspot.com/2013/06/six-quotes-hint-why-marget-sanger.html
https://www.lifesitenews.com/news/breaking-richard-dawkins-choosing-not-to-abort-baby-with-down-syndrome-is-i?utm_source=LifeSiteNews.com+Daily+Newsletter&utm_campaign=40ae1529e7-Breaking_Richard_Dawkins&utm_medium=email&utm_term=0_0caba610ac-40ae1529e7-397575413
http://www.glennbeck.com/2015/01/22/this-is-the-best-argument-made-against-abortion-ever/
http://www.pbs.org/wgbh/amex/pill/peopleevents/p_sanger.html
http://womenshistory.about.com/od/sangermargaret/p/margaret_sanger.htm
http://www.spectacle.org/997/richmond.html
http://www.freerepublic.com/focus/f-news/1145367/posts
https://saynsumthn.wordpress.com/2010/01/25/george-bernard-shaw-hitler-and-margaret-sanger/
http://civilliberty.about.com/od/gendersexuality/tp/Forced-Sterilization-History.htm
http://wholeworldinhishands.com/world/abortion-statistics-by-race.html
http://www.abort73.com/abortion/abortion_and_race/

Disunity Of The Union

http://www.history.com/topics/us-presidents/abraham-lincoln
http://americacomesalive.com/2013/02/12/abraham-lincoln-1809-1865-president-from-1861-1865/#.VN11e0c8KrX
http://www.biography.com/people/abraham-lincoln-9382540#assassination
http://www.civilwar.org/education/history/lincoln-hub/lincoln-ten-facts/10-facts-lincoln.html
http://blog.constitutioncenter.org/2014/02/50-shades-of-abraham-lincoln-2/
http://www.abrahamlincolnonline.org/lincoln/speeches/house.htm
http://www.ushistory.org/us/32b.asp
http://www.history.com/topics/lincoln-douglas-debates
http://en.wikipedia.org/wiki/Slavery_in_the_United_States
http://www.britannica.com/EBchecked/topic/171273/Dred-Scott-decision
http://www.britannica.com/EBchecked/topic/582276/Roger-Brooke-Taney
http://en.wikipedia.org/wiki/Missouri_Compromise
http://en.wikipedia.org/wiki/Roger_B._Taney
http://en.wikipedia.org/wiki/James_Buchanan
http://en.wikipedia.org/wiki/Franklin_Pierce
http://en.wikipedia.org/wiki/Lecompton_Constitution
http://en.wikipedia.org/wiki/Lincoln%E2%80%93Douglas_debates
http://mrlincolnandfreedom.org/inside.asp?ID=60&subjectID=3

Washington, Adams, and Mohammad – Our Founding Fathers
http://www.thegatewaypundit.com/2014/10/john-kerry-lectures-isis-on-appropriate-21st-century-behavior/
http://newsbusters.org/blogs/geoffrey-dickens/2015/02/18/abc-cbs-nbc-skip-marie-harfs-lefty-jobs-isis-idea
http://www.tpnn.com/2015/02/16/isis-beheads-21-christians-on-video-obama-goes-golfing/
http://freedomoutpost.com/2015/02/hey-obama-heres-how-islam-was-woven-into-the-fabric-of-our-country-its-called-the-barbary-wars/
www.history.com/this-day-in-history/to-the-shores-of-tripoli
http://www.usni.org/store/books/history/shores-tripoli
http://en.wikipedia.org/wiki/Marines%27_Hymn
http://www.christianpost.com/news/isis-beheads-21-coptic-christians-in-message-to-nation-of-the-cross-egypt-bombs-terror-group-in-response-134142/
http://lampofhistory.blogspot.com/2008/09/americas-first-war-on-terror-barbary.html
http://americansstandwithisrael.blogspot.com/2011/11/muslims-are-right-they-have-played.html

Net Neutrality - The Tie That Binds
http://www.breitbart.com/big-journalism/2014/04/19/clinton-wh-feared-internet-s-ability-to-democraticize-news-three-years-before-drudge-bombshell/
http://www.britannica.com/EBchecked/topic/474092/Pravda
http://en.wikipedia.org/wiki/Federal_Communications_Commission
http://en.wikipedia.org/wiki/Federal_Radio_Commission
http://techliberation.com/2009/08/10/free-press-robert-mcchesney-the-struggle-for-media-marxism
http://www.jewishworldreview.com/cols/sowell090100.asp
http://dailycaller.com/2013/05/11/top-obama-officials-brother-is-president-of-cbs-news-may-drop-reporter-over-benghazi-coverage/
http://www.nytimes.com/1987/06/21/us/reagan-vetoes-measure-to-affirm-fairness-policy-for-broadcasters.html
http://content.time.com/time/nation/article/0,8599,1880786,00.html
http://en.wikipedia.org/wiki/Fairness_Doctrine
http://www.washingtonexaminer.com/soros-ford-shovel-196-million-to-net-neutrality-groups-staff-to-white-house/article/2560702
http://www.bizjournals.com/philadelphia/news/2015/03/02/coalition-slams-comcast-time-warner-cable-merger.html?page=all
http://content.time.com/time/magazine/article/0,9171,854840,00.html
http://dianawest.net/Home/tabid/36/EntryId/965/-Cronkites-Offensive-History.aspx
http://newsbusters.org/blogs/seton-motley/2009/08/28/video-fcc-diversity-czar-chavezs-venezuela-incredible-democratic-revol
http://www.politico.com/news/stories/0211/49843.html
http://www.biography.com/people/william-randolph-hearst-9332973

The Science Is Settled
http://www.universetoday.com/33113/heliocentric-model/
http://www.tertullian.org/fathers/cosmas_00_0_eintro.htm
http://www.universetoday.com/13573/why-pluto-is-no-longer-a-planet/
http://www.npr.org/2012/12/09/166665795/forget-extinct-the-brontosaurus-never-even-existed
http://phys.org/news/2015-02-big-quantum-equation-universe.html
http://www.chem4kids.com/files/atom_structure.html
http://www.reasonifyouwill.com/2014/03/settled-science-oxymoron.html
http://news.investors.com/ibd-editorials/021015-738779-climate-change-scare-tool-to-destroy-capitalism.htm

http://listverse.com/2009/01/19/10-debunked-scientific-beliefs-of-the-past/
http://www.breitbart.com/big-government/2012/07/30/new-study-crushes-global-warming-data-claims/
http://en.wikipedia.org/wiki/Cambrian_explosion
http://en.wikipedia.org/wiki/Louis_Pasteur

The Birth Of A Nation
http://www.pbs.org/wnet/jimcrow/stories_events_birth.html
https://www.yahoo.com/movies/birth-of-a-nation-100-years-later-the-110826526292.html
http://www.bu.edu/professorvoices/2013/03/04/the-long-forgotten-racial-attitudes-and-policies-of-woodrow-wilson/
http://thequietus.com/articles/12890-birth-of-a-nation-review
http://baltimorepostexaminer.com/happened-ferguson-will-happen/2014/08/20
http://www.pbs.org/wgbh/amex/wilson/portrait/wp_african.html
http://en.wikipedia.org/wiki/Racial_segregation_in_the_United_States

The Science Is Settled, Part II
http://godfatherpolitics.com/21072/fascist-al-gore-wants-to-punish-climate-change-deniers/#
http://mic.com/articles/22334/an-inconvenient-truth-al-gore-sells-current-tv-to-the-emir-of-fossil-fuels
http://hotair.com/archives/2015/03/18/late-nights-seth-meyers-sandbags-ted-cruz-on-climate-change/
http://www.politifact.com/truth-o-meter/statements/2015/mar/20/ted-cruz/ted-cruzs-worlds-fire-not-last-17-years/
http://www.cnn.com/2015/03/22/politics/ted-cruz-2016-election-global-warming-jerry-brown/index.html
http://www.csmonitor.com/USA/Politics/Decoder/2015/0317/Ted-Cruz-to-Seth-Meyers-I-m-not-Freddy-Krueger-video
http://freedomoutpost.com/2015/03/by-hook-and-by-crook-you-are-going-to-pay-for-climate-change/
http://www.astronomy.ohio-state.edu/~pogge/Ast161/Unit3/response.html
http://www.fsmitha.com/h3/copernicus.htm
http://www.wsj.com/articles/SB10001424052702303480304579578462813553136
http://washington.cbslocal.com/2013/12/05/global-warming-scientist-accused-of-falsifying-data-on-drowned-polar-bears-retires/
http://www.thefederalistpapers.org/political-cartoon/global-temperature-data-falsified-for-years-to-show-warming-cartoon-reveals-why
http://newsbusters.org/blogs/tom-blumer/2015/03/20/politifact-rates-cruzs-truthful-statement-17-year-global-warming-pause
http://www.salon.com/2014/02/06/house_gop_overrides_endangered_species_act_protections_to_pass_calif_water_bill/

What's So Good About Good Friday?
http://www.thesacredpage.com/2008/12/christmas-star.html
http://www.gotquestions.org/Old-Testament-Christ.html
http://www.ehow.com/info_7918203_swaddling-clothes.html

The Crucifixion of America
http://www.bible-studys.org/Bible%20Books/John/John%20Chapter%2011%20Second%20Continued.html

Holocausts: Then and Now
http://www.dbonhoeffer.org/
http://www.britannica.com/EBchecked/topic/73037/Dietrich-Bonhoeffer

http://www.britannica.com/EBchecked/topic/131892/Confessing-Church
http://www.history.com/topics/world-war-ii/the-holocaust
http://historynewsnetwork.org/article/1796
http://www.northjersey.com/news/coptic-christians-beheaded-in-libya-1.1272136
http://www.nbcnews.com/storyline/missing-nigeria-schoolgirls/boko-haram-200-000-christians-risk-massacre-nigeria-n306211
http://www.nbcnews.com/storyline/missing-nigeria-schoolgirls/boko-haram-violence-has-forced-800-000-children-their-homes-n340406
http://www.dailymail.co.uk/news/article-2097252/Kill-Jews-annihilate-Israel-Irans-supreme-leader-lays-legal-religious-justification-attack.html
http://cnsnews.com/news/article/melanie-hunter/netanyahu-iran-s-ayatollah-tweets-israel-must-be-destroyed
http://www.theblaze.com/stories/2015/04/05/one-of-the-gunmen-in-kenyan-massacre-was-a-law-school-educated-son-of-a-government-official/
http://www.theblaze.com/stories/2015/04/05/one-of-the-gunmen-in-kenyan-massacre-was-a-law-school-educated-son-of-a-government-official/
http://www.cbsnews.com/news/the-coptic-christians-of-egypt/

War On Women
http://www.thepoliticalinsider.com/must-watch-rand-paul-owned-gotcha-segment-with-nbc-savannah-guthrie/
http://townhall.com/tipsheet/cortneyobrien/2015/04/09/rand-the-press-should-ask-dems-if-its-ok-to-kill-babies-in-the-womb-n1982525
http://www.glennbeck.com/2015/04/20/this-is-the-1-reason-people-are-voting-for-hillary-clinton/
http://www.politifact.com/wisconsin/statements/2015/apr/20/reince-priebus/hillary-clinton-took-money-kings-four-countries-go/
http://lastresistance.com/11220/ted-cruz-answers-gay-marriage-question-brilliantly-some-conservatives-upset/
http://www.thereligionofpeace.com/Quran/002-rape_adultery.htm

The Great American Melting Pot
http://www.glennbeck.com/2015/04/27/leftists-turn-on-jenner-when-he-reveals-he-is-conservative/
http://www.glennbeck.com/2015/04/27/tolerance-gay-hotel-owners-face-boycott-over-hosting-ted-cruz/
http://news.bbc.co.uk/2/hi/americas/4931534.stm

Separation Of Church And State
http://www.patheos.com/blogs/bristolpalin/2015/04/hillary-clinton-religious-beliefs-have-to-be-changed-so-women-can-get-abortions/
http://godfatherpolitics.com/21996/hillary-clinton-wants-to-put-an-end-to-religious-freedom-in-favor-of-abortion/
http://www.mlive.com/news/detroit/index.ssf/2015/04/supreme_court_justices_press_g.html
http://freedomoutpost.com/2015/04/will-christians-be-fitted-with-yellow-crosses/
http://canadafreepress.com/index.php/article/55208
http://candst.tripod.com/tnppage/baptist.htm
http://www.usconstitution.net/jeffwall.html

I Am Garland
http://thedailydan.tumblr.com/post/118286584668/he-pushed-forward-brave-garland-police-officer
http://www.glennbeck.com/2015/05/06/the-pathetic-comments-by-this-charlie-hebdo-cartoonist-will-make-your-head-explode/
http://godfatherpolitics.com/22232/isis-in-america-calling-for-death-of-free-speech-activist-pamela-geller/

http://godfatherpolitics.com/22221/cowards-trip-over-themselves-to-blame-geller-not-terrorists-in-texas/
http://www.thepoliticalinsider.com/cnn-presses-carly-fiorina-to-attack-pamela-geller-but-her-response-isnt-what-the-host-wanted-to-hear/
http://www.dailymail.co.uk/news/article-2914785/Thrown-death-gay-s-latest-abomination-one-expert-argues-images-betray-radical-Muslims-new-thirst-killing-justice.html
http://www.aol.com/article/2015/05/06/garland-attack-cartoon-contest-winner-speaks-ut/21180562/
http://www.theblaze.com/stories/2015/05/12/texas-police-change-major-detail-in-story-of-how-muhammad-cartoon-contest-gunmen-were-killed/?utm_source=Sailthru&utm_medium=email&utm_term=Firewire&utm_campaign=Firewire%20-%20HORIZON%205-12-15%20FINAL

Useful Idiots
http://insider.foxnews.com/2015/05/05/officer-charged-freddie-gray-death-says-arrest-was-legal
http://freedomoutpost.com/2015/05/freddie-gray-race-nope-baltimore-is-about-increasing-federal-power/
http://freedomoutpost.com/2015/04/report-presence-of-professional-protesters-to-incite-more-violence-in-baltimore-and-ferguson/
http://conservativebyte.com/2015/05/angry-president-blames-slavery-jim-crow-for-baltimore-riots/
http://politicaloutcast.com/2015/05/why-were-baltimore-police-ordered-to-stand-down/
http://theeconomiccollapseblog.com/archives/12-unanswered-questions-about-the-baltimore-riots-that-they-dont-want-us-to-ask
http://politicaloutcast.com/2015/05/we-dont-know-right-verdict-for-freddie-gray-prosecutions/
http://dailycaller.com/2015/05/14/most-baltimore-cops-are-minorities/
http://www.thepoliticalinsider.com/baltimore-cops-are-tired-of-their-treatment-so-they-fought-back-with-this/
http://www.thepoliticalinsider.com/army-sergeant-posts-powerful-message-to-baltimore-thugs-now-hes-under-attack/
http://politicaloutcast.com/2015/05/gods-education-plan/#
http://patriotupdate.com/2015/05/obama-loves-criminals-sends-3-officials-to-freddie-gray-funeral-0-to-nypd-funeral/
http://observer.com/2015/04/al-sharpton-calls-for-fedeal-police-laws-after-south-carolina-killing/
http://www.breitbart.com/video/2015/04/30/sharpton-calls-for-doj-to-take-over-policing-going-to-have-to-fight-states-rights/
http://www.historyplace.com/worldwar2/timeline/roehm.htm
http://www.holocaust-trc.org/homosexuals/
http://www.cnn.com/2014/12/01/politics/obama-police-militarization/index.html

I'm Conservative And Pro-Choice
http://www.thenewamerican.com/culture/education/item/12678-%E2%80%9Cscience-guy%E2%80%9D-attacks-parents-who-teach-children-creation-story
http://www.theblaze.com/stories/2013/11/20/its-kidnapping-hospital-takes-custody-of-teen-because-her-parents-were-too-active-in-pursuing-her-care/
http://abcnews.go.com/Health/justina-pelletier-heading-home-16-month-medical-custody/story?id=24191396
http://www.foxnews.com/health/2013/04/30/baby-taken-from-parents-who-sought-second-opinion-removed-from-protective/
http://www.politifact.com/wisconsin/statements/2013/jul/12/rachel-campos-duffy/more-90-women-change-their-minds-about-having-abor/

Marriage Is What Brings Us Together Today
http://www.sodahead.com/united-states/a-brief-history-of-marriage-licenses-in-
the-us/blog-393357/
http://www.sodahead.com/united-states/5-reasons-why-you-should-not-get-a-
marriage-license/blog-32580/
http://www.foxnews.com/health/2013/06/27/history-marriage-13-surprising-
facts/
http://www.macquirelatory.com/Marriage%20License%20Truth.htm
http://en.wikipedia.org/wiki/Marriage
http://en.wikipedia.org/wiki/Marriage_license
http://freedomoutpost.com/2015/05/alabama-senate-approves-bill-to-abolish-
marriage-licensing/
http://www.alimonyreform.org/content/articles/How%20Did%20Government%20
Get%20Involved%20in%20Marriage.pdf
https://answers.yahoo.com/question/index?qid=20080810054927AAL6HVA
http://definitions.uslegal.com/u/uniform-marriage-and-divorce-act/
http://www.strike-the-root.com/4/newman/newman4.html
http://en.wikipedia.org/wiki/No-fault_divorce
http://en.wikibooks.org/wiki/Cultural_Anthropology/Marriage,_Reproduction_an
d_Kinship
http://spartacus-educational.com/USASmarriage.htm

Walking the Walk
http://conservativebyte.com/2015/06/putting-the-duggar-incident-into-a-natural-
perspective/
http://www.thepoliticalinsider.com/duggar-family-just-made-a-huge-
announcement-liberals-are-freaking-out/

Their Deaths Were Not In Vain
http://www.foxnews.com/us/2015/06/20/survivors-charleston-church-shooting-
played-dead-friends-say/
http://www.infowars.com/charleston-shooter-was-on-drug-linked-to-violent-
outbursts/
http://thegrio.com/2015/06/19/children-forgive-charleston-shooter-singleton/
http://www.dailymail.co.uk/news/article-3130396/Dylann-Storm-Roof-21-glares-
hauled-away-cuffs.html
http://www.dailymail.co.uk/news/article-3129109/South-Carolina-church-shooter-
captured.html
http://www.theblaze.com/stories/2015/06/18/obama-after-charleston-shooting-
america-has-to-reckon-with-the-fact-that-this-type-of-mass-violence-doesnt-
happen-in-other-advanced-
countries/?utm_source=Sailthru&utm_medium=email&utm_term=Firewire&utm_
campaign=FireWire%20-%20HORIZON%206-18-15%20FINAL
http://www.cincinnati.com/story/news/2015/06/19/officer-down-
madisonville/28974101/
http://www.latimes.com/nation/nationnow/la-na-dylann-roof-suicide-attempt-
20150620-story.html
http://www.cincinnati.com/story/news/2015/06/19/madisonville-vigil-tense-
future/29018965/
http://www.wcpo.com/news/local-news/hamilton-county/loveland-
community/fallen-officers-son-shares-powerful-goodbye-to-father-on-instagram

How The South Was Won
http://articles.baltimoresun.com/2013-07-06/news/bs-ed-gettysburg-
20130706_1_slavery-constitutional-convention-secession
http://www.tpnn.com/2015/07/04/brand-new-video-democrats-horrible-racist-
past-bill-whittle/

http://www.washingtonpost.com/posteverything/wp/2015/07/01/why-do-people-believe-myths-about-the-confederacy-because-our-textbooks-and-monuments-are-wrong/
http://www.mrctv.org/blog/cnn-poll-shows-majority-americans-do-not-view-confederate-flag-racist
http://www.cnn.com/2015/07/02/politics/confederate-flag-poll-racism-southern-pride/index.html
http://www.westernjournalism.com/mike-rowe-just-revealed-what-he-wants-to-do-when-he-sees-the-confederate-flag/?utm_source=Facebook&utm_medium=Sponsored&utm_content=2015-06-30&%3Futm_source=Facebook
http://twitchy.com/2014/11/03/dem-campaign-flier-prompts-reminder-kkk-was-militant-wing-of-democratic-party/
http://www.freerepublic.com/focus/news/2309727/posts
http://www.examiner.com/article/rush-limbaugh-confederate-flag-legacy-of-democrats-not-republicans
https://en.wikipedia.org/wiki/Jefferson_Davis
http://www.latimes.com/nation/nationnow/la-na-nn-chicago-shot-weekend-violence-20140707-story.html
http://www.maggiesnotebook.com/2012/08/civil-rights-racism-democrats-controlled-everything-but-would-not-pass-civil-rights-the-history-the-timeline-of-democrat-racism/
http://dailycaller.com/2014/12/31/name-that-klansman-robert-byrd-and-david-duke/
http://www.history.com/this-day-in-history/president-andrew-johnson-impeached
https://en.wikipedia.org/wiki/Ku_Klux_Klan_members_in_United_States_politics

A Crusade For The Truth

http://www.theblaze.com/stories/2015/02/10/verbal-rape-conservative-critic-tears-into-obamas-comments-about-christians-and-the-crusades-with-a-comparison-that-stuns-geraldo-rivera/
http://www.history.com/topics/crusades
http://www.encyclopedia.com/topic/Crusades.aspx
http://www.religionfacts.com/christianity/history/crusades
http://www.lordsandladies.org/cause-of-crusades.htm
http://www.rationalchristianity.net/crusades.html
http://www.allaboutreligion.org/history-of-christianity-in-africa-faq.htm
http://jmeca.org.uk/christianity-middle-east/history-christianity-middle-east-north-africa
http://www.thefinertimes.com/Middle-Ages/christianity-in-the-middle-ages.html
http://www.nullsession.net/2009/the-dark-ages-religion/
http://www.cbn.com/spirituallife/onlinediscipleship/understandingislam/IslamHistory0212.aspx
https://en.wikipedia.org/wiki/Battle_of_Dorylaeum_%281097%29
https://en.wikipedia.org/wiki/Siege_of_Jerusalem_%28637%29
https://en.wikipedia.org/wiki/History_of_the_Church_of_the_Holy_Sepulchre
http://www.thereligionofpeace.com/Muhammad/myths-mu-self-defense.htm

The Axis Of Evil

http://politicaloutcast.com/2015/07/how-deborah-nucatola-will-end-abortion/
http://www.theblaze.com/stories/2015/07/21/second-undercover-video-features-planned-parenthood-abortion-doctor-haggling-over-the-price-of-aborted-fetuses-group-claims/
http://www.theblaze.com/stories/2015/07/14/undercover-video-claims-planned-parenthood-uses-partial-birth-abortions-to-sell-baby-parts/
http://eaglerising.com/21154/princeton-professor-says-the-government-should-use-obamacare-to-kill-disabled-infants/

http://www.catholicnewsagency.com/news/report-shows-adult-stem-cell-research-produces-results-draws-money/
http://www.huffingtonpost.com/entry/joseph-c-phillips-bill-cosby-guilty_55a66025e4b0c5f0322bcd8a
http://josephcphillips.com/2015/07/of-course-bill-cosby-is-guilty/
http://www.theblaze.com/stories/2015/07/21/hillary-supporter-talks-about-bringing-back-internment-camps-segregate-those-who-dont-support-the-united-states/
http://politicaloutcast.com/2015/07/former-dem-presidential-candidate-calls-for-prison-camps-for-the-radicalized/

The Rainbow Connection
http://www.thelondonweekly.net/index.php?option=com_content&view=article&id=107:amy-goodman&catid=34:uk-news&Itemid=61
http://www.noahs-ark.tv/noahs-ark-flood-creation-stories-myths-sumerian-kings-list-sumerian-eridu-genesis-kings-list-instructions-of-shuruppak-atra-hasis-epic-of-gilgamesh-berossus.htm
http://www.nwcreation.net/noahlegends.html
http://reviewofreligions.org/5397/noahas-and-the-flood/
https://askaphilosopher.wordpress.com/2011/08/31/finding-the-story-of-genesis-in-other-cultures/
http://www.theblaze.com/stories/2015/06/26/white-house-lit-rainbow-celebrate-same-sex-marriage-ruling/
http://lastresistance.com/12765/to-christians-who-vote-democrat-homosexuality-gay-marriage/
http://www.nwcreation.net/noahlegends.html
https://answersingenesis.org/bible-characters/moses/did-moses-write-genesis/
http://www.slate.com/articles/life/explainer/2012/06/rainbows_and_gay_pride_how_the_rainbow_became_a_symbol_of_the_glbt_movement_.html
http://trishnicholsonswordsinthetreehouse.com/2012/02/24/how-the-brothers-grimm-came-to-write-fairy-tales
http://www.christianbiblereference.org/story_TowerOfBabel.htm
http://www.israel-a-history-of.com/nimrod.html
https://en.wikipedia.org/wiki/Gilgamesh_flood_myth

When Does Life Begin?
http://www.michigan.gov/mdch/0,1607,7-132-2940_4909_6437_19077_19078-45567--,00.html
http://fellowshipoftheminds.com/2012/04/22/feminist-blogger-fetus-is-a-parasite/
http://thevelvetbrick.org/2013/04/
http://www.ushmm.org/wlc/mobile/en/article.php?ModuleId=10005168
http://www.theapricity.com/forum/archive/index.php/t-56259.html
http://thefederalist.com/2015/08/10/cnns-chris-cuomo-has-absolutely-no-idea-where-babies-come-from/#.VctJ7kNGLCQ.email
http://newsbusters.org/blogs/nb/matthew-balan/2015/07/16/cnn-acclaims-defends-jenners-espy-why-wouldnt-it-qualify
http://www.newsmax.com/Headline/marco-rubio-chris-cuomo-debate-abortion/2015/08/07/id/669075/

Evil Is As Evil Does
http://writingtheholocaust.blogspot.com/2011/01/sexual-violence-against-jewish-women.html?m=1
http://auschwitz.dk/Mengele.htm
http://www.ushmm.org/wlc/mobile/en/article.php?ModuleId=10005168
http://www.theapricity.com/forum/archive/index.php/t-56259.html
http://www.theblaze.com/stories/2015/08/11/watch-how-democratic-senator-responds-when-we-ask-if-she-has-seen-planned-parenthood-videos/

http://www.theblaze.com/stories/2015/08/12/whistleblower-drops-shocking-allegations-about-fetal-tissue-procurement-process-involving-planned-parenthood-these-mothers-dont-know/
http://dailycaller.com/2015/08/04/new-planned-parenthood-transcript-nurse-admits-its-fun-to-dissect-fetuses/#ixzz3idPgXJm1
http://www.breitbart.com/video/2015/08/12/ben-carson-planned-parenthood-clinics-put-in-black-neighborhoods-to-control-that-population/
http://eaglerising.com/22616/bombshell-in-the-latest-planned-parenthood-video-are-babies-kept-alive-for-bigger-profit-margins/

A Change Of Heart
http://conservativebyte.com/2015/08/undercover-video-reveals-the-real-hillary-in-argument-with-black-lives-matter-activist/
http://www.free2pray.info/5founderquotes.html
http://www.rushlimbaugh.com/daily/2015/08/18/undercover_video_reveals_the_real_hillary_in_argument_with_black_lives_matter_activist

Jamestown: A City Upon A Hill
http://www.biography.com/people/pocahontas-9443116
http://www.history.com/topics/native-american-history/pocahontas
http://pocahontas.morenus.org/
http://historicjamestowne.org/history/pocahontas/
http://native-american-indian-facts.com/Famous-Native-American-Facts/Interesting-Pocahontas-Facts.shtml
http://www.encyclopedia.com/topic/Pocahontas.aspx
https://en.wikipedia.org/wiki/Pocahontas
https://en.wikipedia.org/wiki/First_Families_of_Virginia
http://www.politico.com/story/2013/09/this-day-in-politics-096486
http://historicjamestowne.org/history/pocahontas/john-smith/
http://www.history.com/this-day-in-history/smith-to-lead-jamestown
https://en.wikipedia.org/wiki/John_Smith_%28explorer%29
The Founders Bible pgs 37-40
http://genevabible.com/
http://howardsnyder.seedbed.com/2013/12/19/who-was-alexander-whitaker/

Constitution Day
https://en.wikipedia.org/wiki/United_States_Constitution
http://www.britannica.com/event/Constitutional-Convention
http://www.britannica.com/topic/Articles-of-Confederation
http://americanhistory.about.com/od/usconstitution/p/constitutional_convention.htm
http://www.scholastic.com/teachers/article/creating-us-constitution-time-line
http://www.timetoast.com/timelines/events-leading-up-to-and-affecting-the-us-constitution
http://constitutioncenter.org/constitution-day
http://www.constitutionday.com/
http://www.constitutionfacts.com/us-constitution-day/history-of-constitution-day/
https://en.wikipedia.org/wiki/Early_American_currency
http://www.history.com/this-day-in-history/george-washington-is-elected-president
https://en.wikipedia.org/wiki/United_States_Bill_of_Rights

America's Moses
http://www.harriettubman.com/day.html
http://www.biography.com/people/harriet-tubman-9511430
http://www.history.com/topics/black-history/harriet-tubman
http://womenshistory.about.com/od/harriettubman/a/tubman_slavery.htm

http://inventors.about.com/library/inventors/blharriettubman.htm
http://womenshistory.about.com/od/harriettubman/fl/Harriet-Tubman-Day-March-10.htm
https://worldhistoryproject.org/1869/3/18/harriet-tubman-marries-nelson-davis
http://www.compromise-of-1850.org/fugitive-slave-act-of-1850/
http://www.libertyletters.com/resources/civil-war/harriet-tubman-civil-war-spy.php
http://www.blackpast.org/aah/combahee-river-raid-june-2-1863
https://worldhistoryproject.org/1859/us-senator-william-seward-sells-harriet-tubman-house-in-auburn-new-york
http://womenshistory.about.com/od/harriettubman/a/tubman_civilwar.htm
https://en.wikipedia.org/wiki/Harriet_Tubman

Is There Any Intelligent Life Out There?
http://www.rushlimbaugh.com/daily/2015/09/29/what_i_really_think_about_mars
http://www.rushlimbaugh.com/daily/2015/09/28/climate_change_on_mars
http://www.usnews.com/news/articles/2015/09/28/nasa-water-means-life-on-mars-is-possible
http://www.breitbart.com/big-government/2015/09/28/timing-of-nasa-announcement-sparks-conspiracy-theories-about-ridley-scotts-the-martian/
https://www.nasa.gov/press-release/nasa-confirms-evidence-that-liquid-water-flows-on-today-s-mars/
http://www.theguardian.com/film/2015/sep/29/the-martian-ridley-scott-knew-water-on-mars-months-ago
http://www.cnn.com/2015/09/28/us/mars-nasa-announcement/index.html
https://answersingenesis.org/the-flood/global/worldwide-flood-evidence/
http://www.pbslearningmedia.org/resource/tdc02.sci.life.stru.singlecell/single-celled-organisms/
http://www.christianexaminer.com/article/bill.nye.science.guy.calls.pro.lifers.ignorant.but.critics.say.he.has.his.facts.all.wrong/49601.htm
http://lastresistance.com/13966/a-response-to-bill-nyes-smug-defense-of-abortion/

I Am A Christian
http://politicaloutcast.com/2015/10/cnn-radio-gun-free-zone-means-nothing-to-a-shooter/
http://www.thepoliticalinsider.com/video-chris-harper-mercers-religion/?utm_source=SailThru&utm_newsletter&utm_medium=email&utm_campaign=New%20Campaign&utm_term=Friday%20Sends
http://politicaloutcast.com/2015/10/computer-models-for-hurricane-completely-contradict-one-another/
http://patriotupdate.com/south-carolina-cop-viciously-murdered-shot-dead-media-ignores/
http://www.theblaze.com/contributions/why-arent-guns-making-americans-safer/?utm_source=Sailthru&utm_medium=email&utm_campaign=Firewire%20-%20HORIZON%2010-2-15%20FINAL&utm_term=Firewire
http://conservativebyte.com/2015/10/oregon-killer-singled-out-christians-to-shoot-them-in-the-head/
http://godfatherpolitics.com/25441/chicagos-strict-gun-laws-leave-50-shot-for-second-weekend-in-a-row/
http://www.newsmax.com/Headline/US-crime-shooting-Oregon/2015/10/01/id/694326/
http://conservativebyte.com/2015/10/obama-on-confiscating-guns-then-and-now/#
http://patriotupdate.com/cnn-photoshops-image-of-mixed-race-oregon-shooter-turns-him-into-a-white-man-view/
http://time.com/3972713/detroit-satanic-statue-baphomet/

The Forgotten President

http://www.history.com/topics/us-presidents/calvin-coolidge
http://conservativevideos.com/coolidge-the-best-president-you-dont-know/
http://millercenter.org/president/biography/coolidge-life-in-brief
http://www.thenewamerican.com/culture/history/item/14546-calvin-coolidge-and-the-greatness-of-a-not-great-president
http://www.heritage.org/research/reports/2013/02/calvin-coolidge-forefather-of-our-conservatism
http://www.wsj.com/articles/SB10001424053111903520204576484673631290098
https://en.wikipedia.org/wiki/Herbert_Hoover
http://teachingamericanhistory.org/library/document/speech-on-the-occasion-of-the-one-hundred-and-fiftieth-anniversary-of-the-declaration-of-independence/
https://coolidgefoundation.org/quote/quotations-s/
http://www.rarenewspapers.com/view/161328
https://en.wikipedia.org/wiki/Smoot%E2%80%93Hawley_Tariff_Act
http://townhall.com/tipsheet/conncarroll/2014/02/17/the-greatest-conservative-president-in-american-history-n1787876
http://www.theblaze.com/books/coolidge/
https://en.wikipedia.org/wiki/New_Deal

All In Due Time

http://historyguide.org/intellect/press.html
http://www.bl.uk/treasures/gutenberg/makingbible.html
http://www.history.com/news/7-things-you-may-not-know-about-the-gutenberg-bible
http://www.gutenberg-bible.com/history.html
http://www.bible-researcher.com/luther02.html
https://en.m.wikipedia.org/wiki/Hans_Lufft
http://www.avdefense.webs.com/pilgrims.html
https://en.m.wikipedia.org/wiki/Geneva_Bible

The American Inquisition

http://lonelyconservative.com/2015/09/feminism-today-throw-men-in-prison-camps-scrap-heterosexuality/
http://www.wnd.com/2015/03/new-inquisition-punish-climate-change-deniers/
http://patriotupdate.com/scientists-order-obama-to-prosecute-skeptics-of-global-warming/
https://en.wikipedia.org/wiki/Spanish_Inquisition
http://www.newworldencyclopedia.org/entry/Spanish_Inquisition
http://www.britannica.com/topic/Spanish-Inquisition
http://www.strangenotions.com/spanish-inquisition/
http://www.reformation.org/inquisit.html
http://www.christianitytoday.com/ch/131christians/theologians/luther.html
http://www.reformation.org/spanish-inquisition.html
http://www.theblaze.com/stories/2015/09/22/ap-updates-stylebook-with-guidance-on-what-to-call-individuals-who-dont-accept-climate-science/?utm_source=Sailthru&utm_medium=email&utm_campaign=Firewire%20Morning%20Edition%20Recurring%20v2%202015-09-23&utm_term=Firewire_Morning_Test
http://lastresistance.com/14352/john-kerry-belief-in-climate-change-required/
http://www.dailymail.co.uk/sciencetech/article-3300063/Antarctica-GAINING-ice-s-losing-10-000-year-old-trend-reverse-Nasa-warns.html
http://i100.independent.co.uk/article/bill-gates-says-that-capitalism-cannot-save-us-from-climate-change--b1xNpbL8O_x
http://content.time.com/time/specials/2007/completelist/0,29569,1661031,00.html
http://www.rushlimbaugh.com/daily/2015/11/02/mind_boggling_gates_bashes_capitalism

http://www.glennbeck.com/2015/10/29/ted-cruz-climate-change-is-not-science-its-religion/
http://www.breitbart.com/big-government/2015/10/07/ted-cruz-destroys-sierra-club-presidents-global-warming-claims-senate-hearing/
http://www.cnn.com/2013/01/07/opinion/kurtz-gore-al-jazeera/index.html
http://www.britannica.com/event/Reconquista
http://www.britannica.com/topic/Marrano
http://www.britannica.com/biography/Tomas-de-Torquemada

The Forgotten General
http://www.history.com/topics/world-war-i/john-j-pershing
http://www.arlingtoncemetery.net/johnjose.htm
http://www.firstworldwar.com/features/pershing.htm
http://www.usa-hero.com/pershing_john.html
https://en.wikipedia.org/wiki/1st_Infantry_Division_%28United_States%29
http://www.1stid.org/historyindex.php
http://www.skylighters.org/225thmemorial/memsite/1sthistory.html
http://www.armystudyguide.com/content/Unit_history/Division_history/1st-infantry-division.shtml
https://en.wikipedia.org/wiki/John_J._Pershing
http://militaryhistory.about.com/od/1900s/p/pershing.htm
http://www.eyewitnesstohistory.com/roughriders.htm
http://history1900s.about.com/cs/panchovilla/p/panchovilla.htm

Everything Free But Speech
http://godfatherpolitics.com/26366/african-american-journalist-exposes-the-hypocrisy-and-foolishness-of-the-mizzou-protests/
http://j.school/post/133025099640/crying-wolfe-exposes-real-problem
http://godfatherpolitics.com/26396/read-unbelievable-comments-that-mizzou-protesters-said-about-paris-terror-attacks/
http://dailysignal.com/2015/11/09/university-of-missouri-and-yale-shows-what-mob-rule-looks-like-in-higher-education/?utm_source=heritagefoundation&utm_medium=email&utm_campaign=saturday&mkt_tok=3RkMMJWWfF9wsRous63BZKXonjHpfsX57usoWKKzlMI/oER3fOvrPUfGjI4AT8FmPa+TFAwTG5toziV8R7jHKM1t0sEQWBHm
http://minutemennews.com/the-entitled-generation-is-now-marching-to-get-more-free-stuff/
http://conservativevideos.com/asian-student-steps-into-safe-space-says-people-shouldnt-be-judged-by-race-gets-this-stunning-reaction/
http://www.theblaze.com/stories/2015/11/12/neil-cavuto-repeatedly-confronts-student-pushing-free-college-plan-with-harsh-facts-figures-during-cringeworthy-9-minute-interview/
http://www.examiner.com/article/keely-mullen-million-student-march-spokeswoman-is-the-one-percent
http://www.bizpacreview.com/2015/11/13/unreal-mu-student-body-vice-president-argues-shes-tired-of-hearing-about-first-amendment-protection-273391
http://politistick.com/mizzou-student-body-president-invents-huge-lie-to-push-racism-narrative/
http://www.stltoday.com/lifestyles/columns/joe-holleman/mizzou-hunger-strike-figure-from-omaha-son-of-top-railroad/article_20630c03-2a68-5e63-9585-edde16fe05f3.html
http://www.stltoday.com/news/local/education/mizzou-graduate-students-pledge-to-fight-for-benefits/article_d9c8499d-d204-5f29-a01c-bc584ba55760.html
http://www.thenewamerican.com/usnews/politics/item/2455-obamas-friend-ayers-kill-25-million-americanshttp://www.thenewamerican.com/usnews/politics/item/2455-obamas-friend-ayers-kill-25-million-americans

*http://www.americanthinker.com/blog/2015/11/dartmouth_official_apologizes_to
_protesters_for_negative_media_coverage_of_library_demonstration.html*
http://www.dartreview.com/eyes-wide-open-at-the-protest/
*http://www.usnews.com/news/blogs/press-past/2013/06/11/george-wallace-
stood-in-a-doorway-at-the-university-of-alabama-50-years-ago-today*
*http://www.theblaze.com/stories/2015/11/16/black-lives-matter-mob-invades-
dartmouth-library-reportedly-harass-white-students-relentlessly-f-your-white-
tears/*
*http://www.thesocialmemo.org/2015/10/black-lives-matter-leader-demands-
new.html*

Wolves In Sheep's Clothing
*http://www.breitbart.com/big-government/2015/11/19/trey-gowdy-im-afraid-
foreign-policy-creates-widows-orphans/*
*http://www.mediaite.com/online/rand-paul-boston-bombers-were-coddled-as-
refugees-but-still-attacked-us/*
*http://www.rushlimbaugh.com/daily/2015/11/23/obama_finally_bombs_isis_oil_
tankers_after_giving_the_terrorists_a_45_minute_warning_to_get_to_safety*
http://www.jewishvirtuallibrary.org/jsource/Holocaust/stlouis.html
*http://www.mediaite.com/tv/whoopi-on-calls-for-only-christian-refugees-there-
are-monster-christians-like-hitler/*
*http://www.newsmax.com/Newsfront/dianne-feinstein-isis-isil-paris-
bombings/2015/11/16/id/702350/*
*http://www.realclearpolitics.com/video/2015/11/13/obama_on_isis_we_have_con
tained_them.html*
*http://www.theguardian.com/us-news/2015/nov/17/republicans-congress-syrian-
refugees-us-paris-attacks*
*http://thehill.com/homenews/administration/260542-obama-gop-refugee-
opponents-scared-of-widows-and-orphans*
*http://www.youngcons.com/pilots-confirm-obama-blocked-75-percent-of-
airstrikes-against-isis/*
*http://www.glennbeck.com/2015/11/24/obama-was-right-glenn-rethinks-what-he-
told-megyn-kelly-last-week*

Walking To Freedom
http://rosapark.com/rosaparks.htm
https://www.thehenryford.org/exhibits/rosaparks/story.asp
http://www.history.com/topics/black-history/rosa-parks
http://www.biography.com/people/rosa-parks-9433715#synopsis
*http://kingencyclopedia.stanford.edu/encyclopedia/encyclopedia/enc_montgomery
_bus_boycott_1955_1956/*
http://www.history.com/topics/black-history/montgomery-bus-boycott
http://www.montgomeryboycott.com/
http://www.biography.com/people/ed-nixon-21308863
http://www.montgomeryboycott.com/e-d-nixon/
http://www.gosanangelo.com/news/national/killingsbypolicechicago_07148225
*http://nypost.com/2015/11/27/arrest-made-in-case-of-9-year-old-killed-as-
gangbangers-revenge/*
*http://www.ammoland.com/2015/11/2703-shootings-440-deaths-year-to-date-in-
heavily-gun-controlled-chicago/#axzz3t2CVQXNA*
*http://chicago.cbslocal.com/2015/11/30/8-killed-20-wounded-in-thanksgiving-
weekend-shootings-across-chicago/*
*http://www.breitbart.com/big-government/2015/11/29/tyshawn-lee-real-hands-
dont-shoot-black-lives-matter-ignores/*

It's Not What's In Your Hand, It's What's In Your Heart
http://www.theblaze.com/stories/2015/12/03/scumbags-new-york-daily-news-

*slammed-for-offensive-cover-following-san-bernardino-
shooting/?utm_source=Sailthru&utm_medium=email&utm_campaign=FireWire%
20-%20HORIZON%2012-3-15%20FINAL&utm_term=Firewire*
*http://www.theblaze.com/stories/2015/12/03/u-s-official-california-shooter-
contacted-extremists-under-fbi-scrutiny-on-social-media/*
*http://dailycaller.com/2015/12/03/officer-to-survivors-ill-take-a-bullet-before-you-
do-video/#ixzz3tIFvjoYB*
*http://dailycaller.com/2015/12/03/beck-on-obama-either-delusional-or-the-
dumbest-son-of-a-bitch-on-the-planet-video/*
*http://www.theblaze.com/stories/2015/12/03/see-letter-cruz-sessions-sent-to-
obama-admin-heres-what-they-want-to-know-about-calif-attackers/*
http://www.theblaze.com/contributions/yes-god-can-fix-this-he-already-has/
*http://www.nytimes.com/politics/first-draft/2015/12/04/a-few-house-democrats-
to-attend-prayer-services-at-u-s-mosques/*
*http://dailycaller.com/2015/12/06/ny-daily-news-columnist-sees-social-media-
backlash-after-saying-san-bernardino-victim-had-it-coming/*
*http://www.thedailysheeple.com/why-have-there-been-more-mass-shootings-
under-obama-than-the-four-previous-presidents-combined_122015*
*http://www.foxnews.com/opinion/2015/12/03/facts-shoot-holes-in-obamas-claim-
that-us-is-only-host-to-mass-killings.html*
*http://www.npr.org/sections/thetwo-way/2015/12/03/458321777/a-tally-of-mass-
shootings-in-the-u-s*
http://www.theguardian.com/world/2008/apr/14/barackobama.uselections2008
https://en.m.wikipedia.org/wiki/2014_Kunming_attack
*http://stephenewright.com/fromthebluff/2008/10/23/the-butcher's-bill---non-gun-
mass-murders/*
*http://www.nbcnews.com/storyline/charleston-church-shooting/dylann-roof-
almost-didnt-go-through-charleston-church-shooting-n378341*
*http://freebeacon.com/national-security/democrats-to-attend-prayer-service-at-
radical-mosque/*

The Forgotten Founding Father
*https://raymondpronk.wordpress.com/2010/05/15/glenn-beck-a-founding-father-
you-never-heard-of-george-whitfield/*
http://www.glennbeck.com/content/articles/article/196/39831/
*http://www.foxnews.com/story/2010/05/17/glenn-beck-founders-friday-george-
whitefield.html*
*http://www.glennbeck.com/2015/06/09/there-are-over-40000-preachers-ready-
to-stand-against-the-government/*
https://en.m.wikipedia.org/wiki/George_Whitefield
*http://www.christianitytoday.com/ch/131christians/evangelistsandapologists/whit
efield.html*
http://www.pbs.org/godinamerica/people/george-whitefield.html
*http://www.georgiaencyclopedia.org/articles/arts-culture/george-whitefield-1714-
1770*
http://www.britannica.com/biography/George-Whitefield
http://www.encyclopedia.com/topic/George_Whitefield.aspx
https://en.wikipedia.org/wiki/First_Great_Awakening
http://www.ushistory.org/us/7b.asp
http://www.believersweb.org/view.cfm?id=94&rc=1&list=multi
http://nationalhumanitiescenter.org/tserve/eighteen/ekeyinfo/grawaken.htm
http://www.ccel.org/ccel/edwards/sermons.sinners.html
http://www.newworldencyclopedia.org/entry/First_Great_Awakening
*http://nationalblackroberegiment.com/first-great-awakenings-impact-founding-
fathers/*
http://edsitement.neh.gov/lesson-plan/first-great-awakening
http://liveagreaterstory.com/george-whitefield-preaching-kingswood/

http://www.stevenmosley.com/news/
http://americancreation.blogspot.com/2008/11/great-awakening-1739-1740.html
http://www.ccel.org/ccel/whitefield
http://nationalhumanitiescenter.org/pds/becomingamer/ideas/text2/franklinwhitefield.pdf
http://www.u-s-history.com/pages/h3853.html
http://www.christianity.com/church/church-history/timeline/1701-1800/controversial-george-whitefield-11630198.html
http://nationalblackroberegiment.com/history-of-the-black-robe-regiment/
http://www.weeklystandard.com/the-great-dissenter/article/823810

Peace On Earth, Good Will To Men

http://blogs.thegospelcoalition.org/justintaylor/2014/12/21/the-story-of-pain-and-hope-behind-i-heard-the-bells-on-christmas-day/
http://www.whatsaiththescripture.com/Fellowship/Edit_I.Heard.the.Bells.html
http://emergingcivilwar.com/2011/12/13/i-heard-the-bells-on-christmas-day/
http://www.hymnsandcarolsofchristmas.com/Poetry/christmas_bells.htm
https://en.wikipedia.org/wiki/Annunciation_to_the_shepherds
https://en.wikipedia.org/wiki/While_Shepherds_Watched_Their_Flocks